Holy Spirit

EMPOWERED PRAYER

EMPOWERED PRAYER

BY
DR. DOUGLAS J. WINGATE

All Scripture quotations are used by permission. Unless otherwise indicated, all Scripture quotations are from *The New King James Version of the Bible.* Copyright © 1982 by Thomas Nelson, Inc. All rights reserved. Scripture quotations marked AMP are from *The Amplified Bible.* Copyright © 2015 by The Lockman Foundation, La Habra, CA 90631. Scripture quotations marked AMPC are from *The Amplified Bible, Classic Edition.* Copyright © 1954, 1958, 1962, 1964, 1965, 1987 by The Lockman Foundation, La Habra, CA 90631. Scripture quotations marked EXB are from *The Expanded Bible.* Copyright © 2011 by Thomas Nelson. All rights reserved. Scripture quotations marked MSG are from *The Message.* Copyright © 1993, 2002, 2018 by Eugene H. Peterson. Scripture quotations marked MIRROR are from *The Mirror Study Bible.* Copyright © 2012 by Francois du Toit, mirrorword.net. Scripture quotations marked NASB are from the *New American Standard Bible.* Copyright © 2011 by Hendrickson Publishers. Scripture quotations marked NIV are from the *Holy Bible, New International Version,* Copyright © 1973, 1978, 1984 by the International Bible Society, Zondervan Publishing House. All rights reserved. Scripture quotations marked NLT are from the *Holy Bible, New Living Translation,* Copyright © 1996, 2004, Tyndale House Publishers, Inc., Wheaton, Illinois 60189. All rights reserved. Scripture quotations marked with NOG are from *The Names of God,* Spangler, Ann, Copyright © 2011 by Zondervan Publishing House, Grand Rapids, MI. All rights reserved. Strong, James, *The Strongest Strong's Exhaustive Concordance of the Bible*, Grand Rapids, MI: Zondervan, 2001. Scripture quotations marked TLB are from *The Living Bible Large Print Edition.* Copyright © 2015 by Tyndale House Publishers, Carol Stream, IL. All rights reserved. Scripture quotations marked TPT are from *The Passion Translation.* Copyright © 2017, 2018, 2020 Passion and Fire Ministries, Inc., ThePassionTranslation.com. Scripture quotations marked WYC are from *The Wycliffe Bible: John Wycliffe's Translation of the Holy Scriptures from the Latin Vulgate.* Copyright © 2009. All rights reserved. Scripture quotations marked WBT are from *The Webster Bible.* Eugene: Wipf and Stock Publishers. Copyright © 2016. All rights reserved.

Life Christian University Press
P.O. Box 272360, Tampa, FL 33688 – 813-909-9720

Visit our website at www.lcus.edu

Printed in the United States of America
ISBN: 978-1-6857303-2-1

TABLE OF CONTENTS

Part One:

Holy Spirit-Empowered Prayer

CHAPTER ONE

A VERY POWERFUL, INNOVATIVE, AND TIMELY TOPIC

This book covers a very powerful, innovative, and timely topic. We will be examining how to tap into everything that God has given us in the new covenant, so we can be the most successful and powerful prayer warriors possible; completing what God has for us to do in our assignments. Because we believe that the epoch of time in which we live is the *last* of the last days, it's absolutely essential that we access *everything* that God has for us, and that we use *all* the tools the Lord wants us to be able to use. We will see that although the Holy Spirit has always been here; in these last days, He has been poured out on the Church *without measure*: in tongues, in prophecy, and in giftings.

We will also discover how to receive and use the most powerful new covenant prayer gift ever given: the ability to pray in tongues. When we're praying in tongues, we are allowing the Holy Spirit to pray the perfect prayers through our spirit according to Romans 8:26; covering all kinds of prayer for every situation and need.

I'm not sure you're going to find too many other places that explore the things that we're going to cover in this book. These truths are "hot off the press" and come directly from praying in tongues for two to three hours a day, for the last year-and-a-half. I will share what the Lord is showing me concerning the exact Scriptures that will give you the understanding of why we're praying the way we're praying.

We will also study all the different kinds of prayer so we can pray them in agreement with what the Holy Spirit has already prayed through us in tongues. For many years, I had this backwards. I said that we needed to gain knowledge and understanding of the many different kinds of prayers so we could pray according to our understanding, and then bathe that prayer in the Holy Spirit by praying in tongues. Now, after many, many years of walking with the Lord, He has started showing me much more.

We can start our prayers by praying in tongues first; then we can actually *interpret* what the Holy Spirit is praying through our Spirit. Then we can come into alignment with what the Holy Spirit is teaching us and what He's praying through us. We will find this method to be far more powerful because the Holy Spirit is always going to pray the perfect prayer. He knows exactly which kinds of prayer to pray and He will show us where we need to come into agreement and alignment with Him.

We will explore the many benefits of daily prayer and seeking the Lord continuously. I believe that as you read this book, you will feel drawn into prayer like never before – especially when you begin to see amazing answers to your prayers!

AN ESSENTIAL SOURCE OF POWER

I was baptized in the Holy Spirit three weeks after I was born again. I immediately knew that I had tapped into the power source that God knew would be essential for the days and times in which we live. Once I experienced that power source, I fell in love with it. I started praying in tongues a lot, and I sang in tongues a lot, because I was so enamored with the power that I sensed. Since the beginning of my Christian walk, I have prayed in tongues for about an hour a day – not all at one time, but throughout the day – praying ten minutes here, five minutes there, fifteen minutes there, etc.

I might as well tell you up front: I believe that God wants us to pray in tongues at least an hour a day. Why an hour a day? You will see this if you go back to what Jesus told His disciples in the Garden of Gethsemane. We are talking about just before Jesus was going to go through the crucifixion to pay the price for every human's sin, for all of eternity. He knew He was going to be separated from the Father and the Holy Spirit, which was actually going to be the worst part of His experience. He asked His disciples to watch with Him, but the disciples were tired that night and kept falling asleep.

Then He came to the disciples and found them sleeping, and said to Peter, "What! Could you not watch with Me one hour? Watch and pray, lest you enter into temptation. The spirit indeed *is* willing, but the flesh *is* weak" (Matthew 26:40-41).

But the disciples could not; they weren't born again yet and they weren't baptized in the Holy Spirit. They had no power in their lives other than that which came from following Jesus; and trying to do everything He said to do as He gave them the authority to use His name.

Jesus' request to pray with Him for an hour stuck in my mind – so much so, that from the time that I was born again and baptized in the Holy Spirit, I felt like Jesus must want us all to pray in tongues for at least an hour a day. And now, for me, over the last year-and-a-half, it's expanded into one to five hours a day. That's how long it takes for me to tap into everything God has planned for my life and ministry.

I felt like the Lord was calling me to pray because I'm a watchman on the wall. There's nothing more exciting than being able to be a watchman on the wall; doing what the Lord's called me to do. It's especially exciting when Jesus says, "Doug, I need you now; I need you to pray now. I've got something critically important." We don't even have to know what it is. We just know that God is using us. The Holy Spirit is praying through our spirit, and we're praying the perfect prayer for whatever circumstance God's leading us to pray about.

After reading and applying what you learn in this book, you will find yourself easily praying in tongues for an hour a day. It doesn't have to be all at one time, although you will find great benefits doing it all at one time! You might do a half-hour in the morning and a half-hour at night; whatever is going to work for you.

In this book I am going to tell you all the prayer secrets that I've discovered in the process of praying in tongues for multiple hours at a time. I want you to be able to tap into all the secrets that God has given me. But unless you pray in tongues for an hour a day, you won't be able to relate to the truths in this book. I pray that you'll get the same anointing to pray, that the Lord has given me. Neither God nor His anointing is bound by space or time, so this same anointing to pray can come upon you. It's embedded in the words of Scripture we will be studying, and in the illumination that comes from reading and meditating on these anointed, *rhema* [Greek: "utterance, thing said"] words.

WAIT FOR THE POWER

The first thing you must understand about Holy Spirit-inspired prayer is this: the only person who can really experience the full power of this is someone who's been baptized in the Holy Spirit and who can pray in tongues. That is foundational for all we have discovered during the last year-and-a-half through praying in tongues for two to three hours a day.

Yet, three-quarters of the believers in the Church of the Lord Jesus Christ throughout the entire earth, don't pray in tongues. If you have not yet experienced this miraculous gift, now is the time! Let's look at what the Bible has to say about this subject, and put to rest any doubts you may have about receiving this gift.

> *NOTE: If you have already received the Baptism of the Holy Spirit, the following is an excellent way to minister this gift to others!*

How to Receive the Gift of Praying in Other Tongues

The last thing Jesus told His disciples before He ascended to heaven was:

> **"Do not leave Jerusalem, but wait for the gift my Father promised, which you have heard me speak about. For John baptized with water, but in a few days you will be baptized with the Holy Spirit.... you will receive power when the Holy Spirit comes on you; and you will be my witnesses"** (Acts 1:4-5,8 NIV).

The baptism of the Holy Spirit gives you power: the power to say "No!" to temptation, and the power to live a victorious Christian life. You will be a living witness of a life transformed by Jesus Christ.

Ten days later, on the Day of Pentecost, 120 of the disciples were together in an upper room.

15

And suddenly there came a sound from heaven, as of a rushing mighty wind, and it filled the whole house where they were sitting. Then there appeared to them divided tongues, as of fire, and *one* sat upon each of them. And they were all filled with the Holy Spirit and began to speak with other tongues, as the Spirit gave them utterance (Acts 2:2-4).

The Amplified Bible, Classic Edition says:

And they were all filled (diffused throughout their souls) with the Holy Spirit and began to speak in other (different, foreign) languages (tongues), as the Spirit kept giving them clear *and* loud expression [in each tongue in appropriate words].

When you speak in tongues, you are speaking in a real language, but a different, heavenly language. You will not understand what you say, but God will.

For he who speaks in a tongue does not speak to men but to God, for no one understands *him*; however, in the spirit he speaks mysteries (1 Corinthians 14:2).

You are not talking to men; you are talking to God. And God will understand you because He understands every earthly language ever spoken, as well as the heavenly language of angels.

I want to make sure that you understand up front, that this is *a very sacred subject to the Lord.* Praying in tongues was the primary gift He gave to equip the New Testament Church. It was as if He said to the apostles, "Don't go out and try to represent Me until you receive the power."

"Behold, I send the Promise of My Father upon you; but tarry in the city of Jerusalem until you are endued with power from on high" (Luke 24:49).

Without this power, you will make a mess of things. How can you lead the Church without this spiritual understanding and the power that comes from being baptized in the Holy Spirit?

The early church was established on the power of the Holy Spirit, and it operated that way for the first 300 years, with supernatural success. Then, under the Roman Emperor Constantine, Christianity became the state religion of the Roman Empire. Soon, everyone professed being a Christian. It was the "required" thing to do. Church leadership became a political position held by unsaved men.

Suddenly, the spiritual power of the Church got watered down. The Church lost the power with which it was established: no more healing the sick, casting out demons, or praying in tongues, and it remained nearly powerless until 1600 years later. There were flickers of light in the late 1300s, as John Wycliffe translated the Bible into English – and in the early 1500s, when Martin Luther realized "the just shall live by faith." In the very beginning of the 20th century, a move of God restored the power of the Holy Spirit and tongues back to the Church.

What a mess the church leadership made of it for those 1600 years! The mess occurred because after Constantine, the majority of church leaders went out to represent Jesus; to be His ambassadors, without the power of the Holy Spirit. They couldn't understand the Word of God. They couldn't rightly divide the Word of truth. They taught all kinds of fairy tales and fables. It's amazing that a person could even *find* the Lord in the midst of all of that! It's sad to say, but many didn't. Yet, once we are endowed with power, we can be the ones who come into the full measure of everything we're teaching in this book, and be a true representative of Jesus on the earth today.

GOD NEEDS THOSE WILLING TO PRAY

One of the wonderful things I have discovered is that when you're an intercessor and you take the time to pray; the first thing the Holy Spirit intercedes for through your prayers is *you!* He's never going to leave you out. You're going to receive the first intercession because He's going to pray for you according to the will of God. He's going to pray through your spirit, so all of your needs are going to be covered first. I really liked discovering that. It's good to know!

Then the Holy Spirit's intercession extends to your immediate family and those that you really need to cover with prayer, every single day. From there, it keeps extending out to cover anyone in your sphere of influence. I'm praying for the 21,000 graduates of *Life Christian University*, on five continents around the world, in twenty-four different nations! We have that many graduates out there serving God in the ministry. I'm praying for them an hour or two a day in tongues because I know they're included in the Holy Spirit's intercession.

If you're a pastor or a minister already, and you have a lot of people that you're responsible for, this is so powerful! I can just imagine a person in your church telling their friends, "My pastor prays for me an hour a day in tongues!" Well, maybe not for him or her individually, but the pastor is covering his entire congregation. So yes, they are being covered with an hour of prayer, if their pastor is praying for an hour a day in tongues.

Finally, God is able to extend your prayer out to people that you don't even know. If you're in the Spirit and He's in you and you're yielded, the Lord will make sure you're praying for that need.

One night, four or five months ago, the Lord gave me a strong prompting to get up to pray. At that time, I had become accustomed to praying between one and six o'clock in the morning (and often, that whole time). But this one night when Jesus woke me up, I was just exhausted. I was ready to go back to sleep but I knew the Lord wanted me to pray. I said, "Lord, really? I'm exhausted. Is there any way I can get out of this?"

What the Lord said next got my complete attention; in fact, it rattled me! He said, "I don't have anybody else who will pray right now." I thought, "Could it be – even if it's only for this ten-minute period of time – that I'm the only person on the planet that the Lord can actually prompt to intercede and pray for this situation? It might be for someone on the other side of the world; someone I don't even know. It might be a life-or-death situation. Maybe it's a believer with an important assignment from God on their lives, and it's crucial to the Lord."

The Lord needs to have an intercessor. He's got to have somebody who's willing to stand in the gap for others; allowing the Holy Spirit to pray through their spirit. This prayer would be the perfect prayer for someone's situation – perhaps to save their lives or maybe to help them make the connection they need for the next part of their assignment. Even if it's only for a five- or ten-minute period of time, you don't want to miss an opportunity when Jesus awakens you and says, "I've got nobody else but you, but you can pray this through if you're willing to pray in tongues now."

HOW AND WHY DO WE PRAY IN TONGUES?

Earlier, we saw that the disciples "began to speak with other tongues, as the Spirit gave them utterance." The Holy Spirit doesn't grab your tongue and make it move. He will give you words to speak – sometimes just a few syllables at a time.

Some people first hear these words in their head; for others, the words just tumble out of their mouths. The Holy Spirit's part is to "give utterance." Your part is to open your mouth, and by faith, speak out the sounds the Holy Spirit gives you, trusting that they will have meaning to God.

You may wonder, "If I can't understand what I'm saying, what good is it? Why do I need to speak or pray in tongues?" Because it helps us pray! Oftentimes, we just don't know how to pray as we should. At those times, the Holy Spirit helps us.

> **Likewise the Spirit also helps in our weaknesses. For we do not know what we should pray for as we ought, but the Spirit Himself makes intercession for us with groanings which cannot be uttered... He makes intercession for the saints according to *the will of* God (Romans 8:26-27).**

Another reason we pray in tongues is because it builds up our faith:

> **But you, dear friends, carefully build yourselves up in this most holy faith by praying in the Holy Spirit (Jude 1:20 MSG).**

How Do I Receive?

You may wonder: How do I receive the gift of praying in tongues? Just ask the Father in prayer!

In Luke 11:9-13, Jesus said:

> **"So I say to you, ask, and it will be given to you; seek, and you will find; knock, and it will be opened to you. For everyone who asks receives, and he who seeks finds, and to him who knocks it will be opened. If a son asks for bread from any**

father among you, will he give him a stone? Or *if he asks* for a fish, will he give him a serpent instead of a fish? Or if he asks for an egg, will he offer him a scorpion? If you then, being evil, know how to give good gifts to your children, how much more will *your* heavenly Father give the Holy Spirit to those who ask Him" (Luke 11:9-13)!

I like how Jesus makes it so simple: just ask and you shall receive! It's a gift. You can't earn it, any more than you can earn salvation. Here is a sample prayer:

Father, thank You for sending Jesus. I believe He died on the cross for me. I believe He rose from the dead. Jesus, thank You for giving me new life. You are my Savior and my Lord.

Father, I ask You now for the gift of the Holy Spirit, to give me the power to live the Christian life, and for a miraculous language to pray to You. I will speak and pray in other tongues as the Holy Spirit gives me the words, in Jesus' name. Amen!

Now, take a deep breath and make a sound. Let the Holy Spirit shape that sound into a prayer to God. It may only be a word or two at first. Keep speaking those few words. It's like when a little child first starts to talk. First, he says, "Mama," or "Daddy," and before long, he's saying whole sentences. Say the few little words the Holy Spirit gives, and soon He will give you more and more.

I was baptized in the Holy Spirit while reading a book by Pat Boone, called *A New Song*. He told how his wife really wanted to be baptized in the Holy Spirit but didn't have anybody to pray for her. She was just calling out to the Lord, saying, "Lord, please baptize me with the Holy Spirit. Even if I don't have anybody to lay hands on me, You can cause the anointing to come on me. I want to pray in the Spirit." And she received the baptism of the Holy Spirit and began to pray in tongues.

As soon as I read that, I got excited. In my naiveté I said, "God, that would be so cool. Could You do that for me?" I started to raise my hands and suddenly, this language that sounded like Russian and Chinese blended together was flooding out of my mouth!

Next, I felt like God had literally picked me up and baptized me in a vat of liquid, *living* love. I was consumed with the love of God. I'd never known that you can *experience* and *feel* the love of God. It was like feeling God come down and wrap His arms around me. I remember saying after that, "Thank God, the search is over. I found the answer to life. I found the truth. I know the love of God now."

As you pray in the Spirit, you will tap more and more into His great love for you and know more and more, all that He has made available to you as a spirit-filled believer.

I should share here, one of the enemy's favorite tricks. As soon as you hear some foreign-sounding words coming into your mind, the enemy immediately places these thoughts in your head: "That just sounds like gibberish or baby talk. I must be making this up."

Well, have you ever made that up before when asking the Father for your heavenly language? Did you ever stop to think that if the Holy Spirit is speaking these sounds to your spirit, and your spirit is now saying them out of your mouth, that it is you speaking? It is the *real* you, your spirit man; the new creation in Christ. Just relax and push the words out. Soon, you will be convinced that you are having an encounter with God.

SECTION ONE:

OLD TESTAMENT PRAYER AND THE MIRACULOUS EXCHANGE

CHAPTER TWO

THE LIMITATIONS OF OLD TESTAMENT PRAYER

We must clarify the significant difference in the way that we pray in the new covenant, as compared with the old covenant way. Under the old covenant, prayer was limited to praying with limited understanding, and according to the Law of Moses. In the Old Testament, God spoke to many people, including the patriarchs and many prophets.

They heard from the Lord about what to pray and how to pray for it, so they saw many miraculous results. But the vast majority of people in the nation of Israel did not know how to pray. And certainly, the vast majority of people in the heathen nations didn't know how to pray. They had false, demonic religions, from the fall of man.

The new covenant obviously followed the old, but the new covenant resolved things the old covenant could not. One of the biggest things it resolved was the mending of the division between God and man.

Let's take a look at how this problem was taken care of by the substitutionary sacrifice of the Lord Jesus Christ, and how God was able to add a supernatural prayer gift to the Body of Christ: the ability to be filled with the Holy Spirit and to pray in tongues, the language of heaven. This limitation of the old covenant had to change. God had to repair the breach that had come between God and man – ever since the first man, Adam.

THEY ATE...AND DIED SPIRITUALLY

Before the fall, the Holy Spirit was in Adam and Eve because God had breathed His breath [or Spirit] into them (Genesis 2:7). Adam and Eve had direct communication with God and would walk and talk with God in the cool of the day. Not only did Adam have the Spirit of God in him from his creation; the Spirit of God filled his soul. He could think the thoughts of God and with perfect intelligence, name every living creature that his Father created.

> **Out of the ground the LORD God formed every beast of the field and every bird of the air; and brought *them* to Adam to see what he would call them. And whatever Adam called each living creature, that *was* its name" (Genesis 2:19).**

Just as God formed Adam out of the ground, God formed millions and millions of creatures out of the ground. Then He brought all the living creatures to Adam, to see what he would call them. Whatever Adam called each living creature; that was its name. That includes every beast of the field, every bird of the air, the fish of the sea, and even every creeping thing, like insects and reptiles. Adam named everything he could see. Do you know that there are 400,000 different types of beetles on the planet? That's a creative God!

The Old Testament said that God's understanding is unsearchable (Isaiah 40:28). But in the New Testament, Paul says that believers have the mind of Christ (1 Corinthians 2:16). We can search God's understanding, just as we are now doing as we explore Holy Spirit-empowered prayer. Even so, we could search for all of eternity and never know everything that God knows. We will always be in school and learning.

I have this theory that once we get to heaven, we're suddenly going to get a download of everything concerning this earth — even quantum physics! Then God will say, "Are you guys ready for what's next?" God is so excited about getting us all to heaven and beginning the next phase.

I believe this will all be birthed from God's human family, from planet Earth. I believe He's going to have the human race fill the entire universe — one that's constantly expanding. I believe He'll explain everything to us then, when our glorified minds can handle it. It will be an amazing thing!

The anointing of God filled Adam's soul and his body and made his intelligence work with a perfect brain. Wouldn't that be a nice thing to have? Scientists say that we probably use only between five and ten percent of our brain. What if we could use all of it?

God programmed us to be able to be self-sustaining. We don't have to think about *making* our heart beat. We don't have to think about breathing. Our body just does that and keeps us going. Adam and Eve had bodies that would have lived eternally, because the Spirit of God dwelled in their bodies. They were sinless and were a suitable habitation where the Holy Spirit of God was comfortable dwelling. But everything changed when they sinned. The Holy Spirit departed from them and mankind was separated from God.

God had told Adam:

"...but of the tree of the knowledge of good and evil you shall not eat, for in the day that you eat of it you shall surely die" (Genesis 2:17).

God told Adam this *before* He took Eve out of Adam's body and fashioned her to be the exact, perfect complement to him. *Eve was not there in bodily form to hear God's instructions about the tree, and she misunderstood*, when Satan asked her (Genesis 3:1):

"Has God indeed said, 'You shall not eat of every tree of the garden?'"

She answered:

"We may eat the fruit of the trees of the garden; but of the fruit of the tree which *is* in the midst of the garden, God has said, 'You shall not eat it, nor shall you touch it, lest you die'" (Genesis 3:2-3).

Adam and Eve were *supposed* to *touch* the tree: Adam was put in the garden "to tend [cultivate] and keep it" (Genesis 2:15). They were supposed to tend all the trees — including the tree of the knowledge of good and evil – for the Lord. Then the devil lied to Eve, by saying:

"You will not surely die. For God knows that in the day you eat of it your eyes will be opened, and you will be like God, knowing good and evil" (Genesis 3:4-5).

When Satan told Eve, "If you eat it, you're going to be like God," he implied that God had been holding out. Jesus said, "He [Satan] is a liar and the father of it" (John 8:44). Adam and Eve were *already* like God, but they lost being like God once they disobeyed and ate.

So when the woman saw that the tree *was* good for food, that it was pleasant to the eyes, and a tree desirable to make *one* wise, she took of its fruit and ate. She also gave to her husband with her, and he ate. Then the eyes of both of them were opened (Genesis 3:6-7a).

Their eyes were opened to the knowledge of *evil*. They *already* had knowledge of the *good*. Now they knew the evil and were experiencing it – firsthand!

God had told Adam, "in the day that you eat of it you shall surely die." God couldn't lie to Adam, yet we know that Adam and Eve didn't die *physically*. They continued to live; the Bible tells us they were hiding out from God in the garden (Genesis 3:8).

So, what happened? The Bible says that we are made up of three parts: spirit, soul, and body (1 Thessalonians 5:23). You are a *spirit*. That's the real you. You have a soul, and you live in a body. At this point in time, Adam and Eve died *spiritually* and were disconnected from God. That's what spiritual death is: disconnection from God.

The Holy Spirit had resided in their spirits, but when they sinned, He moved out of them. Their spirits were still there, but in a coma-like state. From this point on, Adam and Eve had to deal with life strictly out of their souls. When they were sinless, the glory of God emanated throughout their entire bodies and shined all around them. They had been cloaked in God's glory. They did not have any knowledge of nakedness or shame:

And they were both naked, the man and his wife, and were not ashamed (Genesis 2:25).

But after they sinned, the Holy Spirit no longer covered them. Suddenly, they knew that they were naked. They came up with a solution: they sewed fig leaves together to cover themselves. When God called out, "Adam, where are you?" (Genesis 3:9), they were hiding because they had sinned and felt condemned. They were afraid and ashamed.

HOW GOD REPAIRED THE BREACH

Throughout all eternity, God was one God, manifest in three persons: God the Father, God The Word, and God the Holy Spirit. The most frequently used Hebrew word for "God" throughout the Old Testament, is *Elohim*, which is plural and actually means "Gods." In other words, the Lord is one God, but shows Himself to us as three persons: the Father, The Word, and the Holy Spirit. John 1:1-3 speaks of two of these persons:

In the beginning was the Word, and the Word was with God, and the Word was God. He was in the beginning with God. All things were made through Him, and without Him nothing was made that was made.

God The Word actually created everything by speaking. Of course, Jesus invented our body, so if *anyone* knows how to heal our body, it's Jesus. He will know by the Spirit of God, what's wrong with it. If we are really walking closely with Him and are yielded to Him, we get a constant infusion of healing from the Holy Spirit, as well as wisdom concerning the natural things we need to do to take care of our body.

We all need this wisdom because Satan has waged war against the human race. He has been able to break down our DNA and cause us to have all kinds of health problems. We have all "de-evolved" from where Adam and Eve were, before "the fall."

Even though we're all individually and wonderfully made, God knows whatever it is that our body needs. He can quicken to our knowledge and understanding, the things we need to eat and do. One thing He told me was, "Eat spinach salads as often as you can." I try to do it every day. I see it as a matter of stewardship. God has made us stewards over our bodies, to prolong our health and well-being.

God formed Adam out of the elements of the ground. When the medical scientists first examined the chemical elements that made up the human body, they said, "Wow, those are all the same elements that are in the earth." That's why our bodies need all the nutrients that come out of the earth through the plants that God has given us to eat – to keep these bodies healthy and fueled.

With faith in the Lord Jesus for healing, and wisdom from the Holy Spirit for everything that we need to eat and do, we have everything we need to be able to go our distance and live up to 120 years — if it takes us that long to complete our assignment.

> *NOTE: An in-depth, scriptural study of longevity can be found in my book "Divine Healing & Health."*

To repair the division between God and man, the Father planned that The Word would take on human flesh and become one with the human race. The Word agreed. I look at it as The Word saying:

> *"Father, I'll become one of them. I'll take on human flesh. I'll pay the price for them. I'll live a perfect human life by the power of the Holy Spirit of the Living God. I'll teach them about Your kingdom and about Us, and the glory that We have here."*

> *"I'll let them know they're going to come into the full glory of being in total union, alignment, and agreement with Us. I'll teach them all those things and then I'll die in their place so that You can remove their sin from them and put it all upon Me. As long as You are able to bring Me back to Yourself, I'm willing. I'll go and fulfill Your plan of redemption and bring the human race with Me to heaven."*

Now, of course every human must believe in Jesus and receive the way that God made for us to *come to Him – through Jesus.* Jesus said:

"I am the way, the truth, and the life. No one comes to the Father except through Me" (John 14:6).

God made only one way for every human to come into His family; it was through the Lord Jesus Christ. He came to His own (the Jews), but they did not receive Him (John 1:11). But the Father never planned that redemption was going to be just for the lost sheep of the house of Israel. Jesus knew that this gospel was going to be for all the nations, because that's what God told Abraham: "All the nations of the earth shall be blessed in you" (Genesis 26:4).

It was the faith of Abraham that carried mankind all the way through to what we have today: through Jesus. Anyone can come in – from any race, creed, nation, or tongue – anyone from all over the planet. We're all one race, really – the human race – and everyone is invited into God's kingdom, through Jesus.

John 1:14 says:

And the Word became flesh and dwelt among us, and we beheld His glory, the glory as of the only begotten of the Father, full of grace and truth.

God, The Word, did not become God the Son until He became the Son of Man. That was the moment He was conceived in Mary. Suddenly, one-third of the Godhead was now dwelling on the earth in a human, physical body — 100% God: both the Son of God, and the Son of Man. The Word came into Mary and became the Son, when He took on human flesh. For eternity, it was the Father, *The Word,* and the Holy

Spirit. Now it is the Father, *The Son,* and the Holy Spirit.

The incarnation was an amazing event and Mary was an exceptional young woman. But I have to say this: in one particular church, they have gone too far to deify Mary and teach that she is part of the Godhead. They call her "Queen of Heaven" and "Queen of the Universe." She was a mere girl who would live holy and pure, and who would dedicate her life to the Lord. When God sent Gabriel to tell her about God's plan of redemption, Mary humbly said:

"Behold the maidservant of the Lord! Let it be to me according to your word." And the angel departed from her (Luke 1:38).

Mary was willing. She didn't fully understand, but she was willing because she knew it was God speaking to her through the angel Gabriel.

In the fullness of time, Jesus came to earth, but He was disguised. He was the Son of God, disguised as a mere man. But praise God, Jesus was God in the flesh: 100% man and 100% God at the same time! Jesus was sinless because He did not have the blood of an earthly father. He had the holy blood of His heavenly Father and the blood of His earthly mother. The sin nature is only passed down through the father's lineage ("through Adam"); thus no sin nature was passed on to Jesus:

...through one man [Adam] sin entered the world, and death through sin, and thus death spread to all men... (Romans 5:12).

For God to restore man back into a right relationship with Him, it was necessary to remove mankind's sin nature and each person's individual sins as well. This would be accomplished when God the Son took humankind's place as a substitutionary sacrifice. The old covenant sacrifices only provided the atoning or *covering over* of sin. The Messiah's sacrifice of His own life would completely remove mankind's sin – which is known as *redemption*, not *atonement*.

I can't tell you how many books I've seen that say, "There is healing in the atonement of Jesus." No, Jesus didn't "atone." There was a healing in the atonement of the Old Testament, the atonement on *Yom Kippur*, the Jew's most holy day. That was the day that the priest would take the animal blood from the sin sacrifice for the whole nation of Israel into the Holy of Holies, and sprinkle it upon the mercy seat. That sin sacrifice was an atonement for the *Jewish* people to be blessed for a whole year.

In our course "The Tabernacles of God," you will find out that there were many different offerings that the Jewish people were required to make, and they received great blessing from doing each of those. This annual sin offering was the most important, because it atoned for any sin offering they might have forgotten to make throughout the year. It removed any curse attached to any offerings they might have missed.

In the new covenant, Jesus' *redemption* is so much better than the *atonement*, which was an annual thing. The *Lord's* redemption was once and for all. Jesus paid the price *once* for all of mankind's sin, for all time. Once a person is born again, no price ever has to be paid again. Jesus *never* has to come back to pay the price for mankind's sin again – not annually, not every thousand years — never! Jesus did it once, and once was a complete redemption for all of mankind.

> **For God made the only one who did not know sin to become sin for us, so that we might become the righteousness of God through our union with him (2 Corinthians 5:21 TPT).**

I like the way *The Passion Translation* says it; pointing

out it's through our *union* with Jesus. Because we're joined with Him, we are completely covered by His sin sacrifice. This is called "the miraculous exchange." Jesus exchanged His righteousness for our sinfulness; He superimposed His righteousness upon us. We became the very righteousness of God, in Christ. In other words, we are the demonstration of what Jesus, the righteousness of God, purchased.

He redeemed our life. Now our life should be a shining light in the darkness, demonstrating what it is to know God and to be redeemed from the kingdom of darkness. We are to "come out from among them and be separate" (2 Corinthians 6:17).

It's not that we're judging other people and looking down on them. It's that we don't want to be partakers of all of the things they do out of ignorance; not knowing there's no blessing in doing those things. It's just the way man – inspired by the devil – tries to escape his problems with drugs, alcohol, or any number of other sins.

WE NEED A NEW NATURE

The reality is that until you're born again, you don't know what it's like to have your conscience washed from the stain of guilt. When I got saved, I didn't realize that I had been a sinner. I started reading the stories of Jesus in the Bible, and I felt so happy. I was thinking, "How cool would it have been to walk with Jesus and watch Him heal all those people, and see all those miracles happen?" I was so enamored with everything He was doing.

I read straight through the Gospels. Then I got to John 16:33, where Jesus said:

"In the world you will have tribulation; but be of good cheer, I have overcome the world."

Right after I read those words, Jesus spoke to me saying, "Doug, I'm alive and I'm the Lord." After reading that much of the Bible, I knew what to do. I got on my knees and prayed. I didn't know how to do an official prayer. I simply said, "Jesus, can You just come into my life and take over?" I had not read the instructions that say to pray:

"Jesus, I believe You are Lord. I believe God raised You from the dead."

I simply prayed from my heart.

It was a couple of weeks before I realized why I had been separated from God; it was because I was a sinner! All the things I had been doing kept me separated from God. I did those sinful things because that was my *nature.* When I was born again, I got a *new* nature, a nature that God planted into my heart; the nature of righteousness. That's because He made me the righteousness of God through my union with Jesus.

In this great exchange, we absorbed His righteousness as He took on our sinfulness. Of course, Jesus was able to jettison the sinfulness and get rid of it by nailing it to the cross. Then He was raised from the dead and restored back into total communion with the Father and the Holy Spirit. This miraculous exchange perfectly fulfilled Isaiah's prophecy:

He was wounded [pierced through] for our transgressions [sins of revolt or rebellion against God, the same way Satan did; our sin nature] and bruised [crushed] for our iniquities [sins of perversion, departing from the good plan of God for mankind; our personal sins] (Isaiah 53:5a AUTHOR EXPANSION**).**

Jesus was pierced through for our transgressions.

36

"Transgressions" is a different Hebrew word: *peša'* [Strong's H6588], the Hebrew word for individual, personal sins. Transgression is the sin of revolt or rebellion against God.

Because of the sin nature that we got from Adam, we sided with Satan and rebelled against God's kingdom. That's what Adam did; he rebelled against God's Word. God said, "Don't eat of that tree." Adam ate it anyway and died spiritually. The same sin nature that Satan had was absorbed by Adam and Eve. Adam passed it on to everyone in the human race. We need to be delivered from that sin nature, as well as our individual sins.

Isaiah continued to prophesy that Jesus would be "bruised" or "crushed." We know His physical body was crushed with the terrible beatings from the Roman soldiers, just before His crucifixion. Isaiah specifies that Jesus was crushed "for our iniquities," our personal sins of perversion. We perverted God's holy plan for the human race.

If we could have been born again at the moment we took our first breath, we would have grown up always knowing God. We would have always chosen to walk away from sin. We would have been just like Adam was at the very beginning, but we didn't have that option. Sin was infused into our DNA. We yielded to our sin nature and perverted the perfect plan of God.

A NATURE OF RIGHTEOUSNESS

As soon as we are born again, we receive a new nature, the nature of righteousness. However, it often takes awhile to recognize our own personal sins. It took me another week before I discovered that drugs and alcohol don't mix with being a Christian. I asked the Lord to take it away from me, and He delivered me from a spirit of drug addiction and alcoholism. I got the One-step program. I partially believe in the Twelve-step program; I just like the One-step program better! Suddenly, in a dramatic deliverance, I was done with all my addictions.

Then, a week later, I was baptized in the Holy Spirit while reading *A New Song*, by Pat Boone. Once I was baptized in the Holy Spirit, the epistles started to make more sense to me. I began to realize, "Man, it was my sin that separated me from God, and that's what the Lord removed from me. That's why I know Him now. That's why Jesus can talk to me so clearly."

I didn't realize then that eventually, the Father and the Holy Spirit would also start talking to me. I started recognizing all the ways God speaks to us. When the Father speaks to you in your spirit, it's commanding and arresting. Other times, you'll know it's the Holy Spirit speaking to you and not Jesus or the Father. Sometimes, you realize it's your own spirit speaking to you. Your spirit is redeemed, and the Holy Spirit dwells in there, so your own spirit can speak to you.

You may say, "Well, it sounds just like me." Well yeah, it *is* you; the *real* you. It's the "you" that was recreated from a coma-like state, when you made the decision to accept Jesus as your Lord. The Holy Spirit washed your spirit clean and moved in. Now you have this consciousness of the presence of the Holy Spirit.

When we get born again, we don't have to repent of each of our personal sins, which is a good thing! God told me, "You couldn't have *remembered* all of those sins." I knew that I had walked away from my past life and I wasn't going to go back into it. The whole point of the redemption that the Lord provides for us is to give us *the power* to come out from the world and be separate from them. I *knew* I was empowered by the Holy Spirit because I could pray in tongues.

Because of my contracts, it took me six months before I could stop playing drums in the nightclubs. During that time, I witnessed to a lot of drunks! Back then, you could still smoke in nightclubs, so all my clothes and my hair smelled like smoke. It got to where I just didn't want to be in a place where I came out smelling like the bottom of an ashtray.

To give up my music career was kind of like cutting off my arm, but I knew I had to pull away from the music industry and the whole world of entertainment. Then, within a year's time, the Lord gave music back to me, but now I was part of a Christian band; I got to do evangelism with my music! I love how God always restores the things He gives you as a gift.

Section Two:

The New Covenant Begins

CHAPTER THREE

THE HOLY SPIRIT
AND THE MESSIAH

We have been looking at how God prepared the way for Holy Spirit-empowered prayer by removing the limitations of Old Testament prayer. We have seen how God the Father repaired the breech by making us righteous through our union with Jesus, the Son. When God began the new covenant, the Holy Spirit became increasingly active.

Here we will be focusing on the ministry of the Holy Spirit: His presence on earth, His ministry throughout the life of the Messiah, and His role in the new birth. Then we will take an in-depth look at the anointing of the Holy Spirit in Scripture, as well as the power the anointing gives to us today – the Church. First, I'd like to clear up a misconception that some folks have concerning *when* the Holy Spirit came to earth. This misconception resulted from what Jesus proclaimed in John 7:38-39:

> **"He who believes in Me, as the Scripture has said, out of his heart will flow rivers of living water." But this He spoke concerning the Spirit, whom those believing in Him would receive; for the Holy Spirit was not yet *given*, because Jesus was not yet glorified.**

Some take this Scripture to mean that the Holy Spirit was not on earth before Jesus was resurrected. Others say that the Holy Spirit wasn't here before the Day of Pentecost. Yet, while ministering on earth, Jesus did miracles by the power of the Holy Spirit, and His disciples performed miracles in His name, by the power of the Holy Spirit. Every old covenant miracle happened by the power of the Holy Spirit. How then, can anyone believe the Holy Spirit was not on the earth during that time? The Holy Spirit has always been here. And after the resurrection of Jesus, the Holy Spirit "was given" in a new way, which resulted in the new birth.

THE ANOINTING WITHOUT MEASURE

Most Bible scholars understand and expound on the fact that the Spirit of God is omnipotent (all-powerful), omniscient (all-knowing), and omnipresent (present everywhere throughout the created universe and the kingdom of heaven at the same time). So, the Holy Spirit was here. He is always here. He will always be here. Where could the omnipresent Holy Spirit of God go to *not* be here? In other words, if He is everywhere already, where else could He go? Also, there isn't any place we can go that the Holy Spirit is not already there. It's impossible!

David wrote in Psalm 139:7,11 (TPT):

Where could I go from your Spirit? Where could I run and hide from your face? ...It's impossible to disappear from you or to ask the darkness to hide me, for your presence is everywhere, bringing light into my night.

For the most part, David wanted that spiritual illumination, but there was a time he fell and wanted to hide from the Lord. David had done things worthy of execution, under the Law of Moses: adultery with Bathsheba; then sending Bathsheba's husband Uriah into the war to be killed. That's the same as murder. But David was a man after God's own heart, and he repented before the Lord. And in the graciousness of God, He forgave him.

David understood, even in Old Testament times, that the presence of God – through the Holy Spirit – was everywhere; we cannot escape the presence of the Holy Spirit and His light that illuminates our darkness.

The Holy Spirit moved throughout the life of Jesus the Messiah. Jesus, the Son of God and the Son of Man, had the Holy Spirit in His human spirit since His inception. Jesus, being both God in the flesh and man at the same time, obviously had the Holy Spirit in Him while He grew up in the house of Joseph and Mary. Growing up as the sinless Son of God, Jesus heard from the Father. By the time He was twelve, He knew He was the Messiah, the Anointed One...but He didn't yet have that anointing.

The *Apocrypha* is a volume of additional writings from biblical times that was *not* canonized as Scripture. There are stories in the *Apocrypha* that tell tales of Jesus healing birds and people, when He was a little boy. But we will see that as a priest of God under the old covenant, Jesus did not go into the ministry or work any miracles until *after* He was baptized in water, and the anointing of the Holy Spirit came upon Him without measure. So, don't believe those *Apocrypha* stories!

OLD AND NEW TESTAMENT BAPTISM

Before we look at the baptism of Jesus, we're going to see what baptism meant in the Old Testament.

Remember how Adam was anointed by God to name all the animals? Others in the Old Testament were also anointed for their specific position of service to the Lord: the priests (including Aaron, his sons, and on throughout the generations), plus all the prophets.

God had His prophets anoint many of the kings, including King Saul, King David, and King Solomon. God anointed musicians to "prophesy on their instruments," for example, the sons of Asaph. God also anointed the craftsmen Bezalel and Aholiab, who built the Tabernacle of Moses, to "know how to do all manner of work" (Exodus 36:1).

Under the Law of Moses, baptism was used to *publicly show that a person was stepping into their ministry.* They were being set apart. Baptism was important in God's scheme of things, and Jesus would not have violated God's purpose in this.

We see that Moses washed Aaron and his sons for their priestly office:

And the congregation was gathered together at the door of the tabernacle of meeting. And Moses said to the congregation, "This is what the Lord commanded to be done." Then Moses brought Aaron and his sons and washed them with water (Leviticus 8:4b-6)

Just as Moses washed Aaron and Aaron's sons with water at the door of the Tabernacle before they began to minister as priests; so Jesus was baptized in water by John, at the beginning of His priestly ministry. Jesus is now our High Priest, who took His own blood into the mercy of seat in heaven, and He is actually that mercy seat, Himself.

So Christ has now become the High Priest over all the good things that have come. He has entered that greater, more perfect Tabernacle in heaven, which was not made by human hands and is not part of this created world. With his own blood – not the blood of goats and calves – he entered the

Most Holy Place once for all time and secured our redemption forever (Hebrews 9:11-12 NLT).

As New Testament believers, we are baptized in water *for the remission of sin.*

Then Peter said to them, "Repent, and let every one of you be baptized in the name of Jesus Christ for the remission of sins; and you shall receive the gift of the Holy Spirit" (Acts 2:38).

The Apostle Paul tells us that Jesus' baptism in water is also a vivid picture for all of us. When we're baptized in water, it signifies being co-crucified with Jesus Christ and then co-raised again with Him, to newness of life.

Therefore we were buried with Him through baptism into death, that just as Christ was raised from the dead by the glory of the Father, even so we also should walk in newness of life (Romans 6:4).

Baptism in water is important. I was baptized in water a year after I was saved and baptized in the Holy Spirit. I had already started in ministry by then. (I didn't really *know* I was in the ministry, but we were out getting lots of people saved, so it was ministry.) Our associate pastor had taken the College and Career group to Fort De Soto Park, on the Gulf of Mexico, for the day. He suddenly asked, "Hey, has anyone here not been baptized in water?" I said, "I haven't," so he baptized me in water.

Since the Gulf of Mexico is the sea, I joke about it, saying, "I got to bury the old man in the sea." I was already a new creation in Christ Jesus, but I wanted to go through the sacred ordinance of baptism. It is important that we make this public declaration of our faith.

Jesus greatly admired John the Baptist. This is what He

said about John, in Matthew 11:11b:

"Assuredly, I say to you, among those born of women there has not risen one greater than John the Baptist."

In other words, no Old Testament prophet was greater than John the Baptist. *Jesus was still ministering under the old covenant, while at the same time, He was ushering in the new covenant.* Of course, Jesus is the greatest of all Old Testament prophets, and the greatest of all New Testament prophets! But John was the one chosen to introduce the world to Jesus the Messiah, and to prepare the way for Him.

THE HOLY SPIRIT DESCENDS AND REMAINS

While the priests, prophets, kings, musicians, and craftsmen were anointed by God for their specific tasks; Daniel predicted the coming of the Messiah, the "Anointed One." Many other Old Testament prophets made predictions concerning Him, including David, Isaiah, and Zechariah, but it was John the Baptist who got to say, "Here He is!"

The next day John saw Jesus coming toward him, and said, "Behold! The Lamb of God who takes away the sin of the world!" (John 1:29).

John was also the one chosen to baptize Jesus in water.

Then Jesus came from Galilee to John at the Jordan to be baptized by him. And John *tried to* prevent Him, saying, "I need to be baptized by You, and are You coming to me?" But Jesus answered and said to him, "Permit *it to be so* now, for thus it is fitting for us to fulfill all righteousness." Then he allowed Him (Matthew 3:13-15).

At first, John resisted baptizing Jesus, saying, "No, You should be baptizing me!" But Jesus talked John into doing it because of the Old Testament tradition concerning those stepping into ministry...and because Jesus knew what was getting ready to happen!

The Apostle John quotes John the Baptist, in John 1:32:

And John bore witness, saying, "I saw the Spirit descending from heaven like a dove, and He remained upon Him."

Now, "the Spirit descending...like a dove" is referring to the way the Holy Spirit descended; it looked like the way you'd see a dove landing. John didn't say that a bird descended on Jesus and John didn't say that the Holy Spirit was a bird. No, he said that the Holy Spirit descended *like* a dove. The anointing without measure came upon Jesus, and John was able to see it physically.

Luke gives us additional information about what happened at that moment:

Jesus also was baptized; and while He prayed, the heaven was opened. And the Holy Spirit descended in bodily form like a dove upon Him, and a voice came from heaven which said, "You are My beloved Son; in You I am well pleased" (Luke 3:21b-22).

After Jesus came up from the water, He prayed. Then the Holy Spirit descended and the Father spoke words of affirmation to Jesus, confirming Him. John the Baptist got to witness all of this.

As the days passed, John received other important revelations concerning Jesus. We will examine two of John's insights: that God anointed Jesus with the Holy Spirit "without measure" (John 3:34), and that Jesus would baptize us "with the Holy Spirit and fire" (Matthew 3:11). What Jesus said about John should cause us to closely examine these revelations!

After this, John's assignment was pretty much done. John was the one sent to prepare the way for Jesus' ministry. As Jesus stepped into His ministry, John completed his own assignment. John the Baptist said in John 3:27,30:

"A man can receive nothing unless it has been given to him from heaven...He [Jesus] must increase, but I *must* decrease."

Soon after this, John was imprisoned, then beheaded by Herod. John had already earned all the rewards for his high-level assignment; rewards he will have for all eternity. John had finished his race and there was no reason for him to have to remain here.

Of course, Jesus was upset when He found out that Herod had beheaded John. Jesus wanted to get away. He wanted to be alone with His heavenly Father. But then a great multitude of people came, following Him. Jesus was moved with compassion for them and healed every single one of them. That was a sharp stick in the eye of the devil – Jesus' "payback" to Satan for having John the Baptist killed.

A profound observation is found in John 3:34:

For He whom God has sent speaks the words of God, for God does not give the Spirit by measure.

In the Amplified, this verse says:

For He whom God has sent speaks the words of God [proclaiming the Father's own message]; for God gives the [gift of the] Spirit without measure [generously and boundlessly] (AMP)!

In other words, God gave the Holy Spirit and placed His anointing upon Jesus without limit. Some Bible scholars miss the significance of God giving Jesus the Holy Spirit without measure. They read it and shrug as if to say, "Whatever!" But the Lord pointed out to me that this means that God gave Jesus the *fullest* manifestation of the presence of the Holy Spirit that any human being could *ever* have upon his life. Wow!

The Holy Spirit rested on Jesus the entire time He was in ministry until His death on the cross. At that time, Jesus was separated from the Father and the Holy Spirit. We know Jesus could not have died physically until He was separated from God the Father, and God the Holy Spirit, because Jesus was personally sinless. Even a Roman crucifixion would not have killed Him. Jesus was immortal. Until He became sin for us, He could not receive the "wages of sin," which is death (Romans 6:23).

When Jesus became sin for us, that meant the Father and the Holy Spirit could not fellowship with Him. They could not even look at Him. Jesus knew ahead of time, that when He became sin, the Father and the Holy Spirit would leave Him. But on the cross, He experienced such a deep anguish in His soul, that He cried out:

"Eli, Eli, lama sabachthani" (Matthew 27:46)?

That is:

"My God, My God, why have You forsaken Me?"

Why did Jesus repeat Himself? I believe He was saying, "My God, *Father*, My God, *Holy Spirit*, why have You *both* left Me?" Jesus knew He was going to physically die and be separated from the Father and the Holy Spirit, for a period of time. He foretold this in Matthew 12:40:

For as Jonah was three days and three nights in

the belly of the great fish, so will the Son of Man be three days and three nights in the heart of the earth.

VICTORY OVER DEATH THROUGH THE POWER OF THE HOLY SPIRIT

The fact that Jesus was raised from the dead is the most foundational doctrine of Christianity. Peter summed it all up in a short sermon, on the Day of Pentecost.

"But God knew what would happen, and his prearranged plan was carried out when Jesus was betrayed. With the help of lawless Gentiles, you nailed him to a cross and killed him. But God released him from the horrors of death and raised him back to life, for death could not keep him in its grip. King David said this about him:...'For you will not leave my soul among the dead or allow your Holy One to rot in the grave.'...David was looking into the future and speaking of the Messiah's resurrection. He was saying that God would not leave him among the dead or allow his body to rot in the grave..."God raised Jesus from the dead, and we are all witnesses of this" (Acts 2:23-25,27,31-32 NLT).

Jesus went to hell, but He didn't stay long. He didn't have to stay in the depths of hell – to be burned, branded, poked, and stabbed by the devil and all his demons – to pay the penalty for every single sin of every human being. No, Jesus had already suffered the worst thing He could ever suffer for us when He was separated from the presence of the Father and the Holy Spirit.

I think Jesus' visit to hell was more like this: Jesus' body died, and His spirit was descending into hell. Satan was down there already, celebrating with all the fallen angels and demon spirits. It's kind of like they were watching an elevator as Jesus descended. They were cheering and shouting, "We won! We killed the Son of God! We beat Him!"

Jesus reached the bottom, and the elevator door opened up. The devil was standing there, ready to grab Jesus. Suddenly, Jesus' foot shot out of the opening of the elevator door; delivering a powerful "karate kick" to Satan's forehead. This should not have taken Satan by surprise, because God the Father had prophesied this exact event to him in the Garden of Eden, right after he had deceived Eve:

"And I will put enmity (open hostility) Between you and the woman, And between your seed (offspring) and her Seed; He shall [fatally] bruise your head, And you shall [only] bruise His heel" (Genesis 3:15 AMP).

Several translations say:

"He will crush your head, and you will bruise his heel."

I'm sure Eve was comforted knowing that one of her offspring would one day settle the score. He would kick Satan in the head and defeat him. Jesus suffered a bruise on His heel, but Satan suffered a crushing blow to the head. Let's look at Scripture:

Then Jesus made a public spectacle of all the powers and principalities of darkness, stripping away from them every weapon and all their spiritual authority and power to accuse us. And by the power of the cross, Jesus

led them around as prisoners in a procession of triumph. *He was not their prisoner; they were his!* (Colossians 2:15 TPT)

This is an amazing picture! It was a custom in Rome to have a procession of triumph, where the victorious Roman general took the defeated enemy's king, generals, and any other prisoners of war, and paraded them in the streets – chained up and shamed, in front of everybody.

In the same way, Jesus chained up the devil and all of the fallen angels and demon spirits, and paraded them around the heavenlies in front of the Father, the Holy Spirit, and the holy angels. Jesus led the defeated forces of evil in His procession of triumph; displaying them, shaming them, and proving they were completely defeated.

After His procession of triumph, Jesus came back to earth and picked up His earthly and now glorified body. Then He appeared to Mary outside the tomb. At first, she thought He was the gardener, but as soon as she realized it was Jesus, she must have tried to hold onto Him, because He said:

"Do not cling to Me, for I have not yet ascended to My Father; but go to My brethren and say to them, 'I am ascending to My Father and your Father, and *to* **My God and your God'"** (John 20:17).

What Jesus told Mary was unheard of! At that time, no Jew ever thought of God *(Yahweh)* as their father. Jesus said, "God is My Father; and now He's your Father. He's My God; and now He's your God." Jesus told Mary to tell this to the disciples, to bring them into the knowledge and understanding of this new relationship.

Next, Jesus went back to heaven again and presented His blood on the mercy seat, before the Father.* Then, that same evening, He appeared to His disciples and breathed upon them. They were born again and a whole new chapter of human life began!

What follows in italics are theological correction side notes.

When Jesus appeared before the Father in heaven, as High Priest for mankind, He didn't go sprinkling His own blood upon the mercy seat. He was the mercy seat. He just showed up with His blood, back in His glorified body. Some people say that Jesus only has flesh and bone, with no blood in His glorified body. No, He is not flesh and bone only; He is flesh, blood, and bone. The life of the flesh is in the blood. That's in the Word of God (Leviticus 17:11 AMP). So, His resurrected body had blood returned to it.

As a matter of fact, bone and flesh are something that goes all the way back to Adam and Eve, just in reference to a physical body. When Adam first saw Eve, he said, "...bone of my bones And flesh of my flesh" (Genesis 2:23 AMP).

Eve was also alive with the blood running through her body; coursing through her veins, pumped by her heart. So, the life of the flesh is always in the blood. You take the blood out of the body, and the body dies. Even in Jesus' glorified body, He retained the blueprint of being flesh, blood, and bone.

THE ANOINTING WITHOUT MEASURE COMES TO THE CHURCH

Once Jesus took His place on His throne in heaven, He no longer needed the anointing without measure, so He was able to release it to the Church. That anointing is what came upon the 120 in the upper room on the Day of Pentecost.

That anointing is demonstrated by the ability to pray in

tongues, so if you have been baptized in the Holy Spirit and you pray in tongues, you have received that anointing. We don't have the *full measure* of what was on Jesus, but we have a *portion* of the anointing without measure, and that anointing without measure can constantly increase in our lives.

The more you and I pray in tongues, the more we study the Word, the more we walk in obedience to the Lord, and the more we come out from among the lost world, the more we're being refined; like silver and gold, by the holy fire burning on the inside of us, when we pray in tongues. Then, more of that anointing without measure can come upon us and the power of God can do more and more through us than we've ever imagined!

SECTION THREE:

UNDERSTANDING THE ANOINTING

CHAPTER FOUR

THE HOLY SPIRIT
AND THE NEW BIRTH

There is a great deal of difference between the *omnipresence* of the Holy Spirit (where He is everywhere), and the *manifest* presence of the Holy Spirit (when He brings or creates a concentration of His presence and power to one place). The Holy Spirit could still be omnipresent throughout all of heaven and the whole created universe, while also coming upon the Lord Jesus and remaining on Him in a manifest presence without measure.

As we have learned, the *manifest presence* was resting completely upon Jesus, which made Him the Messiah or Christ (meaning "the Anointed One"). The word "Messiah" comes from the Hebrew language, while "Christ" is from the Greek. Both of those terms refer to Jesus as the "Anointed One." It was prophesied throughout the entire Old Testament that there was one coming who would be called the "Anointed One," the "Messiah." And as we know, Jesus was that Anointed One who had the anointing of the Holy Spirit without measure.

This unlimited anointing rested upon Jesus the entire time He was in ministry until His death on the cross. Then it came back upon Him again when He was raised from the dead by the Holy Spirit. This anointing was an *earthly* anointing that came upon Him while He was here, in order to be our Messiah, our Anointed One; our Christ. This earthly anointing enabled Him to fulfill everything God asked Him to do in His ministry.

In Acts 10:38, we read:

"how God anointed Jesus of Nazareth with the Holy Spirit and with power, who went about doing good and healing all who were oppressed by the devil, for God was with Him."

Jesus was constantly listening for the Father's marching orders and doing everything God showed Him to do. All of the ministry that Jesus did was directed by the Father in heaven, Who gave Jesus the Holy Spirit *with the power of the anointing* to do the work through Him.

Jesus had previously told His disciples in John 16:7:

"Nevertheless I tell you the truth. It is to your advantage that I go away; for if I do not go away, the Helper will not come to you; but if I depart, I will send Him to you."

If Jesus had not gone away, the anointing without measure would have remained on Him alone, but the Father's plan was always to give the anointing without measure to the Church, the Lord's body on the earth. While Jesus is the head in heaven, His body is here on the earth, and that body needs that same anointing.

Jesus ascended to heaven and has regained His original place at the seat of the right hand of the Father, as King of Kings and Lord of Lords – the highest, most glorified position ever, because of His great conquest over the devil, for all mankind. From His exalted throne, He ever lives to make intercession for us (Hebrews 7:25). Once Jesus took His seat at the right hand of the Father, He released the anointing without measure.

We have seen that the Holy Spirit is omnipresent and He was obviously on the earth throughout the entire time of creation and the time of mankind. He is the power source of the Godhead and accomplished the miracles of Jesus and of His disciples. Now, let's take a deeper look at John 7:39, where John said:

...for the Holy Spirit was not yet *given*, because Jesus was not yet glorified.

I believe that John is telling us here that the Holy Spirit had not been given to man *for the purpose of the new birth*, until Jesus was raised from the dead and given His glorified body. However, once Jesus was in His glorified body, the Holy Spirit *could* come and inhabit the spirits of anyone who believed in Jesus – those whose sins had been forgiven and removed.

Jesus prepared His disciples for this indwelling in John 14:16-17, where He told them that the Holy Spirit, who currently dwelt *with* them, would soon be *in* them.

"And I will pray the Father, and He will give you another Helper, that He may abide with you forever – the Spirit of truth, whom the world cannot receive, because it neither sees Him nor knows Him; but you know Him, for He dwells with you and will be in you."

JESUS GLORIFIED

On the evening of the Resurrection, Jesus appeared to ten of His closest disciples. (Judas had hanged himself and Thomas was not with the others.) John 20:19-20 tells what happened. Let's look at this passage in detail.

Then, the same day at evening, being the first *day* of the week, when the doors were shut where the disciples were assembled, for fear of the Jews, Jesus came and stood in the midst, and said to them, "Peace *be* with you." When He had said this, He showed them *His* hands and His side.

The disciples were in a room with the doors and windows locked. They were afraid the Jews would come and arrest them and kill them as well. Suddenly, Jesus walked into the room in His glorified body. (That tells us that a glorified body can walk through walls, doors, or windows! How cool is that?)

Jesus had repeatedly told the disciples that He was going to be crucified and then raised from the dead, but they couldn't figure out what He meant. They just thought it was another one of His parables. Suddenly, Jesus was there with them!

Luke 24:36-39a says:

...Jesus Himself stood in the midst of them, and said to them, "Peace to you." But they were terrified and frightened, and supposed they had seen a spirit. And He said to them, "Why are you troubled? And why do doubts arise in your hearts? Behold My hands and My feet, that it is I Myself."

At first, the disciples thought they were seeing a ghost! Then Jesus showed them the wounds in His hands, His feet, and His side. They saw the evidence that this really was Jesus, the One whom they had all witnessed being crucified.

John 20:20b tells us:

Then the disciples were glad when they saw the Lord.

Why were they glad? They were glad because they

realized that Jesus was back! When He showed them His wounds, they believed it was really Him. I'm sure they did some serious rejoicing!

It's interesting that at first, the disciples didn't recognize Jesus. That tells me He must have looked different. Remember, Mary didn't recognize Jesus when she first saw Him in His glorified body. We don't know *why* we change in our looks when we have a glorified body, but that's good news for us: we're all going to be perfect!

Our glorified bodies are not going to have any evidence of suffering: no wounds, scars, genetic limitations, or even wrinkles! In fact, Jesus is the only one in heaven with a glorified body, who will have scars; He still has the nail prints in His wrists and in His feet and the wound in His side.

Glorified bodies are perfect bodies, the way God originally designed for a human body to be, without the de-evolution in our DNA that happened from the time of Adam's sin, all the way down to where we are today. We're nowhere close to what Adam and Eve were like when they were first created.

Once we are in heaven, we will go back to being like them – in our glorified bodies. We will all be unique and individual, but we'll still be perfect: perfectly beautiful, perfectly powerful, perfectly healthy in every way, and perfectly happy and full of joy. Glory to God!

After Jesus' resurrection, He revealed Himself over a period of forty days, to a lot of different people, including five hundred believers at one time. The Apostle Paul, having researched the testimony of eyewitnesses of Jesus' resurrection, states:

and that He was seen by Cephas [Peter], then by the twelve. After that He was seen by over five hundred brethren at once, of whom the greater part remain to the present, but some have fallen

asleep. After that He was seen by James, then by all the apostles (1 Corinthians 15:5-7).

NOTE: What follows in italics are theological correction side notes.

Some Bible teachers believe that the disciples chose Matthias to replace Judas, but God chose the Apostle Paul. We don't know that God chose Paul to be an apostle of the Lamb. We do know that they prayed when they were all in one accord – waiting. Jesus told them to wait for the promise of the Spirit of God, the promise of the Father.

In Acts 1:21-22, Peter said it must be somebody that was with us from the time that Jesus was baptized in the River Jordan, all the way until His ascension to heaven. It turns out that Matthias was one of them. Some people say, "You never see his name mentioned in the Bible." Neither do you see the names of six other of the apostles ever mentioned again anywhere in the New Testament, after Acts 1:13. There's no proof that Matthias wasn't chosen to be an apostle of the Lamb.

Paul wrote 1 Corinthians between 53 and 56 AD. Paul states here, that most of the 500 brethren who saw the resurrected Jesus were still alive at the writing of his letter, twenty-some years later. There were plenty of eyewitnesses to prove that Jesus rose from the dead!

John tells us what happened next, when the resurrected Jesus appeared to His disciples:

So Jesus said to them again, "Peace to you! As the Father has sent Me, I also send you." And when He had said this, He breathed on *them*, and said to them, "Receive the Holy Spirit" (John 20:21-22).

When Jesus said, "As the Father has sent Me, I also send you," He was commissioning them as apostles or "sent ones." When Jesus said, "Receive the Holy Spirit," they received the Holy Spirit *for the new birth*. The Spirit of God returned to the spirit of man, with those first ten disciples who were born again on that day. Don't you want to ask them when we get to heaven, "What was it like to be the first humans since Adam and Eve, who had the Spirit of God returned to your spirit?"

TWO SCRIPTURAL STEPS TO GAIN SALVATION

The Holy Spirit was able to enter their spirits because they had now fulfilled all that the Apostle Paul would later say *was necessary to do* to gain salvation:

that if you confess with your mouth the Lord Jesus and believe in your heart that God has raised Him from the dead, you will be saved. For with the heart one believes unto righteousness, and with the mouth confession is made unto salvation (Romans 10:9-10).

Why must you confess with your mouth "the Lord Jesus"? Because that's how you "close the deal." A lot of people who go to Christian churches believe in their heart that God raised Jesus from the dead, but they've never closed the deal *by confessing Jesus as Lord*. They've never said:

"Jesus, I take You now as my own personal Lord and Savior and Master of my life."

They've never taken that step. They just believe that God raised Jesus from the dead. But guess what? Satan believes that! All of the fallen angels and all of the demons believe that God raised Jesus from the dead. They were eyewitnesses to His resurrection, but they're not saved and never will be, so just believing that God raised Jesus from the dead is not enough. *You must also confess Him as Lord.* The Apostle Paul talks about the process by which this happens:

For with the heart one believes unto righteousness" (Romans 10:10).

Now, "heart" can either refer to the soul or the spirit, but in most cases, it's the soul. So, how does your soul come to the place of believing that God raised Jesus from the dead? From empirical evidence and illumination: you either heard it or read it.

Suddenly, illumination came, and you believed that Jesus was raised from the dead. *That proved that He was the only way to get to the Father.* Suddenly, you wanted Jesus to be the Lord and Savior of your life. So, there are two scriptural steps to gain salvation:

Step one is believing.

"...with the heart one believes unto righteousness."

The righteousness comes when you believe.

Step two is confessing. The miracle of the new birth happens when you confess Jesus as Lord. That's when God can place the Holy Spirit into your spirit and close the deal. Once you are born again, your spirit is complete. That's why everyone who is born again gets to go to heaven. Their spirit is a new creation in Christ Jesus.

CLOSING THE DEAL WHEN WITNESSING

Whether I'm witnessing to somebody or preaching the gospel, I want to close the deal — have them make a decision to receive Jesus, and confess Him as their Lord. I like witnessing to people who have been in a Christian church and who already believe that God raised Jesus from the dead. They are the easiest ones to get saved. They see from Romans 10:9-10, that first they must believe, but then they also need to confess Jesus as their own personal Lord.

Always go for closing the deal with people, making sure they know and understand that they must *make a decision to receive Jesus as Lord and confess this with their mouth.* Then, if possible, keep walking them all the way through to getting them baptized in the Holy Spirit and empowered so they can be a powerhouse for God.

CHAPTER FIVE

ACCESS TO THE GIFTS OF THE HOLY SPIRIT

There are nine gifts of the Holy Spirit that are given, according to Scripture. At LCU, we have a whole course on spiritual gifts, but here's a brief overview. The nine gifts of the Spirit are listed in 1 Corinthians 12:8-10. For instructional purposes, we can divide these into three groups: the *revelation gifts* (word of wisdom, word of knowledge, discerning of spirits); the *power gifts* (special faith, gifts of healings, working of miracles); and the *utterance gifts* (prophecy, tongues, interpretation of tongues).

In the Old Testament, only seven gifts of the Spirit were available, and Jesus operated in all seven. The other two, tongues and interpretation of tongues, were added to the Church on the Day of Pentecost.

In this chapter, we're going to address the *utterance gifts*. Let me address two questions that some folks might have. First, people ask: "Can *every* Spirit-filled believer speak or pray in tongues?" In several places in the Bible it says, "all were filled with the Spirit." In three places, we are told specifically that they *were* filled with the Holy Spirit and *they spoke in tongues*. This happened in the upper room on the Day of Pentecost (Acts 2:4):

And they were all filled with the Holy Spirit and began to speak with other tongues, as the Spirit gave them utterance.

Acts 10 reports that it also happened at Cornelius' house. First, Peter saw a divine vision concerning the Gentiles, and then, by a divinely-arranged invitation, he travelled to Caesarea. There, Peter preached the gospel to Cornelius, a Roman centurion, who had gathered his relatives and close friends.

While Peter was still speaking these words, the Holy Spirit fell upon all those who heard the word. And those of the circumcision who believed were astonished, as many as came with Peter, because the gift of the Holy Spirit had been poured out on the Gentiles also. For they heard them speak with tongues and magnify God (Acts 10:44-46).

It happened a third time when all spoke in tongues in Ephesus, when Paul first told some disciples about the Holy Spirit, whom they had not yet received:

And when Paul had laid hands on them, the Holy Spirit came upon them, and they spoke with tongues and prophesied (Acts 19:6).

These believers did not have to wait; neither did they have to achieve some degree of holiness before receiving the gift of speaking in tongues. Some were Roman Gentiles, just moments before. There is no record in Scripture where someone did *not* receive the gift of speaking in tongues after they were baptized with the Holy Spirit. And in my experience with helping hundreds of people receive this gift, I would have to say, "Yes, *every* Spirit-filled believer *can* speak in tongues."

Additional proof that those in the Book of Acts who were

baptized in the Holy Spirit immediately prayed in tongues can be found in Acts 8 and 9.

In Acts chapter 8, Phillip, the deacon-turned-evangelist, went down to Samaria and preached the gospel and many people were saved and healed. Peter and John were sent down to Samaria by the apostles, and they prayed for the people to receive the Holy Spirit or be baptized in the Holy Spirit.

When Simon, the former sorcerer who had believed on the Lord as well, saw something about the Holy Spirit coming on the people; he foolishly thought that he could purchase the ability to lay hands on people and help them receive the Holy Spirit, but Peter rebuked him and told him in Acts 8:21:

"You have neither part nor portion in this matter, for your heart is not right in the sight of God."

The Greek word translated "matter" is the word *Logos*, which is usually translated as "utterance" or "saying." The utterance that Simon heard was the people praying in tongues when they received the Holy Spirit baptism.

Also in Acts chapter 9, when Saul – who would later become the Apostle Paul – was prayed for by the prophet Ananias to receive his sight again and be filled with the Holy Spirit, he obviously received both. The Apostle Paul is the one who taught the Church of the Lord Jesus Christ how to operate in the gifts of the Spirit, including praying in tongues, speaking in tongues, and interpreting tongues (1 Corinthians 12 and 14). In addition, he included the statement in Acts 14:18:

"I thank my God I pray in tongues more than you all."

Another question some folks may have is: "Does every Spirit-filled believer have access to *all* the gifts of the Spirit?" This question comes up because 1 Corinthians 12:11 in the

KJV says:

But all these worketh that one and the selfsame Spirit, dividing to every man severally as he will.

Some have taken that to mean that each believer will only get *one or two* of the gifts. More modern translations support my belief that the Holy Spirit can use *any* Spirit-filled believer in *any* gift at *any* time He wants. Let's look at two of these modern translations:

All these gifts have a common origin, but are handed out one by one by the one Spirit of God. He decides who gets what, and when (1 Corinthians 12:11 MSG).

Remember, it is the same Holy Spirit who distributes, activates, and operates these different gifts as he chooses for each believer (1 Corinthians 12:11 TPT).

I like that: "the Holy Spirit distributes, activates, and operates these different gifts." *The Passion Translation* also has this footnote: "Spiritual gifts are given by the Holy Spirit at any time to anyone He chooses" (g 12:11).

It has been said, "Praying in tongues is the gateway to all the other gifts of the Spirit." It is where we all start, and being filled with the Spirit is the gateway into all miracles. Then, we see in 1 Corinthians 14:13 that Paul says:

...let him who speaks in a tongue pray that he may interpret.

Scripture also instructs us to pray for, and desire the spiritual gifts.

Pursue love, and desire spiritual *gifts*, but especially that you may prophesy (1 Corinthians 14:1).

In Mark 11:24, Jesus said,

"Therefore I say to you, whatever things you ask when you pray, believe that you receive *them*, and you will have *them*."

Putting all these verses together, it is clear to me that the Lord has given *every* Spirit-filled believer access to *all* the gifts of the Spirit. He *wants* us to ask for them and then be *willing and available* for Him to activate and operate whichever spiritual gift is necessary at the time.

TONGUES AND INTERPRETATION OF TONGUES

The early church met mostly in homes, and occasionally, in synagogues. In these small, more intimate environments, everyone could easily hear if someone had a tongue and an interpretation of tongues. In home Bible studies and prayer groups today, the same type of environment should exist, making this the better place for the use of those gifts of the Spirit to function together. Unfortunately, large church auditoriums make it more difficult to effectively have those two gifts in manifestation.

However, I remember when I was first saved, we'd be in house meetings or prayer groups, and it was very common to have someone give a tongue and someone else interpret the tongue. This was during the early part of the Charismatic Renewal. I was a member of the premier Charismatic church in Tampa, at the time. We often had tongues and interpretation of tongues during the Sunday morning church services, with 800 members in attendance. Back then, we thought the biblical limit was three messages in tongues, based on 1 Corinthians 14:27:

If anyone speaks in a tongue, *let there b*e two or at the most three, *each* in turn, and let one interpret.

I now understand it's not limited to three tongues and three interpretations of tongues. It's limited to three tongues *before you have an interpretation.* For example, you might have a tongue, another tongue, and then a third tongue. Then you would need to have an interpretation. Verse 28 says:

But if there is no interpreter, let him keep silent in church, and let him speak to himself and to God.

In other words, if there's nobody to interpret in the church service, then stop the tongues. However, anyone who has a tongue and can sense the presence of the Holy Spirit *could* pray that they would be able to interpret their own tongue – *right then!*

I'd like to point out here that it's not the *translation* of tongues; it's not word-for-word of what's been said. It's an *interpretation* based on what the Spirit of God is saying. So, you might have a long tongue and a short interpretation of the tongue, or you might have a short tongue and a long interpretation. It doesn't matter. What's important is getting the gist of what the Holy Spirit was saying, at that moment in time. The Holy Spirit wants to get these encouraging, prophetic messages to the Church.

Praying in Tongues vs Speaking in Tongues

Although the Apostle Paul has a lot to say about using the gifts of tongues and interpretation of tongues in public; for almost all believers, in the last days of the Church, tongues will be more for their personal prayer life than for use in church services. In 1 Corinthians 14:2,13-14, when Paul gave instructions on the use of tongues and interpretation of tongues, he said:

For he who speaks in a tongue does not speak to men but to God, for no one understands *him*; however, in the spirit he speaks mysteries (1 Corinthians 14:2).

When we speak to God, we call that praying, right? So, you could also be totally correct in saying, "For he who *prays* in a tongue does not speak to men but to God, for no one understands him, however in the Spirit he *prays* mysteries."

Whenever you're praying in tongues, you're praying mysteries. The mysteries are being prayed back and forth between you and God. If we continue substituting "praying" for "speaking," verse 13 would correctly say:

Therefore let him who *prays* in a tongue pray that he may interpret.

Verse 14 already makes the substitution, saying:

For if I pray in a tongue, my spirit prays, but my understanding is unfruitful.

I have discovered that you can get your understanding to be fruitful *if you pray for the interpretation!* You can ask for the interpretation of your own prayer language in tongues.

Discovering that I have the ability to interpret a prayer I pray in tongues has made a profound difference in my prayer life! I don't have to know in advance what I need to pray about. I just know I need to pray, so I pray in tongues. Then I pray to interpret what I have prayed in tongues.

This discovery came gradually to me when I started

praying two to three hours at a time. The longer I prayed in tongues, the more it just started sinking in that the Holy Spirit was showing me what I'd been praying about; or more accurately, what the Holy Spirit had been praying through my spirit.

Once I was in that third hour, it became so clear that in the first few hours, I had been pushing back against the kingdom of darkness. Then, I felt like I was praying through for the victory. Finally, I realized what the Holy Spirit was praying through me: I was getting the gist of what the Holy Spirit was saying! When this happened, my *understanding* could come into agreement with what I had prayed in tongues.

That's why you want to interpret your tongues: to get your mind engaged and be in faith. That way, you will know exactly what you and the Holy Spirit are believing God for. Then you will understand it and receive it.

Every gift that God gives us should be approached and considered as a *sacred endowment* from God the Father. We should value it highly and desire to be obedient and yielded to the Lord so that we would freely move in that gift, to minister to others.

PROPHECY: FOR EDIFICATION, EXHORTATION, AND COMFORT

As we can see, if you pray in tongues, you can pray and ask for the gift of interpretation. The initial use of the gifts of tongues and interpretation of tongues was to get believers accustomed to fulfilling their purpose in prophesying in public services. God wanted everyone to be able to prophesy.

Some have said that tongues and interpretation of tongues together is the same thing as a direct prophecy, just as two nickels together equal a dime, and that's true. That's what Paul is saying in 1 Corinthians 14:3-5:

But he who prophesies speaks edification and exhortation and comfort to men. He who speaks in a tongue edifies himself, but he who prophesies edifies the church. I wish you all spoke with tongues, but even more that you prophesied; for he who prophesies *is* greater than he who speaks with tongues, unless indeed he interprets, that the church may receive edification.

So, if you pray in tongues and then interpret your tongues – to God's way of thinking – it's the same as getting a direct prophecy. I need to mention here that these New Testament prophecies do not *necessarily* include *anything* about the future.

When we hear the word "prophecy," we often think of messages that predict the future; perhaps because many Old Testament prophesies did just that. And many modern-day ministers prophesy about when Jesus is coming back or about the future of America. But much of it is "pie in the sky guessing." I don't listen to them.

What we really need to know is that – in the midst of anything – we can fulfill our ministry. Jesus ministered when Israel was occupied by Rome – an evil, godless empire – yet He *never* focused on prophesying about the end of Rome's occupation. He simply fulfilled His ministry in the middle of it.

What about modern-day countries, where the devils are definitely running the country continually, as in communist China or in Muslim nations; anywhere there are godless, anti-Christ governments? Christians there can still fulfill what God has called them to do, by operating through the underground church – sometimes deep underground – but they're still getting it done. In the same way, all of *us* can fulfill *our* ministry, whether the devils are running the government or not, because God is making a way for us.

No, a prophecy doesn't need to include *anything* about

the future. That's done by a *different* spiritual gift: *the word of wisdom*, one of the *revelation* gifts. The *word of wisdom* is a supernatural revelation by the Spirit of God, concerning the divine purpose and plan for the future.

In contrast, *the word of knowledge* is the supernatural revelation by the Holy Spirit, of certain facts in the mind of God: facts about people, places, or things in the past or present, that God releases to someone who is ministering. God still reveals both words of wisdom and words of knowledge today. According to 1 Corinthians 14:3, *New Testament* prophecies are simply for "edification, exhortation, and comfort."

YOU CAN PROPHESY TO YOURSELF

I don't know why this isn't taught more! It seems obvious to me now, that if a believer is able to interpret tongues for public use, there is no reason to think they could not interpret their own private prayer in tongues. This means that every believer can be their own prophet for their own personal life. This is what the Lord had in mind all along! So, "to seek the best gift," as the Apostle Paul instructs us to do, we'd be asking to interpret our tongues and then to be able to prophesy to ourselves. God doesn't want us to *need* to get a word from someone else.

Now, when you're a younger Christian and it's all new to you, it's fine if the Lord *confirms what He has been showing you, with a prophetic word.* That's a way to be guided by the Holy Spirit. But if someone prophesies to you and *it's not* something that the Holy Spirit has already spoken to you, I would just put it on the back burner. Don't jump out and change your life. Don't do anything based on somebody's prophecy to you. That's because God will usually show *you* first and then He will *confirm* it through someone else.

Personal Prophecies Should be a Confirmation

I remember Brother Kenneth E. Hagin, whom I regard as the premier prophet of the 20th century. He said that he very seldom gave out a personal prophecy – even though the Lord quite often revealed things to him about people's lives. So, why wouldn't Brother Hagin prophesy to them? He said, "Because, in many cases, the word of prophecy had to do with a calling on their lives. If I prophesied that call to them and they hadn't already heard it from the Lord, they might have just stepped out *because I said it to them*, rather than knowing they were *called by God*."

Brother Hagin said that often, church members would come to him later and say, "Brother Hagin, I feel like the Lord has been saying this to me." Brother Hagin would say, "You know, God spoke that to me, too. I want to confirm what you have heard. I believe the same thing that you believe about what the Lord's given you for direction for your life and ministry." We have to hear from the Lord *for ourselves*. Never, ever, step out to do anything because someone has prophesied to you, because they can miss it.

When Brother Hagin had a word for someone concerning healing, he would often say, "Now, I've got this word, but I could miss it because I'm human. So, if what I say doesn't bear witness to you right now, just put it on the back burner." Then he would tell them what the Lord said.

When he was ministering, especially under a powerful healing anointing, quite often that prophetic word was something that *propelled* the person into receiving their healing, so Brother Hagin would go ahead and give out *those* personal prophecies. But he wanted folks to know that if they hadn't heard it from the Holy Spirit already, concerning direction from the Lord, to wait until they absolutely *knew* that what they were hearing was indeed the Lord speaking to them.

When we are prompted to pray by the Holy Spirit, we pray until we complete the prayer assignment given to us by Jesus. This is really important, because none of us want to miss an assignment from the Lord – especially a prayer assignment. If you think about it, our most important assignment from God is probably our prayer assignment; because really, we're going to have to pray through *everything* He's given us to do.

We must pray out our assignment day to day, every single day. Prayer becomes the key foundation. This even applies to what we do at church. In Matthew 21:13, Jesus said:

"My house shall be called a house of prayer."

It's important to know and understand that the church should be a house of prayer for us. Praying is what we should be doing in church. That's where we learn to pray: both in the Spirit and with our understanding. Then we pray at home on our own time. We surrender.

We mentioned earlier that when a person prays in tongues, he speaks mysteries to God (1 Corinthians 14:2). A mystery is something that has been hidden, but is now brought out into the light. The mysteries are being prayed back and forth between you and God, but the reality is that God already understands all the mysteries; we're the ones who need understanding. God is not hiding the mysteries *from* us; God is hiding the mysteries *for us to discover*. They are hidden from the devil because he has no way to perceive the truth, since the truth is simply not in him (John 8:44).

When you pray in tongues long enough and interpret your prayers, you will definitely receive a revelation of the mysteries. Everything you get from God as you pray in tongues and interpret is going to be *truth*. You're going to pray *truth*. The mysteries you pray are declaring *truth* over situations. And what you pray is going to come to pass according to the *truth* from heaven that God wants to be manifested on earth. You will find things get better and better in your own life as you start praying the truth, which is God's goodwill that He wants prayed over your life and *through* your life, into the lives of others.

God wants to reveal His mysteries to us because He desires to lead us and safely guide us. He desires to reveal His truths to us, to enhance our faith in His promises. He desires to reveal His great love for us; a love that is beyond anything we could have imagined before.

I've been aware of God's love ever since I was dipped in that "vat of *living* love," when I first prayed in tongues. Now, as I pray in tongues for extended periods, this experience of God's love keeps expanding. It's overwhelming! You'll tap more and more into His great love for you, as you pray in the Spirit and come to know more and more about what is available to you.

SECTION FOUR:

HOLY SPIRIT-GIVEN PRAYER

CHAPTER SIX

THE HOLY SPIRIT COVERS EVERY NEED

It wasn't until I started praying in tongues for prolonged periods, that I really understood that the Holy Spirit is actually praying through our spirit, but He doesn't get a chance to do that *until* we pray in tongues. At that point, we're able to allow this *supernatural* flow that comes from the Father, through Jesus, through the Holy Spirit; then through our spirit, which we pray out of our mouth.

When we pray in tongues, the Holy Spirit prays through our spirit, and He prays every known form of prayer that is available to us. Later on in this book, we will look at ten different forms of prayer that the Lord wants to be able to pray through us.

PRAYING THE PERFECT PRAYER

First, let's explore the idea that the Holy Spirit covers *everything* that we need to pray for, and that He does this *perfectly*. Romans 8:26a says:

Likewise the Spirit also helps us in our weaknesses. For we do not know what we should pray for as we ought...

The "weakness" referred to here, is not knowing off the top of our head – in our natural mind – exactly how we should pray about everything. But guess what? The Holy Spirit knows! Romans 8:26b says:

...but the Spirit Himself makes intercession for us with groanings which cannot be uttered.

P.C. Nelson, a well-known Greek scholar, tells us that the Greek reads, "groanings that cannot be uttered in articulate speech." The phrase "articulate speech" means our normal way of speaking. Nelson adds that the Greek stresses that this includes both groanings escaping our lips in prayer, *and* praying in other tongues.

Now, there *is* a groaning in the spirit, which is what we sometimes call "travail." I have been in travail a number of times. There is also praying in tongues, which includes prayer outside our normal way of speaking. Some people speak four or five languages, but their prayer tongues are still different than one of those learned languages. The Holy Spirit prays through us with a language we never learned. It could either be an ancient or current language from an earthly nation, tribe, or people. It could also be the language of angels (1 Corinthians 13:1). The Holy Spirit knows every language and He always prays the perfect prayer.

YOUR NEEDS ARE COVERED – FIRST!

Even though we do not always know what we should pray about and how we should pray, we do know that the Holy Spirit will intercede for us and cover us with prayer. It is important to note that everything that you need to pray for yourself will be covered by the Holy Spirit. There is no need to be concerned that you will not be included, even if you pray and intercede for others in long, extended times of prayer. The

Holy Spirit is never going to leave you out. You're the first one who will be covered.

Why? God knows you need to have a full cup to be able to pour out to other people, so He is going to make sure that you're ministered to first; and from that, you are able to minister to other people. After the Holy Spirit intercedes for you, He then covers those closest to you, like family and loved ones. Next, He begins to extend your prayers outward until you are covering those you don't even know, anywhere on the earth. Romans 8:27 adds:

Now He who searches the hearts knows what the mind of the Spirit is, because He makes intercession for the saints according to *the will of God*.

God searches everyone's heart and knows *everything* about *each of us*. It is interesting that God the Father knows all of this through the Holy Spirit, Who dwells in us. And when the Holy Spirit prays for us – and for any other Christian – He prays according to the will of God, which is always good, as promised in Jeremiah 29:11 (TLB):

"For I know the plans that I have for you, says the Lord. They are plans for good and not for evil, to give you a future and a hope."

God's plans for us are for a *good* future; they give us a *good* hope. We can rest assured that the will of the Father – relayed to us through the Lord Jesus and carried right into our lives by the Holy Spirit – is always based on God's gracious promises in His Word.

DO ALL THINGS WORK TOGETHER FOR GOOD?

In the middle of this passage on praying in the Holy Spirit, we find an often-quoted verse. Romans 8:28 says

(AUTHOR PARAPHRASE):

And we know that all things work together for good to those who love God and are called according to His purpose.

Some theologians have taken this verse out of context, which has resulted in great misunderstandings and perverted theology. Some have taught that *everything* that happens in someone's life will *somehow* work out for their good. But how can having a car wreck and experiencing massive physical injuries work out for your good? What if some of your family members died in the accident? How does that work out for your good? No, it doesn't work for your good; Satan uses such events as a way to come in and destroy something in your life.

I've had car accidents. One of them happened before I knew how to protect myself using Psalm 91. It totaled my car and severely injured all of us, and without divine intervention, it would have killed me and my two friends.

After I went to *Rhema Bible Training College*, learned Psalm 91, and had my faith working; the devil tried to kill me again in another car wreck. I don't know how I avoided the collision, but I was protected by the Lord so that the accident didn't even happen!

No, it's obvious that *all things don't work together for our good!* We must look at Romans 8:28 *in context*. In the preceding verses, Paul has been discussing the blessings of having the Holy Spirit praying the perfect prayers for us. Then he says, "all of these things work together for good." What things? *The prayer realities.* We know that when we're praying the perfect prayer – in tongues as given by the Holy Spirit – *all of these good things that we're praying* will work together for those who love God and are called according to His purpose.

However, as a result of taking this verse out of context,

some folks feel they can't trust the will of God. How could you, if you believe that even tragic things are God's will? Jesus made it very plain: *God's will for you is only good.*

In John 10:10, Jesus said:

"The thief [Satan] does not come except to steal, and to kill, and to destroy. I have come that they may have life, and that they may have *it* more abundantly."

We want to hold onto these words of Jesus: *abundant life is the will of God.* Good things in life will come to you. Success at what God has called you to do in life will come your way; so will provision for your needs, healing for your body, and peace that passes understanding in your home. All those good things will take place in your life because that's the will of God.

The Holy Spirit will always pray for us and through us, according to the *goodwill* of God, which is revealed in the Scriptures. As you pray in tongues, you are praying for yourself and for others, knowing it's going to work everything out, turn things around, give victory, see breakthroughs, and provide everything else needed in your life, as you couple your prayers with faith.

TIPS FOR EXTENDED PRAYER TONGUES

We've seen that when you were baptized in the Holy Spirit, you got a *portion* of the anointing without measure. You can have that anointing without measure constantly increasing, the more you pray in tongues. You get to be useful to the kingdom of God, as a watchman on the wall. Whenever the Lord calls you to pray, you can pray specifically, and effectively "pray through" what God wants you to pray about. You *can* get into the habit of praying at all times in tongues.

Tip 1: In the Middle of the Night

Now, this is not an absolute for everybody, but you *might* find the Lord waking you up in the middle of the night. You may say, "Oh yeah, I usually wake up and I have to get a drink of water and then I lay down and go back to sleep." But what if you lay back down and you can't go to sleep? After reading this book, you will know to ask, "Lord, do You want me to pray now?"

Perhaps you are thinking, "I might need my sleep. I might have a long, hard day tomorrow." Then Jesus will say, "It's okay. I'll give you strength. I'll give you a supernatural ability." Just obey the prompting of the Lord.

There's something special about praying in those quiet hours, when nobody else is awake. Whenever I pray in the middle of the night, I don't run through the house praying loudly in tongues, disturbing everybody. Most of the time, I will pray under my breath in a whisper. Still, I find that if I walk and pray, I stay more alert. If I sit down, I get sleepy again, so I walk a little path inside my house.

Even though the lights are low, sometimes I'll pass by a picture of my wife and realize I'm praying for her. Or I may realize, "Okay, I'm praying for my sons and my daughter." Your prayer assignment starts with you, then your family, and then it starts going out to other people. Before long, you're praying for people on the other side of the planet! I find myself devoted to, and passionate about what God is praying through me.

Some people have asked me, "How do you know when you are finished?" You'll know that you have prayed through when you feel a release in the Spirit. Once you finish your prayer in tongues and God has revealed to you what you prayed for through the interpretation, you can go back to sleep and sleep like a baby. When you've been obedient to the Lord, you'll experience supernaturally awesome rest!

TIP 2: PRAYING IN TONGUES IN YOUR MIND

Here's another secret I've learned about praying in tongues for extended periods of time. Did you know that you can pray in tongues *in your mind?* You can! Now, some may say, "When I pray in tongues, I don't know what it will sound like until it comes out of my mouth." When you've prayed in tongues long enough, you'll be able to *think* in tongues.

It's important to know that when you think in tongues, God hears you. It tells us in Psalm 139 that God knows *every single one of our thoughts.* If He can know what you think, He can hear when you think in tongues. Praying in tongues in our mind gives us a way to "pray without ceasing," as Paul instructs us to do in 1 Thessalonians 5:17. That's available to us. Plus, we'll be praying the perfect prayer all of the time!

I found out I can pray in tongues in my mind even while I'm having a conversation with someone. Sometimes, I feel I need to pray for them while we're talking. I'm not ignoring them. I can still listen to them while I pray in tongues; then I might respond. Quite often, you will then have the opportunity to agree with them in prayer concerning a need that they have. And you can have a great confidence of faith that the Holy Spirit has already prayed this through for them, as you prayed in tongues in your mind.

> *NOTE: While praying in tongues in your mind can be handy at times; praying in tongues out loud is also important. That's because you are commissioning angels while you pray in tongues out loud. They are listening and they hear you! We will go into the details of this in a later chapter.*

TIP 3: PRAYING IN TONGUES IN YOUR SLEEP

Did you know that you can pray in tongues in your sleep? There are times when I feel there's *something* going on that the Lord wants me to pray about, whether I'm conscious of what it is exactly, or not. When this happens, I'll get restless in my sleep and keep coming back to consciousness. At such times, I realize I'm praying in tongues throughout the entire night. Great victories can be purchased and wrought by praying in tongues throughout the night, because it's such a long period of time.

Other times, when I have been up praying at night, after I *do* lay down, I want to pray in tongues while I'm falling asleep. I certainly don't want to disturb my wife, so I'll pray in tongues in my mind while I'm going to sleep. (She does the same thing if she wakes up to pray.) I found out when I do this that when I wake up, I am often aware that I have prayed through the whole night in tongues.

TIP 4: PRAYING IN TONGUES WHILE BREATHING IN

There's something else I discovered while praying quietly in tongues in my house at night. When you're praying in tongues *out loud*, you can only do it when exhaling, because of the interaction of your breath and your vocal cords. But whispering doesn't have anything to do with *exhaling*. I found out that you can pray in tongues in a whisper, both while you're exhaling *and* while you're inhaling. Now, that might not seem like a big deal on the surface, but when you think about it, you are doubling your time of actually praying in tongues! I like maximizing my time.

I WANT TO INSPIRE YOU!

As we finish this first section on discovering Holy Spirit-empowered prayer, I want to inspire you: seek God out! Pray in tongues as often as you can. The Holy Spirit helps us receive guidance from the Lord. When we don't know how to pray, the Holy Spirit prays the perfect prayer – for us and through us.

The more we pray in tongues, the more we study the Word, the more we walk in obedience to the Lord, and the more we come out from among those who are in the world (2 Corinthians 6:17), the more of the anointing without measure that can come upon us. Then the power of God can do amazing things through us – just like He did through the early church!

I also remember when I was ushering at the healing school services with Brother Hagin when I was attending Rhema; each day, Patsy Behrman-Cameneti would lead us in worship. Then, Brother Hagin would walk in and step up on the platform while we were worshipping.

Most of the time I was right up front, where I could easily see his lips moving slightly, and I could tell he was praying in tongues in a whisper. I feel quite sure that he stayed in a state of praying without ceasing. Witnessing this powerful man of God actively demonstrating continual prayer – praying without ceasing – certainly inspired me to do the same!

Part Two:

The Ten Forms of Prayer

CHAPTER SEVEN

PRAYING WITH FAITH AND PURPOSE

There are ten *forms of prayer* found in Scripture, and each one has a different purpose and gives different results. We are discovering how, through tongues and interpretation of tongues we can come into agreement with all ten different forms of prayer that we need to pray – all the while understanding that the Holy Spirit has already prayed those prayers through our spirit and they were the perfect prayers!

The first four forms of prayer that the Holy Spirit will pray through our spirit, are found in Jesus' greatest teaching on faith, seen in Mark 11:22-26. In these passages, Jesus covers the prayers of *consecration, authority and dominion*, and the prayers of *faith*, and *forgiveness and release*.

FAITH IS THE FREE GIFT OF GOD

Faith is the *free gift of God*, which is given to us when we *believe*.

For by grace you have been saved through faith, and that not of yourselves; it is the gift of God (Ephesians 2:8).

Your salvation began when you surrendered your life to the Lord, having believed in His resurrection from the dead. When you chose to believe His promises from His Word, He poured His faith into your heart. From that time onward, you are privileged to use His faith. Your salvation came through faith, and that faith didn't come from you. It was the *gift* of God.

All faith comes from God. We don't have faith of our own. We have God's faith, to use in every circumstance and situation in life. As you see the Word or hear the Word preached, you meditate on it and you believe it. As soon as you believe it, God pours *His* faith into your heart, giving you the ability to believe and to be fully persuaded. It's *His* faith. Faith is the gift of God, to be able to access *all* the grace that He has.

God keeps on pouring His faith into your heart: every time you meditate on a passage of Scripture, faith comes and you feel like you hear Jesus whisper, "This one's for you." All of a sudden: "Bam!" You understand and receive. You have God's faith! That's the faith that God has poured into your heart. It's the gift from God.

God has spoken some promises in His Word — the Bible — and we can have faith in those promises. But He will also speak some *specific* things to us *today* that we get by having the mystery revealed to us as we pray in tongues. The current word from God can come to pass, just as well as the written Word, because the miraculous power of God produces all of it.

JESUS' GREATEST TEACHING ON FAITH

You may remember the story from Mark 11. After Jesus' triumphant entry into Jerusalem on Palm Sunday, He went to Bethany for the night. On Monday morning, Jesus was on His way back to the city and He was hungry.

And seeing in the distance a fig tree [covered] with leaves, He went to see if He could find any [fruit] on it [for in the fig tree the fruit appears at the same time as the leaves]. But when He came up to it, He found nothing but leaves, for the fig season had not yet come (Mark 11:13 AMPC).

Jesus invented and created the fig tree, okay? He knew that once the leaves were full, fig trees should have figs. And even though it wasn't yet the *season* for figs, *this* particular tree was covered with leaves. Jesus walked the distance over to it only to discover it was "all show and no go." It looked promising on the surface but failed to deliver. He said to it:

"Let no one eat fruit from you ever again." And His disciples heard *it* (Mark 11:14b).

Once Jesus reached Jerusalem, He went directly to the Temple and overturned the tables of the money changers and those selling doves. Maybe He was a little cranky, having missed His fig breakfast. Then, Jesus taught the people. That evening, He returned to Bethany. Mark tells us the next morning, as Jesus and the disciples were coming back to Jerusalem:

they saw the fig tree dried up from the roots. And Peter, remembering, said to Him, "Rabbi, look! The fig tree which You cursed has withered away" (Mark 11:20b-21).

Recognizing a teachable moment, Jesus launched into His greatest teaching on faith. Here, Jesus unfolded four distinctive things about faith that relate to our first four forms of prayer. Jesus taught His disciples how to pray in faith; basically saying, "If you knew how to pray in faith, you'd see all kinds of things happen! So, let Me show you how faith works and how the things that come out of your mouth can change and transform what you see, based on your faith."

When Peter noticed that the tree had dried up from the roots, Jesus replied in Mark 11:22 to "Have God's faith." Most translations say, "Have faith in God," or "Have the God kind of faith." These are weak translations; there are very few translations that get it right. The original Greek says, "Have *God's* faith." Why is this so important? Because without God, we can have no faith at all.

PRAYER FORM 1 –
THE PRAYER OF CONSECRATION

The first form of prayer we are looking at is the *Prayer of Consecration*. There are several prayers of consecration using God's faith. Each is an important step of surrender and transformation in a believer's walk with the Lord. The prayers of consecration include: the *believer's* prayer, the *disciple's* prayer, the prayer to be *baptized in the Holy Spirit*, the prayer of *consecration to the will of God*, and the prayer of *consecration for transformation*.

The prayer of consecration is where our salvation began; when we surrendered our lives to the Lord, having believed in His resurrection from the dead. At the time you received Jesus as Lord, you consecrated your life to Him as much as you knew how to. But as time goes on and you learn more and more of all that is required to live a life in the "narrow way," you will find yourself praying many prayers of consecration to His will. Consecration is a continual process.

I know how important it is for me to stay in the center of God's will. As I write this, I'm in my thirtieth year of ministry in higher education. That straight, narrow way seems to be more and more like a tight rope; I feel like I can't falter to the right or the left. Today, we have 21,000 graduates all around the world.

Plus, many of the greatest ministers alive on earth today, have their doctoral degrees from *Life Christian University*. (We gather their many published works and award them academic credit towards their earned degrees.) I've awarded doctoral degrees to the presidents of most of the greatest ministry schools out there right now. Our distinguished degree-holders are champions! If I brought a reproach to the name of the Lord in my life – in any way – I feel like I would be failing all these great men and women of God. I feel responsible to *Life Christian University* because my name is attached to their degrees.

The Lord is calling us to a straight and narrow way. The further we go down this road, the narrower it gets, and the more critically important it is to stay right in the center of God's perfect will for our life. But God has given us the tools with the Word and the Spirit to stay there, so it's not a bad thing. It's something we need to actively pursue.

THE BELIEVER'S PRAYER: JESUS AS SAVIOR

<u>Step 1: Believer's Prayer</u>. As we saw, the first *prayer of consecration* is the *believer's prayer*. It is a great and miraculous beginning in the kingdom of God. It's the prayer that gained us our salvation and the very first prayer that we ever prayed, that did us any eternal good! Some call it the "sinner's prayer," but no one calls upon the Lord until they believe. First, you hear and perceive God's Word as truth concerning Jesus Christ, and the reality that He was, and is, the Son of God who came to redeem you back to God. And, as soon as you believe, you are no longer a sinner.

The new birth happens when you believe the gospel story of Jesus, believe that God raised Jesus from the dead, and you now want Him to be your Savior and Lord. You suddenly believed these truths in your conscious mind. You then received faith to pray a prayer to receive Jesus as Lord.

Next, God starts working within you to prepare you to receive His Holy Spirit into your spirit. He is washing your spirit clean to make it a suitable habitation for Him. Then, when you confess "Jesus as your personal Savior," the Holy Spirit moves into your spirit. *This is when you are born again.* This *prayer of consecration* is that first step toward the kingdom, our first surrender to the Lordship of Jesus: receiving Him as Savior.

THE DISCIPLE'S PRAYER: JESUS AS LORD

Step 2: Disciple's Prayer. The second step we take to represent the Lord is the second prayer of consecration called the *disciple's prayer.* God expects every believer to *continue* to grow in knowledge and understanding of His Word and to become a true disciple. A true disciple is a "disciplined one" who is constantly *listening* to the Lord and *learning* from both the Holy Spirit and from the Word. Jesus said:

"If you abide in My word, you are My disciples indeed. And you shall know the truth, and the truth shall make you free" (John 8:31b-32).

We all want to know the truth that will set us free, but it comes from *abiding* in His Word. Abiding in His Word means to "live" in it. We can do so because we're born again and empowered by the Holy Spirit. The truth will come and set us free in every area of life. Remember, someone can simply pray the believer's prayer, desiring to gain salvation and go to heaven after they die, and some people do that. They just pray to get saved and then continue to live any way they want to. But we need to receive Jesus as Savior *and Lord of our life.* There's a big difference between praying:

"I want to go to heaven. I believe in You, Jesus. Come into my heart and life so I can go to heaven."

And praying:

"Jesus, I surrender my life to You. I know You are Lord. I want to go to heaven to be with You, but I also want Your Lordship to begin now. I want You to rule and reign in my life, so I surrender it all to You, completely."

The latter is the prayer of a true disciple. The true prayer of a disciple should be one of total surrender to the Lordship of Jesus. When we do this, we will receive rewards in this life. We want to be disciples so we can make disciples, as Jesus told us to do in Matthew 28:19:

"Go therefore and make disciples of all the nations, baptizing them in the name of the Father and of the Son and of the Holy Spirit."

I like to say that life on this earth is not really about life on this earth. This is just a test to determine how we're going to spend the rest of eternity. Once you are born again, you start finding out that everything that happens in this life is all a test. The Lord expects you to respond to, and get victory over these challenges. It's like a big, long, faith test about fulfilling God's purpose in putting us here.

God knew us – every single one of us – before we were even formed in our mother's womb, and He had a plan for us. As a matter of fact, going back to Psalm 139:16, we read:

Your eyes saw my substance, being yet unformed.
And in Your book they all were written,
The days fashioned for me,
When *as yet there were* none of them.

God wrote a book and included all of us, with exactly what He's called us to do and exactly why He put us on this planet. He wrote it all down; He wrote the whole story of our life, all the way to the end. Now it's up to us to live it out the way He planned it. If we do that, we get rewarded – both in this life and for all of eternity.

The disciple's prayer, where you surrender to the Lordship of Jesus, starts you on your path to a fulfilling life that brings honor and glory to the Father and His Son Jesus, and brings you great rewards.

PRAYER TO BE BAPTIZED IN THE HOLY SPIRIT

Step 3: Prayer of Consecration and Baptism in the Holy Spirit. The third step we must take to represent the Lord, and third prayer of consecration is to be baptized in the Holy Spirit, with the evidence of the ability to pray in tongues. We cover this in-depth in this book.

Being baptized in the Holy Spirit gives us the power we need to live the Christian life. *Praying in tongues* is the primary supernatural gift God gave to equip the New Testament Church. And it is essential for enjoying a powerful prayer life, for it is through praying in tongues that God reveals His mysteries to us. We have also discovered that the Holy Spirit actually prays through our spirit – covering everything we need to pray for – and He always prays perfectly!

PRAYER OF CONSECRATION TO THE PLANS AND PURPOSES OF THE FATHER

Step 4: Prayer of Consecration to the Will of God. The fourth kind of prayer of consecration is based on our *being yielded and obedient to the Lord.* This should be a *continual* prayer of consecration that we pray regularly, as more and more is revealed to us by God about His plans and purposes for our life.

Some people say, "I'm consecrated to the will of God as far as I know it, but I don't know what else He wants me to do." Others never even think to ask God about His plans for them. You're only going to find the answers when you press into God, in prayer and in the Word; then He will begin to reveal things.

I don't know how many times I've had *Life Christian University* graduates tell me, "I enrolled in LCU because I promised my mom I would finish my bachelor's degree. I had all this secular education but I never finished. Then, an LCU campus came to our church and I thought, 'I really enjoy studying the Bible and I can actually earn a degree, so maybe – for my mom's sake – I'll finish that bachelor's degree she always wanted me to finish.'"

So, they started to study. As they were studying the Word of God, they found themselves being drawn in; they were learning faith, learning how to pray, and learning how to hear the voice of God. Even if their goal was just to get their bachelor's degree, about six months into the program they realize and say, "God has called me to the ministry. I started hearing His voice specifically speaking to me."

You see, all these things are not revealed and unfolded to us right up front, when we first get saved. We must be consecrated to the will of God, and *then* He will keep unfolding more and more. We must consecrate our life to what He unfolds to us so that it will come to pass. We must yield to that. God told me, "Life is all about yielding to Me." It's about yielding to the Spirit of God and to the will of God for our life. The more we pray in tongues, the more the Lord reveals His mysteries to us, and the more we can consecrate our lives to His divine purpose for us.

PRAYER OF CONSECRATION FOR TRANSFORMATION

Step 5: Prayer of Consecration for Transformation. The fifth step and prayer of consecration is for *transformation*. So far, we have seen how praying in tongues helps you become more deeply aware of the truth of the Word of God and the mysteries hidden there. Next, increased spiritual maturity comes as you lay down your will for God's will.

Now comes the process of the renewing of your mind; when your spirit and your soul start to come into alignment and agreement with each other. When you continually pray in tongues, your soul goes through a process whereby it begins to resemble your spirit, the real you. This results in a completely transformed life, as your soul becomes more and more like your born again spirit.

YOUR SPIRIT – THE REAL YOU – IS NOW PERFECT

What does your spirit, the real you, look like? Your born again spirit is filled with the Holy Spirit. Here is what 1 Corinthians 6:17 says:

But he who is joined to the Lord is one spirit *with Him*.

That's what took place on the day you were born again. That's why your spirit is called a "new creation" in 2 Corinthians 5:17. Your spirit, with the Holy Spirit dwelling in it, was suddenly a new creation that did not exist anywhere before in space or time. You are a new being with the Holy Spirit living in you. Your spirit became perfect.

We see this in Hebrews 12:22-24:

But you have come to Mount Zion and to the city of the living God, the heavenly Jerusalem, to an

innumerable company of angels, to the general assembly and church of the first born *who are* registered in heaven, to God the Judge of all, to the spirits of just men made perfect, to Jesus the Mediator of the new covenant, and to the blood of sprinkling that speaks better things than *that of* Abel.

In this wonderful passage, we see several marvelous events that happen in the realm of the Spirit when we are born again. First, we come to the eternal city of God, the heavenly Jerusalem. That's our eternal abode with the Lord. Suddenly, we find we have fellowship with an innumerable company of angels; we were birthed into the kingdom where they live. Then, we come to the general assembly, the Church of the firstborn.

All born again people are "registered in heaven," yet some of us still live on this earth, while some already live in heaven. This verse tells us we're in fellowship with both the ones in heaven, as well as with every born again believer here on earth. Next, we come into the presence of God, the Judge of all.

But who are the "spirits of just men made perfect?" These are the Old Testament saints who died in faith, before Jesus came and paid the price for mankind's redemption. This includes the heroes of faith, as well as countless other faithful Jewish men and women. These righteous dead could not go to heaven until Jesus paid for their sin. They were saved on credit, based on what Jesus was going to do when He came. They were just.

You and I are living almost 2,000 years after Jesus died on the cross. For all these years, people have been getting saved and coming into the fullness of all that God has planned for them. But these Old Testament saints didn't have that; they never saw the promise of it fulfilled; they died before Jesus came. They were held in a place called "Abraham's Bosom," or "Paradise." When Jesus ascended on high and led captivity captive (Ephesians 4:8), He led all the Old Testament saints into the presence of God.

What a glorious moment! Moses, who so wanted to see the glory of God, finally got to see God face-to-face and still live! Now Moses is residing with God the Father for all of eternity. When Jesus led captivity captive, the spirits of these Old Testament saints became perfect – just as our spirits are made perfect when we are born again.

Next, Hebrews 12:24 says that we've come into the presence of Jesus, the Mediator of the new covenant. We are in complete communion, and face-to-face fellowship with Jesus! Finally, we see:

the blood of sprinkling that speaks better things than *that of* Abel.

This is in reference to the blood of Jesus. We are now in full fellowship with the blood that purchased our way into all of these awesome realities in the realm of the Spirit.

Aligning Your Soul with Your Spirit

Your spirit is perfect and now your soul can come into alignment with your perfected spirit – and into complete alignment and agreement with the Lord. God will continually transform your life by transforming your soul. The more your soul knows the Word of God, is sensitive to the Spirit of God, and hears the Spirit of God, the more this transformation takes place.

Paul tells us in Romans 12:2:

And do not be conformed to this world, but be

transformed by the renewing of your mind, that you may prove what *is* that good and acceptable and perfect will of God.

In other words, your transformed life *proves* God's will. I want to point out that this verse is *not* saying there are three levels of God's will. No, His will is always good, acceptable, and perfect: it's good for you; it's acceptable to Him; and it's perfect for His kingdom. As your life gets transformed, you are living proof that God's will for you is always for your good.

You live differently than everyone else, but you live *more blessed* than everyone else! You live healthier than everyone else and more prosperous than everyone else. All the good things start coming into your life because you separated your life out for God's purposes, and He says, "I will protect you." Satan is still going to keep throwing stuff at you – he will try every problem in life, but you'll get the victory over everything that comes down the pike.

For example, I have passed up the flu for forty years – and counting. I was supernaturally healed of the flu when I was a student at Rhema in 1980. And although I had previously suffered from the flu every year, I have not had it one time since then! So, when COVID-19 came along, I said, "I'm not going to have COVID-19 or COVID-20 or -21." Other variants are going to come next year: maybe COVID-23 and COVID-24. There will always be some kind of flu or pox coming along, but we can have the victory over every single one of them!

YOUR LIFE IS AN EXAMPLE

Praying in tongues is going to do a lot to "tune you up" and have you receiving a regular flow of the mysteries of God. You will be getting fresh insights as you interpret your prayer in tongues. You see, the Holy Spirit has been praying for every need that you have. He's been praying for all those to whom you are ministering, and all those in your sphere of influence whose lives you influence for the sake of the gospel.

They are going to be greatly impacted by the transformation that you go through. And as you are transformed, you become much more of an example that God can shine His light on to say, "Follow him as he's following Christ," as the Apostle Paul said in 1 Corinthians 11:1 (EXB):

Follow my example [Imitate me], as I follow the example of [imitate] Christ.

We know that if we stay on target following the Lord, as we go through this transformation process, we will have more to give to more people.

YOUR FAITH IS UNLIMITED

In fact, your spirit begins to convince your soul that your faith is unlimited when trusting the promises of God's Word. This becomes extremely essential. Maybe you always wondered, "Why do some people have faith to do all kinds of things that I haven't been able to get done?" It's because they're constantly increasing in faith by being in that place of hearing from the Lord.

It's one thing to read the Word, meditate on the Word, speak the Word to yourself, and be convinced, "That's in the Bible. That is God's Word, and that's the truth." There's a big difference between that and hearing Jesus speak directly to you by the power of the Holy Spirit, where He'll tell you, "You've got this, this is yours. I have delivered it to you." Now, pray the prayer that the Holy Spirit has already prayed – come into agreement with Him that this is on its way!

CHAPTER EIGHT

CONTINUAL PRAYER TRANSFORMS

So far, we have looked at prayers of consecration found in Jesus' greatest teaching on faith (Mark 11:22-26). As we are learning, there are different forms of prayer to help establish a believer's faith and purify their life as they learn to walk as disciples of Jesus. In each one, we pray using God's faith. In this chapter, we continue examining forms of prayer and begin to understand how a continual prayer life is vital for complete transformation in a believer's life.

WHY IS IT SO VITAL TO PRAY IN TONGUES?

As we have seen, the Holy Spirit will always pray the will of God through your spirit, when you are praying in tongues. But the Holy Spirit cannot pray through your spirit if you don't pray in tongues. And if you take the additional step to interpret your prayer in tongues, your soul can agree and then act on it – and amazing, supernatural things will happen!

Unfortunately, it's just one of those things that people know about; they want the results, without taking the time to actually do it. Of the major Pentecostal denominations founded at the beginning of the 20th century, less than 50% of their members actually pray in tongues. I feel like I'm on a quest to get everyone who *has already been* baptized in the Holy Spirit, to pray in tongues at least an hour a day. Plus, for everyone who goes to a Pentecostal church and believes in tongues but hasn't been baptized in the Holy Spirit yet; they need to just go ahead and receive.

There's no reason to tarry. Jesus told the disciples to tarry those first ten days while waiting for the Day of Pentecost. Since that time, we can just receive, so don't tarry at all! Receive now! It's a matter of getting people to plunge themselves into the presence of God, to hear from the Holy Spirit, and start using the tool; the very gift that God has given us in the new covenant, to change the world!

I'm convinced that if we got everyone throughout the entire earth who has the ability to pray in tongues but hasn't been doing so, to pray in tongues an hour a day, it would completely change the world we live in. It would probably stop all wars. The Holy Spirit would pray so many things through Christians who were yielded to Him, that everything we need to see change would be changed!

What if everyone who *attends* a Pentecostal church actually got baptized in the Holy Spirit and they too started praying in tongues an hour a day? What if some of us yielded to the Lord and we started praying in tongues for two, three, or even four hours a day? It doesn't have to be every single day. If we're at least yielded to Him enough that when He needs us we are willing; we will be able to pray through our prayer assignments.

As you pray in the Spirit, you are continually drawn into the presence of God, where the surrendered soul delights to be completely consecrated or dedicated to the will of the Lord. As you continue to consistently pray in tongues, you will come to realize that the Holy Spirit is praying the prayer of consecration *through your spirit*. In other words, the Holy Spirit is praying your prayer of consecration *for you*, concerning surrendering more and more, yielding more and more to the Lord, and being refined more and more. It's like silver and gold being refined by the holy fire as you're praying in the Spirit.

Then, when you ask for the interpretation of your prayer in tongues, you find yourself being *conscious* of what the Holy Spirit prayed. That's when you'll say, "Yeah, Lord, I see what the Holy Spirit prayed for me and I agree: I want to be consecrated to Your purposes. I yield to You; I die to *me* so that I can live *for Christ.*"

HEARING SPECIFIC DIRECTIONS FROM GOD

Praying through is really important when it comes to receiving specific directions from God. By the phrase "praying through," I am referring to a concept that I heard explained by Brother Hagin. He said that those who prayed in tongues in bygone eras – whom he referred to as "old-timers" – knew how to pray through.

Brother Hagin said, "I can't explain that to you, other than this is something that you know spiritually, when the Lord has asked you as a watchman on the wall, to pray in the Spirit until you have prayed through it – until you've prayed to the point where everything you needed to pray, has been prayed."

That means praying long enough to gain a sense of release from the Holy Spirit, or when you sense a note of victory in your spirit. This may be described differently by various people who pray, but anyone who is an intercessor will know what you are talking about. You must be experienced in order to truly understand.

That's what we're really talking about. You pray through until you know the Holy Spirit has prayed through everything that needed to be prayed through for that day. Then, every day is another day of prayer. Some days you'll pray that hour – maybe ten minutes here, fifteen here, twenty there, or whatever. You'll realize throughout the day, that you've prayed and you've covered about an hour. Then there are going to be those times when you say, "Man, I had this whole hour, and I prayed straight through."

One time, I really needed an answer from the Lord. I was young in this and I didn't know the Word of Faith, but I was in the ministry doing evangelism outreach through a music ministry. Our band had a big decision to make.

You see, there was a traveling group that came to Tampa and our band was playing for a lot of their services. They had a tent ministry and they were winning souls and doing a great job. We loved what they were doing and saw a lot of great things happen when we went out with them. They wanted us to join them full-time. The rest of our group wanted to join them; I was the only one in our band who didn't have peace about it.

So, I went up into the mountains to pray, in a cabin my parents had built up there. I spent eleven days praying in tongues and fasting. Now to me, the only purpose for fasting is to take that time for prayer. After eleven days, the Lord finally spoke to me and said, "No, you are not to join that ministry. It will be a bad testimony to your father (who I worked with every day). Go back and tell him this. He'll get born again and you'll stay on the course that I have for your life."

I went back and told our band, "I'm not going to join the traveling group. I won't stop you from joining them, but you'll need to get another drummer." Then I told my dad what the Lord showed me. It was within that year that my dad got saved. Praise God!

DON'T EVER DO THAT AGAIN!

I'm not a big guy. After eleven days of fasting, I got down to 103 pounds. It was not healthy; I don't need to do eleven days of fasting. The Lord actually rebuked me. He said, "Don't ever do that again." Now, that was amazing to me. I thought the Lord would always tell people to fast. There are some people who could fast forty days and just barely get to the right weight for their body. But I can't fast for even ten or eleven days; for me, it's unhealthy.

Fortunately, I found out that God is more interested in my prayer time than He is in my fasting. He wants me to consistently pray every single day. Sometimes, He prompts me to pray for two, three, four, or even five hours at a time – which I've done many times over the last year and a half. I've been having these incredible encounters with the Lord, and I get great direction from Him. I don't have to fast to get clear guidance. Actually, when I pray in the middle of the night, I'm praying during a time of fasting, because you're *automatically* fasting at night if you're not eating! I don't eat; I just drink water and pray through until the early morning hours.

IT TAKES DISCIPLINE

It takes discipline to consistently pray in tongues. Your body will not always want to shake off tiredness and sleepiness. There are going to be times when you have to tell your body, "No, you can't go back to sleep. I know the Lord wants me to pray *now*. I'm going to pray." It's not a legalistic or a religious thing; it's by the prompting of the Holy Spirit. As we begin to understand the power that comes to us, we start getting addicted to praying; to having the Lord interpret our tongues, show us what we've been praying for, and show us how it's all going to come to pass. It's exciting to see that great things are going to happen because of our prayer time! It *is* a discipline but not a *legalistic* discipline; it's a passion discipline.

Your mind will easily wander until you discipline it to stay focused on your prayer assignment, to pray through. This is the breakthrough zone where the mysteries that you have been praying begin to be revealed to you. A lot of people say, "I need a breakthrough." Well, just pray long enough and you will get to the breakthrough zone where the mysteries are revealed to you. We have to get to that place and we can! People say, "I really don't hear from the Lord very well." That's basically calling Jesus a liar because in John 10:27 He said:

"My sheep hear My voice, and I know them, and they follow Me."

Jesus was making a statement about you, but it's a *faith statement*, until you come in alignment and agreement with Him. Jesus makes this same faith statement about every single Christian: it's up to *us* to follow through and make it not be just a faith statement, but a statement of fact. Then Jesus can say, "Oh, you see that sheep of Mine? He hears My voice; I know him. He's convinced Me that he's always going to be following Me, all the way through."

Another thing that happens as you pray in tongues for awhile, is that you become conscious of the demonic opposition that you are pushing back against. Many times, you will sense that your prayer in the Spirit is what is gaining the victory over all opposition to your life's assignment. All of this adds to the consecration of your life to the Lord's plans and purposes for you.

WALKING IN THE HOLY FIRE

Why does praying in tongues lead us into deeper consecration? It all has to do with the revelation given to John the Baptist – that Jesus would baptize us with the Holy Spirit and holy fire.

> **"I indeed baptize you with water unto repentance, but He who is coming after me is mightier than I, whose sandals I am not worthy to carry. He will baptize you with the Holy Spirit and fire"** (Matthew 3:11).

We have covered being baptized in the Holy Spirit in detail, but what does it mean to be "baptized with fire?" "Baptism by fire" is a phrase used in the military and refers to a soldier's first time in battle. In other settings, it's when any person like an employee is going through a difficult transition or learning something the hard way. But John was referring to something different here. I believe both subjects are holy: the Holy Spirit and the holy fire. We see a reference to this holy fire in the fiery stones mentioned in Ezekiel 28:

> **"You *were* the anointed cherub who covers;**
> **I established you;**
> **You were on the holy mountain of God;**
> **You walked back and forth in the midst of fiery stones.**
> **You *were* perfect in your ways from the day you were created,**
> **Till iniquity was found in you.**
>
> **By the abundance of your trading**
> **You became filled with violence within,**
> **And you sinned;**
> **Therefore I cast you as a profane thing**
> **Out of the mountain of God;**
> **And I destroyed you, O covering cherub,**
> **From the midst of the fiery stones"**
> **(Ezekiel 28:14-16).**

This passage is referring to "the anointed cherub" Heylel (Hebrew: Helel, or Halel), who used to walk in the holy fire of God on the holy mountain. I believe there were three high-ranking angels whose names included God's name "El": Gabri-el, Micha-el, and Heyl-el.

I believe each one of those three high-ranking angels (probably archangels) were assigned to each one of the three persons of the Godhead. I also believe that Heylel was the one assigned to The Word (Who would become Jesus). Heylel was given the assignment to go to earth and prepare the way for God to be able to create His human. Heylel failed in that process: instead, he began to amass a great deal of wealth. The business term translated as "trading," expresses Heylel's means of gaining his riches by conducting business with a pre-Adamic humanoid race that was living on earth at that time.

At first, God told Heylel, "You were perfect in your ways...till iniquity was found in you...by the abundance of your trading." The business deals that Heylel was doing caused him to become puffed up. Suddenly, he wanted everything that God had; he wanted to usurp the throne of God (Isaiah 14:13-14). He sinned against God, so God had to judge him and cast him down from the midst of the fiery stones. After Heylel fell, he lost the name Heylel and became Satan, which means "the adversary."

Note that the Hebrew name "Heylel" appears only once in the original Hebrew Scriptures, in Isaiah 14:12. When the Hebrew Scriptures were translated into Latin, Heylel was translated as *Lucifer*, which means "light-bearer." The *King James Version* kept this translation. Satan likes that name: he thinks he brings light, but he hasn't done that in a long, long time. I don't call him Lucifer; I only call him Satan. It's interesting that Satan was perfect, as long as he walked among the fiery stones. It was when he got distracted by his business dealings on earth, that iniquity was found in him.

The fiery stones are in the presence of God, on the Holy Mountain of God. It's the fire of God that brings everything to a place of total purity. Everything in the kingdom of God has this unquenchable fire. If you're in the natural realm, this unquenchable fire burns up the chaff. But if you're in the realm of the Spirit, it's the presence of holiness; the holiness of God, the holiness of the Holy Spirit.

MOSES AND THE FIERY STONES

It's interesting that God brought these fiery, sapphire stones to earth when He came to give Moses the Law. In Exodus 24, God told Moses to come up the mountain and bring Aaron, Aaron's sons (Nadab and Abihu), and seventy of the elders with him. The others stayed back while Moses stepped over into the presence of God. Exodus 24:10 tells us something very interesting:

And they saw the God of Israel. And *there was* under His feet as it were a paved work of sapphire stone, and it was like the very heavens in *its* clarity.

It seems that in order for God to come to earth, He had to bring His own holy, fiery sapphire stones to stand upon. The planet was already that demonized, fallen, and perverse, so God brought His own holy pavement to stand upon, to be able to be among the people of earth.

The sight of the glory of the LORD was like a consuming fire on the top of the mountain in the eyes of the children of Israel (Exodus 24:17).

Earlier in Exodus 20:18-19, the people were afraid of the presence of God:

119

Now all the people witnessed the thunderings, the lightning flashes, the sound of the trumpet, and the mountain smoking; and when the people saw *it*, they trembled and stood afar off. Then they said to Moses, "You speak with us, and we will hear; but let not God speak with us, lest we die."

When the people experienced these things – they both saw and heard – it scared them witless. They did not *ever* want to hear the voice of God. They told Moses, "You go and you talk to God. You listen to Him for us and come back and tell us what He said."

Moses stayed there on the mountain with God, for forty days. God wrote the Ten Commandments on two tablets of stone. God gave Moses many more commandments and instructions. Then Moses went back down the mountain and discovered that the Israelites had sinned. He got so angry that he threw the tablets down and broke them (Exodus 32:19).

After this, God called Moses to go back up the mountain with two stone tablets, for God to write the Ten Commandments on, a second time (Exodus 34:1-4). Moses was on the mountain for *another* forty days. This time, the Scripture says that Moses was there with absolutely no food or water.

So he was there with the LORD forty days and forty nights; he neither ate bread nor drank water. And He wrote on the tablets the words of the covenant, the Ten Commandments (Exodus 34:28).

GLOWING WITH THE GLORY OF GOD

Moses was in the presence of God, which tells you the presence of God will sustain life. He had nothing to eat and nothing to drink. This was not just a forty-day fast – it was a forty-day fast *without water*. You can't go forty days without drinking water! It took the supernatural glory of God to keep Moses' body alive. When Moses came down from the mountain, his face glowed from being in the presence and the glory of God.

Now it was so, when Moses came down from Mount Sinai (and the two tablets of the Testimony *were* in Moses' hand when he came down from the mountain), that Moses did not know that the skin of his face shone while he talked with Him. So when Aaron and all the children of Israel saw Moses, behold, the skin of his face shone, and they were afraid to come near him (Exodus 34:29-30).

This time, it was *Moses* who scared the people witless, not God! Moses put a veil over his face so that people couldn't see the glow (Exodus 34:33). And, in the process of time, that glory began to fade. Moses kept wearing the veil for awhile so the people didn't notice that the glory was fading. Then of course, there came a time when Moses took it off completely.

What a transformation took place in Moses! He was standing in the holy fire of God and listening to God's Holy voice. Moses was so consumed with the glory, that he came down from the mountain looking as Adam looked before the fall, when he was clothed in the glory of God.

Holy Fire Burns Impurities Out of Our Soul

When we pray in tongues, not only does the Holy Spirit pray through our spirit, but the holy fire of God burns in us; burning all the dross or impurity out of our soul. If you really want to be used of God, your soul has to go through this transformation in order to be in complete agreement with your spirit. And part of the tool to get this transformation is to pray in tongues for extended periods of time!

Alignment of Soul and Spirit, Not Soul and Flesh

The Lord wants us to have our soul come into alignment with our spirit so much that our transformed soul actually starts to look like our spirit. Our soul and spirit start to be a mirror image of each other (Romans 12:2). It's really all you of course: you are a spirit, you have a soul, and you live in a body. But the reality is that your soul can actually follow the dictates of your spirit, and be in absolute alignment with the Holy Spirit and doing what the Holy Spirit wants you to do.

The *last* thing people should do is neglect the Word and prayer. When they do, before long, they're ruled by all the sensory input that constantly surrounds them. It's an ugly, demon-infested world, and there's a lot of bad news out there! It's your choice: are you going to arrange your life based on all that bad news; or on what the Lord is showing you and the influence you can have in the midst of all the bad news? If you choose to come out from among the world and be separate, then you're going to have a powerful life in the midst of it all.

You can have success; all the while enjoying the provision of the Lord, health in your body, wellness in your family, and the peace that passes all understanding. It's going to require dedication to God's purpose in your life; meditating on the Word, and being in prayer so as to not be ruled by the senses and swayed by all the predictions that bad things are coming. Another pitfall of listening to your flesh is that it puts you in a place where you can be tempted.

Someone who has been baptized in the Holy Spirit but is not praying in tongues enough to remain Spirit-filled, can fall into sin and there's no need for it! Praying in tongues allows the holy fire to burn in you enough to make you focus on the question: "Why would I do anything that the devil would tempt me with? I need to follow after *everything* God has called me to do, in order to accomplish that in my lifetime." We must be driven by the purpose that God has placed on our lives, so we can fulfill our destiny and receive all His rewards – both here and for eternity.

PURIFIED FOR MINISTRY

John the Baptist was the fulfillment of the prophecy given to Malachi, about being the messenger sent to prepare the way of the Lord. Then, Jesus the Messiah came to purify a Church for Himself from among the people.

"Behold, I send My messenger,
And he will prepare the way before Me.
And the Lord, whom you seek,
Will suddenly come to His temple,
Even the Messenger of the covenant,
In whom you delight.
Behold, He is coming,"
Says the Lord of hosts.

"But who can endure the day of His coming?
And who can stand when He appears?
For He is like a refiner's fire
And like launderers' soap.
He will sit as a refiner and a purifier of silver;
He will purify the sons of Levi,
And purge them as gold and silver,
That they may offer to the LORD
An offering in righteousness" (Malachi 3:1-3).

In the new covenant, the born again believers are the sons of Levi. We have all been made kings and priests, according to Revelation 1:6. As the Lord's New Testament priests, we too must be cleansed. The Holy Spirit is a sanctifier who refines, cleanses, purifies, and purges dross and evil out of the human soul; as a fire purifies silver and gold. We must be this separated, purified Church.

The last part of this passage makes an interesting point: we must go through this cleansing process so that all the things we do for the Lord – even the things He's instructed us to do – will be a *true* offering in *true* righteousness. That way it will be an offering that can be rewarded by God, and not a work of the flesh, done with motives of pride and self-righteousness, like the deeds of the Pharisees.

Brother Hagin showed us that so well, in his life of ministry: he spent a lot of time praying in tongues. He told us in class, "It's so essential to pray in tongues, that I do most of my praying – 90% of it – in tongues." Now, he knew how to pray the prayer of faith and the other prayers we cover in this book. He knew how to pray in agreement with God and in agreement with the Word, but he didn't do that until he had broken through by praying in tongues. We're going to see that this has an impact on all of us.

CHAPTER NINE

A HIGHER LEVEL OF CONSECRATION

FACE-TO-FACE COMMUNION WITH GOD

We have been talking about the *prayer of consecration for transformation*. This prayer of consecration is a continual prayer, and an active process through which the Holy Spirit works with us and through us, to transform our soul to match our spirit so we may live set apart and holy unto the Lord. But this transformation process is not just for a season; it is a *lifestyle* of holiness that is witnessed by all those we encounter. Many people will be able to sense the Holy Spirit's manifest presence in and around us; some will still sense God's peace upon them even after we have gone. What an exciting walk it is!

This type of prayer of consecration brings us into a *higher* level of consecration. It's a place of face-to-face communion with our Father and His Son Jesus. It is a prayer that causes us to be submitted to the Lord in all things. This produces a heart for prayer without ceasing, where you're just drawn in and you say, "How can I *not* desire to pray?"

I put on prayer music in my car. I have a fifteen-minute ride to the office, but often I've got to do some other things on the way, so I might have an hour of driving in my car. I put on prayer music that reminds me to pray in tongues the whole time I'm driving, so I can get in an hour of prayer almost any day, just in my car. When you add this driving time plus other moments throughout the day to a concentrated time when you have been praying at home, you'll find it all adds up to what you need to get this breakthrough. This heart for prayer without ceasing is the kind of prayer that brings us into the miraculous exchange.

For He made Him who knew no sin *to be* sin for us, that we might become the righteousness of God in Him (2 Corinthians 5:21).

This exchange started when we received the righteousness of the Lord Jesus when we were born again, and continues as we receive everything Jesus paid for us to have. We surrender all that we have and are, and we gain everything that He has and is. All of His presence, His power, and His best become ours. We're here representing Him as His ambassadors; He wants us to live like royal ambassadors, having every tool we need to be able to represent Him well!

If It Be Thy Will

The prayer of consecration is the only prayer that could include the words, "If it be Thy will." This is an expression of our surrender to God's plans and direction. Jesus prayed this way *only* when He was facing death on the cross and separation for a time from the Father and the Holy Spirit. That was the *only* time Jesus prayed:

"Father, if there's any other way to do this, Let's do it that way. Yet not My will, but Your will be done."

Jesus knew what lay ahead, but in His soul as the Son of Man – 100% God, yet 100% man – He still needed to pray that. Over the history of mankind, He had seen God do many miracles and come up with amazing interventions at the very last minute.

For example, remember Genesis 22:2, when God told Abraham, "Sacrifice your son to Me, the son of promise"? At that point, Abraham's faith was at a level where he didn't even bat an eye. He told Isaac, "Son, we're going up to the mountain of God and we're going to sacrifice and worship the Lord." Isaac went with him carrying the wood, but they didn't have any offering to sacrifice. Abraham tied his son up and was about ready to sacrifice him.

All of a sudden, God supernaturally stopped everything. He sent an angel to say, "Do not harm the lad. Now I know that you'll do anything I ask." Suddenly, God provided a ram in the thicket. Earlier, Abraham had told Isaac, "God Himself will provide the offering. He will provide the sacrifice" (Genesis 22:8). God did indeed provide; the sacrifice didn't have to be Abraham's own son.

"By Faith" Abraham Offered Up Isaac

The Bible says that "in a figure," Abraham received Isaac back from the dead (Hebrews 11:19). *The Mirror Bible* gives us an interesting insight into Abraham's "calculation":

> **...Inspired by what faith saw, Abraham was ready to do the ridiculous; to sacrifice his only son, convinced that not even Isaac's death could nullify the promise that God had made to him.... He made a prophetic calculation by faith to which there could only be one logical conclusion based on the word he had received: that God would raise the promise from the dead (Hebrews 11:17,19 MIRROR).**

In other words, Abraham "saw" – in a figure, like a faith vision – God raising Isaac from the dead. Abraham believed God was able to raise Isaac up out of the ashes, even after being a burnt sacrifice. That's faith! I always wondered if God was saying, "Abraham, I've got to find somebody who's willing to offer their son as a burnt offering to Me." Right after this event, God told Abraham:

"In your seed all the nations of the earth shall be blessed, because you have obeyed My voice" (Genesis 22:18).

If Abraham *hadn't* been willing to offer his son, God would have had to find somebody else who *was* willing to do that. Then God would make *that man* the father of our faith. But because His covenant partner Abraham was willing to offer *his* son (Isaac), God could send *His* Son (Jesus) to bear the curse and release the blessing of God upon all the nations of the earth. Abraham showed the pattern of faith; for him, it was unquestionable: "Whatever God says, we're doing that, and nothing else."

We want to get to that same place of faith where Abraham was, and where Jesus was when He prayed the prayer of consecration in the Garden of Gethsemane. We want to do what God wants, not what we want. And praying through in tongues is a great tool to get us to that same place of consecration.

I want to tell you something I recently received in prayer, concerning total consecration to the will of God. But first, I have to revisit one of the trances that I have had. Many times, a person will only have one trance in their life. Some people have never had a trance, and many have only had one trance; but I found out you can have more. I'm going to keep praying through in tongues as much as necessary, because I want more visitations and trances!

A *trance* is one of the highest levels of *spiritual vision*. An open vision is the only spiritual experience I know of, that is higher than a trance. A trance is when your senses are completely suspended. You're still conscious and awake, but you're suddenly in another place from where you are physically, on the earth. You're in another place spiritually, with the Lord.

"He's Right There in You!"

I experienced my first trance when I was a student at Rhema; it was a season of total immersion in the Lord. That first year, I didn't have to work, so I spent all my time going to class, studying the Word, praying, and attending healing school, every afternoon with Brother Hagin.

This was an unparalleled opportunity because Brother Hagin only ran it himself for about six years, and I was able to go for two of those years. I watched intently as Brother Hagin operated in the spiritual giftings he taught us about in the morning classes. For me, going to healing school was like having Holy Spirit School every day, because Brother Hagin would flow in demonstration of the Spirit and of power.

My first year as a new student, I got healed from the flu in November, and I started walking in divine health. After that, I felt guilty about simply attending healing school; I thought, "I need to help out," so I volunteered and became an usher; taking up offerings and doing camera work. Then I started "catching" in Brother Hagin's healing lines – that was certainly the School of the Holy Spirit of God!

During that time, my life was totally consecrated to the call of God. I had just discovered in August of that year, that I was called to the ministry. Then God made a way for me to go to school without having to work. I was going to take advantage of every moment. I was totally dedicated. I didn't own a TV;

I didn't care about owning a TV. I was "all in." I didn't even know what was going on in the news; I was disconnected from everything in the rest of the world.

One day, Brother Hagin came into healing school and said, "I really feel today that we need to pray." We all turned around and knelt down at our chairs. As soon as my knees hit the floor, I was in a trance. I was no longer in healing school; I didn't hear anything anyone else said or prayed. I wasn't there!

In my trance, I was in what looked like my apartment. I was sitting on the couch in the living room, reading my Bible. There was a knock at the door, and when I opened the door, there stood Jesus. I saw His white robes, but when I tried to look at His face, it was full of the *shekinah* glory (divine presence). It was like looking at the sun but it didn't hurt. I noticed that in His right hand, He was holding a letter. There He was in His robes and sandaled feet, with a letter; it seemed out of place. I asked, "What is that?" Jesus answered, "It's a love letter from the Father."

He handed it to me and I started reading. It said, "Doug, I love you with an undying love. If you'd been the only person on the planet, I still would have sent Jesus just for you." I started weeping and weeping. There was more in the letter, but I can't tell you what it said. I'm not sure I even read it: I just read that first line. That was the core part of what God wanted to get across to me.

Then, all of a sudden, the trance repeated itself. I was sitting there reading my Bible. Once again, I heard a knock at the door. I opened the door and there was Jesus, with a love letter in His hand. I read it and started weeping. Then the trance repeated itself a third time. I found out that most trances repeat three times. Remember Peter's "sheet" trance in Acts 11:4-10, that repeated three times?

The third time, I was sitting there reading the Bible and there was another knock at the door. I opened the door and saw Jesus again, but this third time when I looked down, there was no letter in His hand. He simply asked, "Are you ready?"

I asked, "Ready for what?"

He said, "Let's go see the Father."

The next thing I know, we were in the throne room of God. There was a white stone wall all the way around it – like a radius wall. Leaning against the wall were solid gold "bucklers," the kind of shield that you wear on one arm for hand-to-hand combat, while you wield your sword with the other hand.

Then I looked and saw a rectangular table with chairs around it. The table came to an end in front of me, with one chair at the head of it. Have you ever seen that painting of the Marriage Supper of the Lamb? It shows a table that goes on for eternity; this table looked like that. I didn't look down the length of the table, but I was sure it looked like the painting. Jesus led me to a chair. As soon as I got to the chair, I was instantly sitting down.

Then, Jesus walked behind the chair at the head of the table. As soon as He got to the other side, He was also instantly seated. As I saw Jesus sit down, I looked to my right and saw the hands of the Father on the table. He had taken His place at the head of the table with Jesus, the Son of God, who was now sitting at His right hand, and I was sitting at His left hand.

Now, I was absolutely in shock. I can't describe it any other way. It was one thing to have a vision of Jesus – I'm familiar with Jesus – but to be sitting there with the Father to my right hand and to be looking at His hands on the table, I was dumbfounded. I looked up to see Him and He looked just like Jesus. I was looking at two identical people! I couldn't see the Father's face because it too was like looking at the sun, but it didn't hurt. I was just looking back and forth between the Father and Jesus.

Finally, it dawned on me: I see both of Them, but I don't see the Holy Spirit and I thought, "Something's missing!" So, I decided to ask the Father about it. I said, "Father, I'm amazed that I'm sitting here. What an honor to sit with You and with my Lord and Savior Jesus."

I looked across the table again to see Jesus, and that's when I saw the nail prints in His hands; the scars that are still there because He paid the price for every one of our sins. Well, I started weeping again. I realized that once we get to heaven, all of us will be in our glorified bodies. Jesus Himself is the only One who will be scarred for all of eternity; having paid the price for all of us. We'll always be able to recognize the Lamb of God in heaven!

After I regained my composure but still being in shock, I said, "Father, I see You. I see Jesus, but where's the Holy Spirit?" I'll never forget the Father's response. When I repeat it, it's as if it just happened yesterday. This was the purpose of the trance. He reached His hand out about six inches from my chest. He pointed to it and said:

"Why, He's right there in you."

I suddenly got it. Even when we get to heaven, we're not going to see the Holy Spirit. He's the invisible One who dwells inside of every single believer. Although He fills the entire universe and the entirety of heaven, He's invisible. We'll see the Father manifest because we're actually created in His image. Once we are in heaven, we'll see God the Son (Jesus), who is the image of the invisible God, who won't be invisible to us then, but we won't see the Holy Spirit. He's on the inside of each one of us.

I instantly became aware of two truths. Because the Father, the Son, and the Holy Spirit are in constant communication with each other, and because the Holy Spirit is on the inside of each and every born again Christian, we are all drawn up to the table of fellowship. The second truth is what freed me from all fear, once and for all. Again, this was the real purpose of the trance.

From that time on, I have always had a unique sense of the presence of the Holy Spirit in my spirit. I have never felt alone. In fact, I have travelled to 25 different countries around the world and I have never felt alone and never felt any fear. Some of the places that I have travelled mostly by myself were where I would have probably felt fear before the trance. But after having heard the Father say, "Why, He's right there in you," with His finger pointing right at my chest; I have never experienced a sense of fear no matter where I have gone.

As soon as the Father spoke, the trance was over and I was back at healing school. I realized I had been kneeling for 45 minutes! My knees hurt and my metal folding chair was filled with a pool of tears. It felt to me like the whole trance only lasted five minutes and yet it actually lasted 45 minutes. It seems time is different in the heavenly realm: earth's time and heaven's time do not track with each other.

IN THE BODY OR OUT OF THE BODY?

Being in the body or out of the body seems to make a difference. For example, when author and speaker Dr. Kevin Zadai went to heaven, he said he was out of his body for 45 minutes but felt like he was in heaven for a much longer time. Kevin actually died: they accidentally overdosed him with anesthesia when they were pulling his wisdom teeth. Jesus came into the operating room and took him to heaven.

It was the same 45-minute period of time for both of us. I was still *in my body* in a trance for 45 minutes, and it seemed like five minutes. Kevin was *out of his body* for 45 minutes, and in heaven for what seemed to be anywhere from five days to two weeks. Another interesting difference that Kevin reported was that he could see the face of Jesus. I couldn't see the face of Jesus; I only saw the *shekinah glory*. Perhaps this was because Kevin was out of his body, while I was still in my body.

Jesus told Kevin, "You can see the Father, but you can't see His face. When you get a chance to see the Father, if you see His face, you don't go back to the earth; you stay here. But We're going to send you back because it's not your time. We still have a divine assignment for you." So, it seems that if you see the Father's face in heaven, you're permanently there. You're never going to be coming back. I believe once we're in heaven in our glorified bodies, we're going to be able to see Jesus and the Father face-to-face. I wasn't able to see the Father's face and I'm glad, because I was able to come back to finish my assignment!

"Just Keep Coming up Here"

Thirty-six years after that first trance, I was talking to the Father about trances. I told Him, "I haven't had another trance like that. I've had all these encounters with You: I've heard the Word spoken to me; I've had angelic visitations and dramatic healings, but nothing like *that*. Father, have I done something to displease You or dishonor You? Is that why I haven't had another experience like that again?"

Then the Father spoke to me. What He said shows me that the Father has a sense of humor. He said, "What do you mean? I showed you more than I showed Moses. What do you want?" I laughed when He said that. I said, "Well, yeah, okay. I don't want any more."

You see, as a born again Christian, in my experience with the Father, I got to see more than Moses did while he was on the earth and saw the Father. I got to see God's *front* side, while Moses could only see His *back* side. That's because Moses wasn't born again; he didn't have the Spirit of God inside him. God had shown me more than He showed Moses!

Even so, I want to meet Moses! There is something amazing about being in the glory of God for forty days on the top of the mount – twice in a row – and hearing the voice of the Lord and then writing the Law (the first five books of the Bible). We will all get to meet Moses face-to-face one day. We get to meet *everybody* up there, so start preparing your questions! When we get to heaven, we know we're going to recognize the heroes of faith and they're going to recognize us. We're not even going to need name tags. It's going to be awesome to be there!

I met Kevin Zadai the day before he ministered in Tampa for the first time. We had lunch together and started sharing stories about the presence of God, the glory of God, angelic visitations, and such. What was going to be a short lunch turned into three and a half hours! Afterwards, we were "drunk in the Holy Ghost" – just like the apostles in Acts 2:15! And we both had to have help getting to our cars.

As Kevin was ministering that night under the anointing, I was suddenly so envious of dying and going to heaven that I said, "Jesus, I want to die and go to heaven and then come back." I was 70 at the time. Then I realized, "Wait a minute! At 70, maybe I wouldn't be coming back, so scratch that!" Then Jesus spoke to me, "Wait a minute. I took you to heaven and introduced you to the Father. Just keep coming up here."

Suddenly, I got it! I realized I could go back to heaven again; all I had to do was keep on praying through in tongues. About six months later, on one of those nights when I was praying through in tongues, sometime in the fifth hour of prayer, I went back to heaven! I was praying straight through in tongues: I walked and prayed for a couple of hours and then

I got tired of walking, so I sat down but I didn't get sleepy at all. I was in the presence of God, praying through.

All of a sudden, I was back in the throne room. As soon as I got there, I was sitting in my chair next to the Father at the head of the table, with Jesus across the table from me. I was sitting there just like before, but instead of saying anything in English, this time I just kept praying in tongues.

As I did, it was as if I was watching the Holy Spirit pray through my spirit. I was watching the words come out and go to the Father's ears and to Jesus' ears. As the Holy Spirit was praying, I sensed He was pleading my case before the Father and before the Lord Jesus. All of a sudden, the prayer stopped. Then both the Father and Jesus simultaneously said, "That's exactly what We've planned, right from the very beginning!"

Suddenly, the prayer started again in tongues, as the Holy Spirit pleaded my case. When He stopped, both the Father and Jesus said, "That's exactly what We've planned from the very beginning!" This happened three times in a row.

Here is what I discovered: because the Father and the Son and the Holy Spirit are always in communion, They are constantly communicating. They are always talking about Their plan for mankind, as well as Their plan for each individual. God has placed the Holy Spirit on the inside of us and He draws us up to the table to sit there and commune with Them. When we're praying in tongues, we're communing with the Father and with Jesus.

The Holy Spirit is relaying the things that They are talking about. These are the same things that the Holy Spirit is praying through us about our circumstances, our situation, and everything pertaining to our assignment. They know we're bound by space and time, yet every single one of us who needs to hear something can hear it, if we just simply take our place in prayer and pray it through.

RESTORATION!

Those three times that I prayed in tongues and where the Father and the Son both said, "That's exactly what We've planned from the very beginning!" I sensed something exciting! You see, there are a lot of things that the devil has stolen from all of us. I believe God will restore in a Jubilee, the year of Restoration, as set forth in the Law of Moses (Leviticus 25:10b WYC):

(And thou shalt hallow the fiftieth year, and thou shalt proclaim remission, *or forgiveness*, for all the inhabitants of thy land; for that is the Jubilee Year, *that is, the Year of Restoration;* a man shall return to his possession, and each man shall go back to his first family.)

The Jubilee Year was the fiftieth year, which started as soon as Israel passed the forty-nine-year mark. As New Testament believers, I believe we can have a *spiritual* Jubilee. November 11, 2022 marked my forty-ninth year of being saved, and I'm believing that everything the devil has stolen from me will be restored in this one year – especially everything God has called me to do. Anything that has been delayed in any part of the ministry that I need to fulfill; I expect it to be restored and to come into full measure.

ACTIVATING THE WILL OF GOD

Those three times I prayed in tongues, I sensed that the Father and Son were saying that the plan was now activated: The Holy Spirit had prayed it through and it was activated. In other words, it was the "Amen!" to my prayer. The Father and the Son were both saying, "It's on its way now. We've released it from heaven. It's going to show up. It's going to be manifest in your life." I realize I have to stay in the Spirit; I have to keep walking in the holy fire; I have to pray every part of my assignment through, every single day. I've got to pray it through, in order for it all to come to pass.

That's what it means to be a disciple: we're stewards of all of the promises of God. In order to steward it properly, we have to pray it through. We have to stay in the Word and believe all the truths that God reveals to us out of the Word. Now, I have been studying the Word for *over* forty-nine years. I've been studying intensely, especially while at Rhema and in the last forty-two years of ministry since graduating from Rhema. I understand the Word, but I'm still learning; I'm *constantly* learning new things from the Word of God.

In this book, I desire to pass on these "hot off the press" insights into Holy Spirit-empowered prayer. Brother Hagin used to tell us, "I hope to take my fifty-five years of ministry experience and impart it to you in the two years you're a student here." In a way, that was wishful thinking, because what took him fifty-five years of ministry to get, was going to take us more than two years to walk out and do everything he was telling us to do. But he wanted to cram that knowledge into us and give us that encounter with the presence of God.

In a way, these things *are* imparted, and people can take them and run their race; fulfilling the course God set before them, but it will take each one of us spending our years being faithfully yielded to the Lord, in order to fulfill our destinies.

That's what we want to do here at *Life Christian University*. I want to impart these truths to everyone who will listen. I'm praying for anyone who reads or hears these words, that you will receive the full measure of everything God has for you. I'm praying that you will come into that place of being transformed by the renewing of your mind and transforming your soul, until it becomes identical to your spirit.

Then, you can run with your body being totally subject to what your spirit and your soul are saying, and fulfill everything God is calling you to do. Even if it takes 120 years to fulfill your assignment; you'll be able to do it in health and provision, praising God the whole way, in Jesus' name.

THE FULL ARMOR OF GOD

Using God's faith will be involved in every prayer that we pray from now on. When the Apostle Paul was teaching the Ephesian church, he elaborated on dressing in the full armor of God before going to prayer. Ephesians 6:13-17 lists the armor that we should have on:

Belt of Truth: We gird our waist with the belt of truth, the Word of God. Everything Jesus spoke to us in the gospels, and the things He speaks to us now, and which are relayed to us through the Holy Spirit, are truth.

Breastplate of Righteousness: The belt of truth holds our breastplate of righteousness in place. The breastplate of righteousness is our salvation. When we were born again, we were suddenly given the breastplate of righteousness: we have been made the righteousness of God in Christ. The thing that holds our consciousness of our righteousness in place is the belt of truth. If we don't continue in the Word of God, it is possible to let our consciousness of that righteousness slip. That's why Jesus warned us:

"If ye continue in my word, *then* are ye my disciples indeed; And ye shall know the truth, and the truth shall make you free" (John 8:31b-32 KJV).

Gospel Shoes: Next, Paul instructs us to have our feet shod with the *preparation of the Gospel of Peace*. That means every born again Christian has the ability to win souls to the kingdom. We're all representatives of the Lord, to take the good news to others so we say, "My feet are shod with the Gospel of Peace: every place I go could be an assignment."

We always need to be in the Spirit to see what doors God will open to us to be able to witness to someone, pray with someone, or share a gospel tract with someone. If you can't find a tract you like, then write your own. Write down your own testimony. At a restaurant, tell the servers who are waiting on you, "We're about to pray over our meal. Is there anything we can pray for you about?"

There are a lot of ways to open the door. When I feel prompted to witness, the Lord usually has me say, "Can I ask you a question?" If they say, "Yes," I ask them, "Do you believe in your heart that God raised Jesus from the dead?" This locates people immediately! If they say, "I absolutely *do not* believe that," just reply, "Okay, I was just curious." But if they say, "I've gone to church my whole life. Yes, I believe that," then say, "Have you confessed Jesus as your own personal Lord and Savior?" That question helps you close the deal!

Shield of Faith: We take up the shield of faith and quench the fiery darts of the enemy. That's defensive: it's faith that stops all the opposition of the enemy against our lives.

Helmet of Salvation: We put on the helmet of salvation, which is a saved and renewed mind. Of course, we renew our mind by meditating upon the Word of God (Romans 12:2).

Sword of the Spirit: We also take up the sword of the Spirit, which is also the Word of God. We've seen that the Word is the belt of truth that holds the breastplate of righteousness in place; it's also the sword of the Spirit, our offensive weapon, our weapon of warfare.

After this armor is in place, we're now dressed for our prayer warfare against the enemy; on behalf of ourselves – and other saints.

praying always with all prayer and supplication in the Spirit, being watchful to this end with all perseverance and supplication for all saints (Ephesians 6:18).

Brother Hagin always used this for the foundational Scripture for his prayer seminars. He would always say, "Praying with all prayer is the same thing as praying with all kinds of prayer." The Apostle Paul adds, "in the Spirit," because you have to be in the Spirit, praying in the Spirit. Next, Paul says, "being watchful to this end." Why did Paul throw in the word "watchful"? It's because we're watchmen on the wall. Our prayer life is part of being a watchman on the wall and overseeing – as stewards – everything God has assigned for us to do.

The last part of this passage says, "to this end with all perseverance and supplication for all saints." We are praying for *all saints*; that's how we can know that we start off praying for ourself and for those in our family; then for those in our sphere of influence; all the way out to praying for all the saints on the planet, the body of Christ.

I have come to understand this about ministry: we're not servants of God, because God doesn't need us to serve Him. We're sons and daughters of the Most High; we're kings and queens on the earth. That's our relationship with our Father and with our Lord Jesus. However, we *do* serve Them by serving the body of Christ. That's why I say, "Pray for all the saints; serve the saints." Even when we're doing evangelism and we minister to unbelievers, we are serving the saints because we're believing that these people will come into the kingdom and become part of the Church.

CHAPTER TEN

YOUR FAITH AND AUTHORITY PLEASE GOD

We are taking a close look at the four forms of prayer that spring from Jesus' greatest teaching on faith, found in Mark 11:22-26. We have been exploring the prayers of consecration. Now let's move on to the next form of prayer mentioned in this powerful passage: the *prayer of authority and dominion.*

PRAYER FORM 2 – THE PRAYER OF AUTHORITY AND DOMINION

If we don't understand the hierarchy of the kingdom that God has established, we'll struggle in every area of our life – especially our prayer life. It is therefore not only vital to every believer's walk to meditate on the Word and pray in tongues; but critical to our prayer life that we understand the wonderful gift of authority and dominion that we have been given freely from God through His Son Jesus Christ, and that we exercise our gifts daily. When we believe God and exercise His Word by faith, our faithfulness is pleasing to God and He will reward us.

Levels of Reward and Authority

Our obedience is so important! I believe there will be levels of *reward* and *authority* for every born again believer when we get to heaven – rewards that will be based on our *consecration* and *fulfillment* of the Lord's plan for us on earth. Jesus often spoke about receiving rewards from God in the afterlife. For example, He told a parable in Matthew 25:21, where the master said to his faithful servant:

"Well *done*, good and faithful servant; you were faithful over a few things, I will make you ruler over many things. Enter into the joy of your lord."

If we're faithful over a few things here, God will make us rulers over many things in heaven. It seems there are going to be different levels of authority and dominion that we will enjoy for eternity; based on how we walked in authority and dominion – by faith – while we were on earth. Before we cover how we are to become faithful rulers of a "few" things here, let's touch on some other kinds of authority that are really important for us to understand.

Four Levels of Angelic Authority

As listed in Scripture, there are four levels of angelic authority and four levels of demonic authority. The four levels of authority among the holy angels that the Son, The Word, created in heaven, are listed in Colossians 1:15-16a:

He is the image of the invisible God, the firstborn over all creation. For by Him all things were created that are in heaven and that are on earth, visible and invisible, whether thrones or dominions or principalities or powers.

As The Word, Jesus spoke and created all things. God the Father thought it, The Word spoke it, and the Holy Spirit empowered it. The Holy Spirit is the enforcer, the one Who made the things the Father thought and The Word spoke, come to pass.

The invisible things Paul mentions in this passage refer to the holy angels of God. "Thrones or dominions or principalities or powers" are the divisions of authority among the holy angels. These thrones, dominions, principalities, and powers are the "powers of good" behind everything. I believe that the listing of angelic powers starts with the highest first: thrones, then proceeds to the lowest, the powers. Colossians 1:16b continues:

All things were created through Him and for Him.

All of the holy angels were created for the Lord Jesus Christ, to serve Him for eternity. They also serve God the Father and the Holy Spirit – and the Bible says they are here to serve us, too! Hebrews 1:14 says the angels are:

all ministering spirits sent forth to minister for those who will inherit salvation.

Yes, as angels, they are more powerful than we are, while we are here on the earth, but they are "sent forth" to help us and to serve us. In 1 Corinthians 6:3, we find out that we will be over them in heaven! Paul writes:

Do you not know that we shall judge angels?

Peter also tells us something interesting about the angels: he says they are curious about the mysteries of the new creation realities we have experienced.

What the prophets had spoken, the Holy Spirit,

**who was sent from heaven, has now made known
to you by those who spread the Good News among
you. These are things that even the angels want to
look into (1 Peter 1:12b NOG).**

They desire to look into our lives to see why we were
created in God's image to be His exact likeness, and how He
gave us dominion. Maybe they are curious about how we were
redeemed and restored to our original design by the blood of
Jesus. Now that we are born again and filled with the Holy
Spirit, they look at us and say, "Wow, those humans are just
like God!" They see the heavenly realities already, just as God
and Jesus do.

The angels know their assignments. Every one of us had
an angel assigned to us as soon as we were conceived. Jesus
spoke about the children's angels in Matthew 18:10:

**"Take heed that you do not despise one of these
little ones, for I say to you that in heaven their
angels always see the face of My Father who is in
heaven."**

There is no indication in the Word of God that the
angels who were assigned to individuals leave them when they
become an ornery teenager or an even more ornery adult!
We know the angels are with us. Once we are born again and
flowing in the things of God, they are happy to help us.

FOUR LEVELS OF DEMONIC AUTHORITY

While there are four levels of angelic authority, there are
also four levels of demonic authority. In the *Book of Ephesians*,
we find that the angels who rebelled with the devil against
God were judged by God, kicked out of heaven, and they fell
to the earth. Yet, they seem to have remained in the rank of

authority that they had in heaven. Ephesians 6:11-12 says:

Put on the whole armor of God, that you may be able to stand against the wiles of the devil. For we do not wrestle against flesh and blood, but against principalities, against powers, against the rulers of the darkness of this age, against spiritual *hosts* of wickedness in heavenly *places*.

Paul is writing here about the spiritual forces that are the invisible part of the kingdom of darkness. He lists four divisions: principalities, powers, rulers of the darkness of this age, and spiritual hosts of wickedness in heavenly places.

When we compare the two lists, we see four ranks of holy angels and four ranks of fallen angels. I see a direct correspondence between the two lists. I believe Paul starts listing the ranks of the holy angels with the highest in place first: thrones, and then dominions, and then principalities and powers.

When he talks about the ranks of the fallen angels – in a reverse order – he lists the lowest first: principalities and powers. These two correlate directly with the lowest ranks of the holy angels: principalities and powers. Next in the ranks of fallen angels come the rulers of darkness of this age, then the spiritual hosts of wickedness in the heavenly places.

At the Resurrection, Jesus won total authority in heaven and on earth:

And Jesus came and spoke to them, saying, "All authority has been given to Me in heaven and on earth" (Matthew 28:18).

Jesus now gives this authority to all who believe in His name.

"And these signs will follow those who believe: In My name they will cast out demons" (Mark 16:17a).

We read earlier in Ephesians 6:12, that "we" are the ones who wrestle against principalities, against powers, against rulers of the darkness of this age, and against spiritual hosts of wickedness in heavenly places. God fully intends for us to have dominion in this age – not the devils!

Four Levels of Reward and Authority for Mankind

We've seen there are four levels and ranks of authority for the heavenly angels and for the fallen angels. I believe there will also be four levels of reward and authority for humans in heaven. There is no reason to believe that the human race will not follow God's pattern of delegated authority, as a reward for faithfully fulfilling all of our assignment while on earth.

God Is a Rewarder

The great heroes of faith are listed in the "Faith Hall of Fame" of Hebrews 11; it is in the middle of this passage that we read:

But without faith *it is* impossible to please *Him*, for he who comes to God must believe that He is, and *that* He is a rewarder of those who diligently seek Him (Hebrews 11:6).

If you're a diligent seeker, you can expect rewards. Some are not diligent seekers because they don't "give a rip." Others aren't diligent seekers because they don't know it's available to understand what God is calling us to do; why He put us on the planet. If you are *not* a diligent seeker, you're *not* going to get any rewards. That means we'll get *no reward*s down here on earth, and *no eternal rewards* in heaven. There are a lot of Christians who are going to enter heaven on what I call "the bottom rung of the ladder."

Our reward is based on how diligently we pursue the assignment and yield to the Lord's positioning of the assignment. It's about finding our place and doing what God has called us to do.

If God calls someone to be the most faithful janitor of a local church and they fulfill their call with total abandonment to the task and with a right heart attitude, they may receive the same level of reward and authority as the Apostles of the Lamb (the original disciples); or any founding apostle such as Paul, Barnabas, James, or Jude.

It seems that the reward is given for diligently seeking God and fulfilling His assignment for your life, *not* for the magnitude of fame that your assignment holds. Fame has nothing to do with it – only faithfulness.

A Christian who was satisfied with being barely saved; simply receiving Jesus as Savior to take the fire escape from this life and get to heaven, but who refused to seek God for His divine purpose for their life, will simply enter heaven at the lowest level of reward and stay there for eternity. It will certainly be way better than being in hell; they will still experience heavenly peace and have a wonderful, glorified body and other blessings, but they will be aware that they are in the lowest place.

I picture it like this: those in the lowest rank of heaven who did *not* fulfill their divine assignment will only get to take a bus tour every million years, to observe what those who *did* fulfill their divine assignment on earth will be doing – special assignments with the Lord and the apostles throughout the created universe! (I'm just kidding, but you get the point!)

I want to inspire you to fulfill all God has called you to do. Seek Him out; fulfill His purpose for your life. He's given you the tools; praying in tongues is one of the main tools. It's going to take you through a constant consecration to the will of God and help you pray continual prayers of consecration. As you yield to what the Lord unfolds to you and pray it through, it will come to pass. Then the Lord will keep unfolding more and more.

WE SPEAK TO THE MOUNTAINS

After Jesus said, "Have God's faith," the very next thing that Jesus told His disciples to pray using God's faith was the *prayer of authority*. It's actually a prayer even though it sounds like you're just speaking out; commissioning and commanding things.

> **"For assuredly, I say to you, whoever says to this mountain, 'Be removed and be cast into the sea,' and does not doubt in his heart, but believes that those things he says will be done, he will have whatever he says" (Mark 11:23).**

This is an amazing truth from God's Word. Most people think that when praying, the first thing we should do is ask God to meet one of our needs. That is a *prayer of petition*. Instead, Jesus is in effect saying, "Since you have God's faith to work with, and since the devil is holding back your blessings and trying to put all these negative things into your life, you must *first* take authority over the devil and cast his mountains of opposition into the sea."

In other words, here's the first thing you need to do: identify what's in the way, and then start commanding that mountain of opposition to get out of the way because you have the faith of God to use.

WE SPEAK TO OURSELVES

Let me explain here, that this same verse 23 *also* applies to speaking the Word while meditating on the Scriptures. Brother Hagin told us, "In this one verse of Scripture, Jesus said, 'Say it' three times more than He said, 'Believe.'" Biblical meditation literally means to keep speaking the Word to yourself. When you're meditating on the Word of God, you keep repeating the promises of the Word. For example: "By His stripes, I am healed. By His stripes, I am healed," or "My God shall meet all my needs according to His riches in glory, by Christ Jesus."

You also study the whole passage; you read it out loud and you memorize specific verses. That's all part of your meditation. You keep saying the promises to yourself, and before long, God shines the light on that truth. Suddenly, you believe it; it becomes internalized.

I remember hearing one famous Word of Faith teacher say, "That's a problem with a lot of Word of Faith Christians. They're just confessing the Word and trying to believe it." I thought to myself, "That's what we're *supposed* to do: say it until we believe it." We meditate in order to believe it.

But speaking to the mountain is different from speaking the Word for meditation. Once we believe it and we've internalized it, we've got the faith: we "have God's faith!" Now, we use that faith to cast the devil's mountains of opposition out of our life! A mountain in your life is any opposition against your well-being.

We all have things in our life that need to be taken out of the way. It could be a mountain of bills and a corresponding lack of provision. It could be a mountain of sickness in your body or the body of a family member. It might be division in your family or strife in your home. Now we're making a declaration of faith and authority against the oppositions that are in the way. We're going to use Mark 11:23 from that perspective and remove anything that is limiting us or holding us back.

This is so powerful! *Before* we pray the *prayer of faith* – that's the request to bring in the replacement to the mountain and receive what God wants to bring into our life – *we cast the mountain of opposition out first.* Only then can we receive the replacement for the mountain. Suddenly, we find that we've got the provision of God in every area of life!

We Speak to the Devil

Remember Jesus' words when identifying the source of all problems in life:

"The thief does not come except to steal, and to kill, and to destroy. I have come that they might have life, and that they may have *it* more abundantly" (John 10:10).

I like to combine this with what Jesus' half-brother James said in James 4:7:

Therefore submit to God. Resist the devil and he will flee from you.

A lot of people try to resist the devil, but they've never really been submitted to God. Once you're submitted to God, you have His power and might working in you; combine that with a revelation of the promises of God that this will work! That's why James says to *first* submit to God; *next*, resist the devil, *then* the devil has to flee.

The Apostle Paul said in Ephesians 4:27:

nor give place to the devil.

The devil has had a place in all of our lives; we've allowed it, but now we have come to the place where we're not going to give any place to the devil ever again. We're going to get *all* of his problems out of our life and receive healing for our bodies, healing for family members, and for other people, and receive the provision we need.

I say this in our *Divine Healing* course: the number one thing you must have in your life in order to fulfill what God has called you to do is a healthy body, a healed body. If the devil can take you out in your health, you'll be going to heaven too early. The devil can't keep you out of heaven, but once you're in heaven you become useless, as far as earth is concerned (unless we still have the ministry of intercession once we get there).

The exception to this is if you've been able to pass on the teachings the Lord has given you. Then your influence will remain as long as people are studying what you've taught. Even so, it helps to have a healthy body!

A fellow once asked me, "What do you think is the key to success in ministry?" I said, "Number one, don't die. Make sure you do not die and that you still have mobility." In other words, you better spend a lot of time learning to exercise faith to receive healing, and then to walk in divine health.

I was so glad that I had almost two years of sitting under Brother Hagin in healing school at Rhema so that I learned to walk in divine health. I've had some opposition from the devil – you're going to have that – but you come out on the other side completely free from it.

I've only missed six and a half days of work in the last 42 years. That's a whole lot better than when I was young and had the flu every single year for a whole week. It was as if I had faith *for* the flu rather than faith *against* the flu. But once I was *healed* of the flu – man, I was *done* with the flu! For 42 years, I haven't had the flu. I'm not going to have any COVID-flu or any other flu that comes down the pike.

After health, you're going to need provision. Now, I'd like to have more provision than what I've had, but I'm coming into a new place of understanding and I'm starting to receive more and more provision. Next comes peace: I walk in peace with my family and all my kids are serving God. Our two sons work for us at the university. Our daughter is now a professional hairdresser. She's a light shining in the darkness; even all of her unsaved hairdresser friends love her. They know she's completely different. She loves the Lord and she just loves them. She has a great influence on their lives.

STEADFAST RESISTANCE

Peter said in 1 Peter 5:8-9a:

Be sober, be vigilant; because your adversary the devil walks about like a roaring lion, seeking whom he may devour. Resist him, steadfast in the faith.

This is the faith that you have been given by God, once you believed His Word and He poured His faith into your heart. *Now* you can resist the devil steadfastly in that faith. The devil is seeking anyone who doesn't have faith so he can take them out of the race and kill them off.

We just had a global pandemic and so many people died. Unfortunately, when people would come down with COVID, they would go to the hospital. I didn't realize for the longest time, that when the doctors said someone needed a "breathing device," that they intubated them. They put them in a medically-induced coma and shoved a breathing tube down their throat. They were unconscious. You can't fight the good fight of faith when you're in a coma! Many of the people died because they were "treated" to death by the medical system. It's a crazy thing.

I just happened to watch a video the other day, of this guy who had the biggest software company on the planet back in 2010, and who said, "We've got *6.9 billion* people on the planet right now. Through the vaccines and modern medicine that we have, we believe we can *reduce* that number by ten to fifteen percent." He was talking about *reducing* the human population by ten or fifteen percent – with vaccines – and guess what? He has the biggest stake in all the vaccines and makes a lot of money off of the vaccines!

Listen, don't trust the world out there! They will kill you. You're going to have to trust in God way more than any other systems. I don't mind putting that on record for people. You have to turn to the Lord Jesus Christ and the Word of God and your Father in Heaven and the Holy Spirit, by praying and tongues a lot, in order to be able to survive this planet and finish your race successfully.

It Takes a Righteous Indignation

You must understand that everything the devil does is illegal – but he's able to get away with illegal things if we don't enforce the law against him. We have the law of the Spirit of Life in Christ Jesus that has set us free from the law of sin and death. We need to be able to enforce that law against the devil so that we can legally get all of his things off of us, and come into the place of legally receiving everything Jesus has purchased for us.

A righteous indignation should rise up within us and cause us to desire to take action. Jesus has given us His name to use against this mountain. Everything we do, we do in the name of Jesus, especially in matters of authority and dominion. That's what takes the awkwardness out of casting a mountain out of your life. Remember, Jesus said to *speak* to this mountain and *command* it to be cast into the sea. Because He's given us that command, you can say, "I'm just obeying Jesus!"

For example, you can say, "Debt, I command you to get out of my life!" My wife and I started commanding the mortgage on our house to be paid off, because that's a debt. We've been declaring, "We call this mortgage paid, in the name of Jesus. Now Father, we believe that we receive all the necessary funding to come in to pay this mortgage off."

We've started to make the payment *plus* extra principal. That is something we can do in the natural to see our mortgage quickly reduced and eliminated. God has been sending in more than what we need so we can pay the mortgage off, beginning with paying extra on the mortgage principle. Still, we don't want to keep doing a little every month. We want to have one final payment that we make and then we can say "Goodbye!" to our debt. So, we just keep commanding our house to be completely paid for and for debt to be removed out of our life.

You need to become very comfortable rising up in your authority and saying out loud, "In the Name of Jesus, debt and lack, I cast you into the sea," or "Sickness and disease, I cast you into the sea." If your mountain involves relationships, you should be saying, "Disagreement and disunity, I cast you into the sea," or "Division and enmity, I cast you into the sea."

All prayers of authority are about demanding changes so the natural realm lines up with the will of God in the Spirit realm. After we get rid of the mountains of opposition, we need to get a vision of all the wonderful blessings of God in the Spirit realm. Then we say, "Now, I command everything in my life to come into alignment with this vision of blessings that I see in the realm of the Spirit."

WHAT GREATER WORKS?

These prayers of authority and dominion are what Jesus referred to in John 14:12-14:

"Most assuredly, I say to you, he who believes in Me, the works that I do he will do also; and greater *works* than these he will do, because I go to My Father. And whatever you ask in My name, that will I do, that the Father may be glorified in the Son. If you ask anything in My name, I will do *it.*"

Jesus was saying that in order to do the works of ministry like He did, we have to use His authority. "He who believes in Me" refers to belief on a level beyond believing for salvation. This belief is on the level of taking our place in the position God has given us. This level of faith is what enables us to do the works of ministry Jesus did – plus *greater* works than these!

Some may ask, "What greater works could we do than what Jesus did?" First of all, our works are greater *in number*, because nobody got born again under Jesus' ministry until He was raised from the dead. After the Resurrection, the Bible tells us He was seen by a little more than five hundred before He ascended to heaven. 1 Corinthians 15:5-7 says:

...He was seen by Cephas, then by the twelve. After that He was seen by over five hundred brethren at once, of whom the greater part remain to the present, but some have fallen asleep. After that He was seen by James, then by all the apostles.

Then, Jesus ascended to the right hand of the Father and released the anointing without measure on the Church. After Peter preached his first sermon in Acts 2:41; three thousand were added to the Church. In Acts 3:12-26, Peter preached his second sermon. Acts 4:4 tells us that about five thousand more believed.

Eight thousand people born again was "greater in number" than what Jesus saw in His earthly ministry. In our day, we have evangelists who have won millions and millions of people to the Lord. It's an amazing thing to see! So, we are certainly seeing works that are greater in number.

Others may ask, "What greater work could we do than raise people from the dead?" Peter raised Dorcus from the dead in Acts 9:36-40. In our day, ministers have also seen people raised from the dead. Plus, the Bible records other works: as far as I can find in any of the gospels, never once did Jesus heal anyone with His shadow, but that happened in Peter's ministry. It's recorded in Acts 5:15-16:

> **so that they brought the sick out into the streets and laid *them* on beds and couches, that at least the shadow of Peter passing by might fall on some of them. Also a multitude gathered from the surrounding cities to Jerusalem, bringing sick people and those who were tormented by unclean spirits, and they were all healed.**

When folks knew Peter was coming, they would put all their sick people out on the street, just in case Peter's shadow might fall on them. Why would they do that? Because somebody had been healed just by being *touched by Peter's shadow*. Just being in close proximity to the anointing upon Peter resulted in healings. This was a case of Peter doing something you could call "greater works" than what we saw Jesus do. Also, Jesus never sent out handkerchiefs from His body like the Apostle Paul did, in Acts 19:11-12:

> **Now God worked unusual miracles by the hands of Paul, so that even handkerchiefs or aprons were brought from his body to the sick, and the**

diseases left them and the evil spirits went out of them.

There were people Paul couldn't get to, so he prayed over handkerchiefs and sent them out. When these cloths were placed on sick people's bodies, they were healed. If their sickness was caused by a spirit of infirmity, the demon spirits were driven out of the sick person and they were healed. I'd say this is in the category of "greater works!"

MAKE A DEMAND

We have been looking at John 14:12a and the greater works Jesus said we would do. Let's take a closer look at the rest of this very important passage.

"because I go to My Father. And whatever you ask in My name, that will I do, that the Father may be glorified in the Son. If you ask anything in My name, I will do *it*" (John 14:12b-14).

Here, Jesus explained *how and why* we can do these exploits: "Because I'm going to My Father." In other words, "I'm going to represent you. Everything you do down here, I'm going to be enforcing from heaven, by the power of the Holy Spirit through you."

Next, Jesus gave us specific instruction concerning using His name. When Jesus said, "Whatever you ask in My name," that word "ask" should be translated as "demand." You see, there are five Greek words that are sometimes translated as "ask" – the word used here is *aitoe* (Strong's G154). *The New Strong's Concise Dictionary of the Words in the Greek Testament* gives the shades of meaning for each of these five words, in the entry for *punthanomai* (Strong's G4441). Here's what it says:

"4441...to question, to ascertain by inquiry (as a

matter of information merely); and thus differing from 2065, which properly means a request as a favor; and from 154, which is strictly a demand for something due; as well as from 2212, which implies a search for something hidden; and from 1189, which involves the idea of urgent need (78)."

In this verse, the Greek word translated as "ask" is "strictly a demand for something due." It's mistranslated here simply as "ask," probably because it seemed offensive, as if we were demanding from God. No, we're not demanding something from God. We're demanding from the circumstances. We're demanding the devil to get his hands off all the provision of the Lord, including what has already been stolen. We are demanding from the natural realm, that things come into alignment with the will of God in heaven.

When Jesus tells us, "If you ask anything in My name, I will do it," it's as if He is saying, "Man, *I'm* on the scene, and *I'm doing it.*" He doesn't have to come back to earth. He can manifest Himself spiritually through the Holy Spirit. Jesus is seated on His throne at the right hand of the Father; ruling and reigning for all of eternity. From that position, when we act in His name, *He* is the one who does it. Here, He was telling His disciples, "Listen, this is not going to happen while I'm still here with you. But once I go to heaven, remember this!"

They *did* remember it, and they used the name of Jesus in authority and dominion. We're going to find a couple of places in our prayers where we will say with authority, "I *demand* that this mountain get out of my life!" And Jesus will say, "Good, I'm getting it out of your life, right now. I can't do it until *you* demand that it go, but once you do that, then I can make it go." That's why He's telling us to take our place of dominion in life.

THIS IS YOUR RHEMA WORD

Some people can read the Bible and memorize it. You think, "Wow, they have to be great thinkers." But sometimes, they just know it in only a superficial way. They've never meditated on it to the point where the light has shined on that Word; where it's become *rhema* to them.

I wish I were a natural genius! From the day I got born again, I've been pursuing the Lord, but I know the limited faculties I've been given. That's why I must spend so much time meditating on the Word, in order to come to that place where I truly believe it and it becomes *rhema*. It is actually better to need to meditate on the Word than to be a genius.

To me, *rhema* means Jesus whispered in your ear and said, "This is yours. I'm doing this for you now." That's what I felt like when I received two dramatic healings in my body. It was amazing! I felt like Jesus said, "This is your *rhema* word. I'm doing this right now."

Taking my place in authority and dominion was so important in these two dramatic healings. Both of these happened in November of 1980. The flu had hit Rhema the week before Dr. Lester Sumrall was scheduled to hold a seminar. I thought, "I'm not going to have a problem with the flu. Brother Hagin has been teaching on "Christ the Healer," and I'm in healing school every day. I believe I'm in faith."

Now, in Tulsa, it can drop forty degrees in an hour. I went to school wearing a light jacket because it was about sixty-five degrees. I went to a restaurant that afternoon, to eat lunch before going back to healing school. They sat me near the door, which was constantly opening as people kept coming in and out. While I was sitting there eating lunch, I felt the temperature dropping. It was freezing by the time I left the restaurant: I had purple lips and I was literally shaking at that point. I went to my car and got warmed up, then I went to healing school, and then home.

I started reading *Christ the Healer*, by F. F. Busworth. Before long, I realized I had all the symptoms of the flu: I had to run to the bathroom, I was throwing up, I had diarrhea, I had miserable sweats, and a fever. I kept praying, "Father, I believe that I receive! I believe that I receive my healing!"

Much later, it dawned on me: the *first* thing Jesus said in Mark 11:23 is to *command the mountain out of the way*. It was four o'clock in the morning before I realized that! But I stood up in the middle of my bed and hollered, "Satan, get your hands off my body. It's the temple of the Holy Spirit!" When I said that, I suddenly felt the power of God come on the top of my head and just course through my body. I still felt sick, but when I felt the power of God hit me, I was at peace. I lay down and went to sleep for three hours; then woke up at seven o'clock, completely healed! I was so excited!

After that experience I thought, "I've got a handle on healing now." Then, a couple of weeks later, I got food poisoning. I found out that food poisoning feels exactly like the flu; with the same vomiting, diarrhea, and everything. I don't know why it took me until four o'clock in the morning again to realize, "Oh, my gosh! I haven't done that first step that Jesus told us to do when we have God's faith – which is to take authority and dominion over the mountain."

I immediately said, "Satan, get your hands off my body; it's the temple of the Holy Spirit," and the power of God came over me. I went to sleep and woke up the next morning at seven o'clock, completely healed. I don't know why it took me two times in a row before I "got" it! But that was pretty much my last real sick day. The devil has attacked my body, but I haven't had anything anywhere like either one of those days, ever again. I've vomited a couple times since then from eating something that disagreed with me, but I didn't stay sick.

What I'm saying is that we must take our place of authority, because the Lord says, "If you don't do it, then I can't. If you don't take authority over the devil, I can't cause him to get out of your way." We have to take our place and demand that Satan and his mountain of opposition get out of the way – and then that mountain *will* move. Hallelujah!

Oppose the Thief!

Satan is the thief that comes to steal, kill, and destroy (John 10:10). *Prayers of authority* are often used to counteract the enemy's opposition in our life when he has stolen from us or other believers. Every one of us has had the devil take things from us. Over the years, we've come into more and more understanding, according to our own learning curve. I'm at a place today that is way different from where I was as a student at Rhema; but that was enough to get me started in ministry, walking in health, and experiencing the provision of God. A lot of things started coming together from that time on, and I've made a lot of strides along the way.

Opposing Sickness

When sickness is in your body, the best way I can think to describe your situation is this: Satan has stolen your health. In other words, God designed you to be healthy and healed and whole; and if you get sick, Satan has suddenly stolen your health.

Health is the natural state of the body, according to the will and plan of God. God's will or plan for any of us is to never be sick, but most of us grew up experiencing sickness. A lot of minister friends of mine are *still* used to experiencing sickness. Thank God, He always heals us after we get sick, but man, I'd rather not even get sick! I like warding it off.

I know the attacks come, but let's attack back! As soon as the attack comes, cast the sickness and the disease, the injury and the limitation, into the sea. I've seen times where injury happened; which was a direct attack to leave someone scarred and slowed down by the devil. And I have seen that injury completely healed: it got cast out of the way so that they could keep moving forward with the plan of God.

OPPOSING DISUNITY AND DIVISION

When lack of peace and disunity are abounding with all division, cast it into the sea. Others might not realize that they are playing into the devil's traps of temptation, self-centeredness, and manipulation. As trained believers, we must be the one to take authority over the spirit of division among our fellow Christians.

There may be a lot of instances with your own family and with co-workers, neighbors, or friends where you're going to have to be the mediator or the peacemaker. You do it in the spirit realm first: you take authority over all spirits of disunity, division, and strife that come in, when people are walking in the flesh.

Yes, you will also need to do some teaching, but you've got to take care of disunity, division, and strife *spiritually*, before others will be willing to receive the ministry you have for them, from the Word of God. We have been given dominion over all the things the devil puts in place to cause division among believers.

OPPOSING POVERTY AND LACK

When the bills are mounting up above the income level, the mountain of lack is in the way. Poverty was included with our sin and sickness, when Jesus went to the cross. The believer must cast poverty and lack into the sea before asking the Father for His provision in Jesus' name.

Removing the opposition in the Spirit by praying in tongues and then coming into agreement with what the Holy Spirit has prayed allows us to move onward, praying in the replacement to the opposition or lack. That's done with the *prayer of faith*. In other words, as we pray in tongues and ask for the interpretation, we find out that the Holy Spirit is commanding the mountains to be removed. He will do that for you! Everything that needs to be prayed, even the *prayer of authority*; He will be praying for you when you pray in tongues enough.

That's why it gets easier. After you've prayed in tongues *for awhile*, you realize, "Wait a minute! That's what the Holy Spirit has been praying; of course, I can do that! Jesus told us how to use His name; the Holy Spirit has prayed it already, now I'm coming into agreement with the Holy Spirit. Satan, get your hands off my money! Get your hands off my provision! It's what God has called into my life."

I remember the time the Lord spoke to me, saying, "Listen, I have already provided every dollar, every euro, every yen, every rand, every peso, every rupee..." and He went on to list a whole bunch of different world currencies. Then He said, "It's already earmarked for you from all over the world, to come into your life to provide for you to fulfill the call that I've placed on your life."

I suddenly saw it: the provision of God to run the ministry that we do, and everything we need. You see, I live off the ministry, my family lives off the ministry – all the people who work for us live off the ministry. So, I have that responsibility to bring all the provision in so that the ministry continues to go forth and the Word goes out. All the training of students all over the world happens because we're able to fulfill that call.

The Lord continued, "I've already provided all that money, but you have to take your place to receive that money in." Sometimes, it comes down to telling the devil to get his hands off your dollars and your euros. (You probably have some euros that God has earmarked for your ministry; not just dollars, but currency from all over the world.)

We've had money come in from all over; from campuses in twenty-four different nations. Even though the campuses pay us in U.S. dollars, the students pay their tuition with the currency of their nation.

So, take your place of authority, remove the mountains of opposition through prayer, praying in tongues, and coming into agreement with what the Holy Spirit has prayed, and watch God's provision replace those mountains!

CHAPTER ELEVEN

POSITIONED BY FAITH

We have been examining the four forms of prayer that Jesus taught His disciples in Mark 11:22-26. We have covered *prayers of consecration* and *prayers of authority and dominion*. Now we'll take a look at the *prayer of faith*, as seen in Mark 11:24a:

"Therefore I say to you, whatever things you ask when you pray..."

This is going to be a prayer *asking* for provision. We are asking the Father, in the name of Jesus. Here, Jesus is telling us that we're now in position: once we've taken authority over the mountain; then we can start praying for the replacement of the mountain.

PRAYER FORM 3 – THE PRAYER OF FAITH

Now is the time for the proper position of the *prayer of faith*. So much of the time, we've thought the prayer of faith was the first thing we were supposed to pray. We need to take the authority and the dominion first. *Before* you pray the prayer of faith, it is essential that you have meditated on the promises of the Word of God enough to believe in your heart, that every promise is God's will for you to have.

In other words, you have already renewed your mind. We can't teach about prayer on this level, to someone who just got saved and who hasn't spent much time in the Word of God. They are still trying to understand the promises of God and starting to walk by faith. The prayer of faith is going to work for those of us who already believe that it is the will of God to do these good things for us. Now we've got some ammunition for using that Word of promise in our request to the Father.

Convinced of God's Love

It would be a fruitless exercise in futility if we are not convinced that the love of God toward us includes every blessing He desires to place in our life. That's why I say it's so important to pray in tongues: we get caught up in the love of God. Being caught up in the love of God is the experience of being in His presence. It's a place!

I've always said that true worship is coming into the presence of God and just sitting there in His presence – even without praying – just to enjoy His presence, just to hear Him speak into your life, and just to sense Him loving you. So, true worship is really coming to that place of pure adoration of your Heavenly Father and everything that He's done to make you part of His family.

The reality is that most people think about going to the Father and praying in Jesus' name for their needs. When Jesus spoke about prayer in Matthew 6:6, He said:

"But you, when you pray, go into your room, and when you have shut your door, pray to your Father who *is* in the secret *place*; and your Father who sees in secret will reward you openly."

What did Jesus mean by "shut the door?" He meant to shut the door on all the problems that you've got, even the things that you need to take authority over. First, you need to know the love of God, so shut the door on your problems. Leave them outside; spend time in the presence of your Father. You'll find out how much He really loves you. You start being convinced: "My Father loves me so much, that every promise He's put in this book is for me. I can receive it. He wants me to have it; it is His desire that it come into my life. I know it's in His grace because I've encountered His love. I know His grace contains everything. It's a free gift for me. I just have to access it by faith."

It's All in God's Grace

Once you've encountered God's love, it's easy to access His grace – and everything you need is there in His grace. We're teaching you how to be able to access all those things by faith because you've got an assignment. You will need to use all the tools of accessing the grace of God by faith. So, most of the prayers that we will study are all basically prayers in the category of the prayer of faith.

If you are a graduate of LCU's Program 1, this place has probably been resolved in your heart a long time ago. But you can understand when you are ministering this to someone who does not have the faith foundation that you have, that they may require some patient instruction from you, in order to come to a level of faith necessary to pray the prayer of faith.

So, you've got to teach people the promises of God's Word enough so that they believe. There are people that have a misunderstanding or a misapplication of Scripture, such as the belief that everything that happens in life is the "will of God."

No, it's not. A lot of the things that happen in many people's lives were never the will of God. Satan was able to work his way in, worm his way in, and wreak havoc in our lives. No, that was never the will of God. His will is *always* the *good* things.

Seeing the Answer in the Heavenly Realm

We looked at this under prayers of *authority and dominion*. The *prayer of faith* brings the replacement for the mountain of opposition that you have just cast into the sea. Jesus said in Mark 11:24b:

"when you pray, believe that you receive *them*, and you will have *them*."

We ask the Father in the name of Jesus, and believe that we receive our request at the time we finish our prayer and say, "Amen." Jesus then promised us, "You will have your requests. They will come into your life." The important truth for every believer to remember, is that we are seeing into the heavenly realm; seeing the promise through our eyes of faith.

We're seeing into the grace of God and all the provision in that grace. When we pray to receive these things to be manifested in our natural life, we must recognize that the answer to our prayer happens at the time we say the prayer.

We are looking into the realm of the Spirit. Healing for our body is from the realm of the Spirit. To me, healing is one of the easiest things to receive because it doesn't require anyone else's faith. God doesn't need to talk to anyone or move all sorts of circumstances and situations around, as He sometimes does in order to get money to you.

God is able to heal you quickly. I've received some almost instant healings before, so I know the Lord is more than able to do that once you are in that place of believing the promises are for you, and that when you pray and you say "Amen" to your prayer, the promise is on its way.

We are looking into the realm of the Spirit, but guess what? A lot of the things that need to come into our life are already here in the natural realm around us. When you're praying for provision or for unity, you're taking spiritual authority over the works of darkness on earth, and spirits that are causing poverty or division. It may take awhile to move the opposition around here, to be able to get all that provision or unity in.

Still, some of it can come pretty quickly. Once you've done the spiritual work, it frees the Lord up to do some supernaturally-fast provision. I've had that happen many times over the years, but praise God, we're coming into a place where I believe that in one year of time, I'm going to have a complete Jubilee.

Proverbs 6:31 says:

Yet when he [a thief] is found, he must restore sevenfold.

That means that *everything* the devil has stolen from me, he will have to replace seven times. That includes a house he stole from me. Even though I've got three houses now, I'm going to have seven houses to replace that one.

You may ask, "Why would you need seven houses?" Well, how about just for investment? How about for rental income? One house that we own is a vacation rental house that I inherited from my parents. We can have those kinds of things.

My parents went the distance, fulfilled their assignments, and then left their children a heritage. There's an inheritance that's passed on to the Christian believer's children. I want to have even more of that, to be able to pass it down to my two sons and my daughter. So, maybe I need at least six houses; to pass down two houses to each of my three kids, and one for somebody else – I don't know! I'm not that close to my departure yet!

THE PROVISION IS ALREADY HERE

We're talking about accessing the good things that God has already placed here on the earth. Some of these things are just in the wrong hands; they're in the possession of the devil's people. I'm not going to covet what somebody else has, but there may be some things that God wants to put in my life that are already on the earth. It's like when the children of Israel went into the Promised Land. Deuteronomy 6:10-11a says:

...the Lord...swore to your fathers...to give you large and beautiful cities which you did not build, houses full of all good things, which you did not fill, hewn-out wells which you did not dig, vineyards and olive trees which you did not plant.

So, whatever buildings you might need, they might have already been built; maybe you won't have to build them. The children of Israel didn't have to build buildings. The parallel for us in the church age is maybe you will find a building that works perfectly for what you need.

Praise God, the provision we need is already there. It just needs to be accessed by us going through this proper process of praying everything through, taking dominion over the mountains, and then watching the Lord replace them as we pray the prayer of faith. We see into the heavenly realm and we recognize that the answer to our prayer happens at the time we pray. Now we can say, "It's activated!"

It's like in my vision, when I felt the Holy Spirit praying through me to the Father and the Son. There He was, pleading my case, and at the end of each of the three petitions, I felt an assurance like, "Okay, now it's activated." I knew the prayer was answered at that time.

We must also understand that in many cases, the promised blessing is not *immediately* manifested in the natural realm. This is the perfect time to use the confession of faith. It may sound something like this: "I believe that I have received my healing when I prayed, knowing my Father in heaven has heard my prayer, in the name of His dear Son Jesus. He was delighted to release my healing when I prayed."

Then we must be willing to keep making this faith confession until the promise is manifested. If we do not relent in our commitment to receive, it will be manifested sooner, than later. God always comes through with the answer, when we stand our ground in faith.

That's what we're going to do after we pray the prayer of faith: we stand our ground. We're not going to give up until we see that prayer answered and manifested in the natural realm. The Lord knows He's out there in eternity beyond space and time. But we still live in the space-time continuum in a natural world, where the things we need have to come into our lives in order for us to run our race all the way to the finish line. Praise God!

IN JESUS' NAME

Prayers that fall into the *prayer of faith* category are all covered by the prayer to the Father in Jesus' name, according to John 16:22-24. Jesus gave us instructions on how to be able to pray. He said:

"Therefore you now have sorrow; but I will see you again..."

Now, He's just told them He's going to be going away. Of course, He's going to go away through crucifixion and then they were going to see Him again in a resurrected state.

"...and your heart will rejoice, and your joy no one will take from you. And in that day..."

From that day forward – we're in that day forward. This is the beginning of the church age – when He came back and the first disciples were born again. We're still living in the church age until Jesus comes back again. He says:

"...in that day you will ask Me nothing. Most assuredly, I say to you, whatever you ask the Father in My name" (John 16:23a).

Now, He's using that term "ask." There is a request or a *supplication*. It's kind of like a requisition. If anybody's been in the military, you know what a requisition is. It's a list of the things that you need. It gets sent and then it gets supplied into your unit. It's the same thing for us; we're in God's army. We've got to send these requisitions to the Lord. It's not a bad thing to write them down and then lay them out before the Lord in your prayer. "Father, in Jesus' name, I believe we need all these things and I believe that we're going to receive them now, in Jesus' name." So, He said to them:

"Most assuredly, I say to you, whatever you ask the Father in My name He will give you. Until now you have asked nothing in My name. Ask, and you will receive, that your joy may be full" (John 16:23b-24).

Now, Jesus knew that in our human condition – the human state that we're in – that we need to have the joy of the Lord. We need to have the joy of having our prayers answered. It's the joy of living in the miraculous realm. That's when you realize that nothing that you see around you that's temporal and that is a hindrance in any way, is permanent. It's temporal; it's subject to change. And when you're constantly walking with the Lord and praying the prayer of faith, then all of the things that you need are going to come into view. They are going to come into your life and will be a blessing in your life – even the house you live in.

God knows you need to have a nice house. If you're going to represent Him, you've got to have a roof over your head that doesn't leak. It's got to be comfortable. He's got to give you a prayer place. If you'll pray, He'll make sure you've got a good prayer place. He'll give you a place to raise your family in and for the family to be in ministry all together, and representing the Lord all together; a place for you all to pray together as a family. You've got to have that. You've got to have transportation, not some clunker that's going to be breaking down once a week. He's going to give you something nice; something that you can depend on.

All of those things are not an attempt to "keep up with the Jones." They're simply the provision of the Lord. There's nothing that is actually "too nice" for the kings and priests that God has down here on this earth, so don't complain about somebody having so much money.

Every time I hear somebody say, "Well, that should be sold by those preachers and put into the gospel" – do you remember who said that to Jesus? Judas Iscariot is the one who came up with that idea! "That should have been sold and given to the poor or put into the gospel for the poor." Well, I'm not going to do *anything* the way Judas Iscariot did, so I'm not ever going to say, "Oh, that money should be put into the gospel." No, if that's a tool that they need to get their assignment done, then so be it!

But if there is anybody out there who is just squandering things just because they've got "stupid" money; instead of the anointed money and wisdom of God to know what to do with it, it's up to them. They are the ones who have to answer to

God. I don't have to answer, but I'm not going to complain about those who have great tools. I can just see it, with all of His tools. Airplanes and jets are tools. Cars and houses are tools. You need the tools of the trade to be able to accomplish what God has called you to do.

In reality, there's no limit. There's nothing that is on this earth that is too good for God's people, so get that out of your head. Take the limitations off.

Again, every prayer in the category of the *prayer of faith* will be a prayer offered to the Father, in Jesus' name. There are only two prayers that I'm sharing with you that have the prayer of authority and dominion. The first one is casting the mountain into the sea.

The second one is actually going to be *prayers of judgment and justice* – probably justice first and judgment after that, and that's done in the dominion authority; things that you demand to take place in the realm of the Spirit. Everything else is going to be in the category of making a request. Jesus says, "You're always going to be requesting of the Father in My name, and He's going to give it to you so that your joy is full."

PRAYER FORM 4 – THE PRAYER OF FORGIVENESS AND RELEASE

Remember that Jesus put four prayer forms together in His greatest teaching on faith. We get them all from Mark 11:22-26. This next prayer form is key. This is the *prayer of forgiveness and release.* A lot of people say, "What do you mean, a prayer of forgiveness?" Other people say, "Well, you just have to ask somebody to forgive you" or "You have to forgive somebody and tell them verbally that you forgive them," or something like that. Listen, unless you've involved God with this – and this is involved as a prayer of forgiveness and release – you never really get to the place that this is intended for, which is that it keeps you completely separate from all the other things that are so divisive in people's lives.

Again, we come to this prayer of instruction of the Lord Jesus that is designed to make sure that we don't undo our prayers of authority and faith that we've prayed. We started with the *prayer of authority* and then the *prayer of faith*; now we've got the *prayer of forgiveness and release*. Let me read this passage in Mark 11:25-26:

"And whenever you stand praying, if you have anything against anyone, forgive him [or her or them], that your Father in heaven may also forgive you your trespasses."

You know, even as Spirit-filled, born again, praying in the Holy Spirit, praying where the power of the holy fire of God is purifying you believers; we're still always going to be human. We can still make little mistakes along the way and sow a little seed of something that maybe we need to be forgiven for – as well as seeing what other people have done to us, and the things they need to be forgiven for. The reality is that there are things that we are always going to need. We're never going to become perfect while we're down here.

That's until you have a glorified body and you don't still have this regular earthly body and the regular earthly brain cells and regular earthly mind that you've got. Even though it's being transformed by the power of God's Word; there's a possibility that you can have little offenses and little trespasses that you need to be forgiven for, from our Heavenly Father. So, I believe in taking care of those every single day. Every night it's, "Father, anything I might have done today to offend anybody, I repent. Forgive me, please." Then you've got forgiveness from Him. Later on, He might point out somebody that you need to ask to forgive you.

It's just like being a parent; you'd like to be the perfect parent. I would love to be the perfect parent to my kids, except that I'm a human being, so nobody's ever done it perfectly. So, I'm asking the Lord to forgive me for not doing everything perfectly and I'm telling my children to: "Please forgive me for any mistakes that you perceive that I've made in raising you." That's because there's no way I could claim that I did it perfectly.

Whatever nurturing deficit that came into your life where you feel like, "I've neglected this," or "I didn't do this," or whatever; God will make up the difference for that nurturing deficit so that you can be whole, mature, balanced, and in your right mind and not crazy. We're always distracted by all the things that people are so distracted by: the drama of people – even Christians or family members that are not walking in the Spirit and pursuing the Lord. You can get caught up in all of that stuff; just don't allow yourself to do it. Be a solution where you can be a solution, but the rest of the time you can say, "It's not part of my assignment; sorry, moving on from that." So, He's telling us:

"But if you do not forgive, neither will your Father in heaven forgive your trespasses" (Mark 11:26).

We need to make sure that all of our trespasses are always being forgiven, and we have to make sure that we are forgiving other people and that we're praying that prayer of forgiveness.

"Father, in Jesus' name, I forgive so-and-so of what they did to me and I release them."

That's why I call it the *prayer of forgiveness and release*; because in the actual Hebrew word it's symbolic of untying a boat in a river and letting it float downstream. Here's the offense. You untie it and just let it float downstream; so it's forgiveness and release. Let it go out of your life. How can you tell that you've really forgiven somebody? I'll tell you how. It's whenever the thought comes to you and you remember it, but it doesn't tap you in your nervous system in any way.

Nothing rises up. You just realize that it's just ancient history, like water off a duck's back. I'm just letting all that stuff go. It's like letting a boat just float down the stream. I'm letting it go. Now I've done that and I'm not going to pull it back up the stream. I'm not going to get back under the water and let that water sit on my back; I'm just going to let it flow off my back. We keep ourselves in that place at all times.

Jesus does not specifically say that your prayer will not be answered, but it is strongly inferred that you would be undoing your prayer of authority and undoing your prayer of faith. Either way, it's recommended that you always walk in forgiveness, for a number of reasons. Here are some of those reasons.

The first and primary reason is that *the entire kingdom of God is based on forgiveness.* If it weren't for God's forgiveness of our sins through the work of Christ on the cross, we would not even be in His kingdom. He forgave us everything. What did we have to offer God? Zero. We had nothing. He had everything; we had nothing. When we came into a partnership with Him, we got everything He has, and He took our "nothing" that we had to add to the equation. Now, all of a sudden, we have everything.

I know He's given you some intelligence. He's given you some talents and all those things, but in a way it's all those things you have to see as a "nothing" that you surrender to Him and watch Him make it a "something," because this temple is anointed by the Spirit of God. It's really nothing; it's just something that's here. It's going to be gone.

You may say, "What about all the great things that people

have done artistically and musically and so forth?" Well, we can remember it for about a hundred years but after that, it's a whole new generation. They're not going to be looking back hundreds of years and listening to the music from hundreds of years ago. They're going to think that what they've got is the best. "Oh, that's funny. Oh, my gosh, what a joke! Wow, they thought that was art. Are you kidding me?" We're going to be moving on with the kingdom of God because the kingdom of God is always in motion, moving forward. So, once again, we're forgiven and we're in the kingdom.

FORGIVENESS COMES WHEN WE REPENT

It's important to know that *God only forgives when someone repents.* Many people need to repent to Him because they have offended God by living outside of His plan and His purpose – until they repent or change their mind. That's what repentance means. The Greek word *metanoeō* (Strong's G3340) means "to change your mind" about what you think.

When you repent to get born again is when you change your mind about God – whatever you thought about Him before and what you thought about Jesus as Lord. Suddenly, you're convinced Jesus died for you so that you could live and be in God's family for eternity, so you receive Jesus as your Lord and Savior.

You change your mind about what you thought about God to come into the kingdom of God. Well, we have to change our mind about all these other things that we didn't know were wrong. Like I said, it took me awhile before I realized, "I've got to change everything in my life." Now, I wanted to be pleasing to the Lord, so I was happy to just suddenly come into alignment.

Forgiveness is always available but it does not go into activation on God's part until repentance or the changing of our mind is offered to God. People have to repent to God, change their mind, and ask Him for forgiveness, in order to get His forgiveness.

We do not have the same capabilities that God has. He's saying, "You don't have the same faculties that I have." So, you have to walk in forgiveness of everyone; even if they haven't asked for forgiveness, because you have to have a clean heart. You have to have a clean conscience at all times.

It doesn't mess God's conscience up one bit if somebody doesn't repent. They just stay in their state of unrepentance, disconnected from Him. Believers don't have that ability. We're not afforded that luxury. We have to be able to have a pure conscience. Therefore, we have to forgive people even if they've never changed their mind and never repented. We are required to forgive to maintain freedom from all the bitterness and the evil intent that is related to unforgiveness.

We need to keep our conscience clean. Unforgiveness in the heart of a human can war against your soul. That's what happens when people find themselves not being able to pray in tongues. Every bad thing that people have done to them suddenly comes to mind. Why?

Satan will make sure that stuff is immediately pushed into your mind when you go to pray. Pray in tongues and keep your focus on the Lord. Satan is just trying to rob you of the ability to pray all the way through and pray into that place where you're walking in forgiveness with everybody. Unforgiveness in the heart of a human can war against your emotional and spiritual well-being. It's like having a cancer in your soul. You need to be free from that.

HONOR YOUR FATHER AND MOTHER

One of the most important areas of forgiveness for most people is the forgiveness of their parents. Even if you had the most loving, committed Christian parents; no parent has ever done a perfect job in raising their children. There's always something that most people need to forgive of their parents.

Many today have parents that have so neglected them and abused them in every evil way; they still have to forgive them because the Bible tells you if you want it to go well for you in this life, you have to forgive (Deuteronomy 12:28). You *have* to forgive because you have to honor your father and your mother. It's the very first place you have to start with. For most people, honoring their father and mother is to forgive them.

I had great parents but they weren't perfect. They weren't even Christians when we started off. They were nice. My dad was one of the nicest guys you're ever going to meet; he just wasn't saved. Then, after he got saved, he became even nicer. It was amazing. My mom was a nice person. She loved people but she could also be very manipulative. I found myself resisting manipulation. I wasn't in rebellion; I was just going to resist manipulation. I still needed to be able to make my own choices.

But my mom was the one who prayed all of us in. She was the first one who got born again in the family, and she got baptized in the Holy Spirit and started praying all of us in. I was the first one to come in. After that, she and I started praying and both my sisters came in. Then my dad finally came in; he was the holdout. But when he got saved, he got baptized in the river Jordan and baptized in the Holy Spirit in the upper room. I said, "Dad, you were the holdout; but man, when you did it, you did it right!" It was awesome.

It was easy for me to honor my parents. I got a lot of reward for having parents who became Christian parents, and who spent a lot of their years as Christian parents. My dad was probably in his fifties when he got saved, but he lived to be almost ninety. My mom got saved much earlier than that;

probably in her early thirties, and then she was baptized in the Holy Spirit, but she lived to be 85.

They never even finished reading my books that I've written. They would have gotten all the wealth of knowledge and understanding that they paid for, so I could get into school and be able to launch into ministry. They were great supporters of my ministry. I wish I could have gotten more faith into them so they would have been healthier and lived longer.

The whole point is that's honoring. Especially when somebody forgives parents that were horrible parents; you still position yourself with God in that you have honored your father and mother. It's going to go well with you and you're actually going to inherit lands and properties and provision because of that. You'll have the provision of the Lord. So again, there's always something that most people need to forgive of their parents. Many today had parents who were neglectful, abusive, and even evil toward them. Forgive. This is how one can fulfill the requirements of the Bible in the way that brings the blessings.

The Apostle Paul wrote in Ephesians 6:2:

"Honor your father and mother," **which is the first commandment with promise.**

He was referring to one of the Ten Commandments in Exodus 20:12 (AUTHOR PARAPHRASE):

"Honor your father and your mother," that your days may be long upon the land which the Lord your God is giving you.

So, if you want some land to be given to you by God; honor your father and your mother by forgiving them.

This is what you're going to be ministering to other

people. They'll have to:

1. Take the faith of God.

2. Take authority over the mountain.

3. Pray the prayer of faith.

4. Make sure you've prayed the prayer of forgiveness.

Make sure you've involved God the Father and the Lord Jesus and the Holy Spirit so they all know you have forgiven others. Involve them in a prayer.

"Father, I forgive. Lord Jesus, thank You that You are the way that I have been forgiven by the Father and that You're empowering my prayer of forgiveness so that there's a release in their lives."

Forgive Those Who Have Passed On

Some people have to forgive parents that are now dead. It's ridiculous. Some people haven't forgiven people that have been dead for twenty years. What's it going to hurt you? They can't do anything about it. There's nothing that would help them, but it helps you. It blesses you and honors them by forgiving them. So, if you want to live long and have some land given to you, honor your father and your mother. Start by forgiving them. It's one of the greatest honors that they can ever receive.

Now, if they're alive, your forgiving them doesn't mean that you necessarily tell them. You just act like you have forgiven them. Some people say, "Well, we're estranged. We don't even talk." Well, then call them up and act like nothing's ever happened. Tell them you love them, in Jesus' name. Make sure you put Jesus' name in there. It's something you're having to do in the power of Jesus' name – to love them – but that's how you honor them.

I've heard so many stories where people have miraculous turnarounds in their families; where they had been horribly treated by parents and then the parents start repenting to them after they treated them well and honored them in an honoring way. Parents start saying, "Listen, I'm sorry. I really was a horrible parent. I was under all of this pressure and I wasn't nice to anybody. And you were probably the first ones to get the brunt of all of it."

With many, this is the beginning of a variety of blessings in restoring relationships with parents. You can forgive, even if a restored relationship is not possible. In some cases, it's not possible to have a relationship restored. God's not going to have you walk into or be a part of something where you're going to be abused (continually). So, you might still have to stay away. You just forgive from a distance. God doesn't expect anyone to move back into an abusive relationship.

Forgiveness will always bring blessings into your life. Sometimes it's important just to forgive other people because there are people that can't be trusted. Some people have proven they can't be trusted. You forgive them, even if you don't go back into a relationship with them. Businesses have broken up because people can't be trusted. It doesn't mean you go back into business with them; you forgive them from a distance. Make sure that forgiveness is there and you're not holding a grudge against them.

FORGIVENESS BREAKS CURSES

Here is a profound word for us all. Forgiveness also disconnects you from any curses that may have come upon the life of the person who is continually offending others. People do come under curses. You want to sever yourself from any curses that the offending person may be carrying on their life. Suddenly, something got attached to you when they offended you, in whatever way they did it. You guard your life by refusing to take offense or by forgiving others of their offenses. You refuse to take offense, now that you're spiritually mature, but you also forgive everybody in the past.

I remember a teaching I heard, by a minister named Larry Lee. He was doing a teaching on "Could you not tarry one hour?" He said this in his prayer for people, every single day. At the very beginning of the day, he would pray:

"Father, I forgive in advance, anybody who might offend me today, so that I take no offense."

There's a pre-forgiveness offered so that you don't take offense. Guess what? Somebody is probably going to come along and try to offend you during the day. Something may happen that you will find is offensive to you. There will be some disrespect of you, so just don't take offense. Forgive them in advance. If you forgot to forgive them in advance in the morning, then forgive them right then so that you don't walk in the offense.

In his defense to Felix, the governor of Israel at the time, Paul said:

"This *being* so, I myself always strive to have a conscience without offense toward God and men" (Acts 24:16).

This was Paul's statement to Felix, the Roman governor. God had prophesied to Ananias, who came to pray for Paul, that he was going to speak before kings, people, rulers, and all these others. He wanted to be the apostle to the Jews, and God made him be the apostle to the Gentiles. But all these other people were the Gentiles; they were the rulers. He got all the way to Caesar.

In Ephesians 5:1-2, Paul said:

Therefore be imitators of God as dear children. And walk in love, as Christ also has loved us and given Himself for us, an offering and a sacrifice to God for a sweet-smelling aroma.

That's what comes before the Lord. It's a sweet-smelling aroma; as a sacrifice where we make our prayer of forgiveness the sacrifice of love.

True liberty of the soul is not possible without forgiveness toward any offending person. So, again, if you want to have a clean conscience; nothing between you and God and the Lord Jesus or the Holy Spirit, make sure you're walking in forgiveness and pray that powerful forgiveness prayer – the *prayer of forgiveness and release.*

CHAPTER TWELVE

PRAYERS TO CHANGE OUTCOMES

PRAYER FORM 5 — THE PRAYER OF PETITION AND SUPPLICATION

We have finally moved into the area of specifics that you need to have in your life, in order to accomplish what God has called you to do. It doesn't matter that it's not always a need. God says, "I'm just going to bless you because I love you. I want to bless you with nice things. I want to restore your joy." Some things can just be a request that doesn't have anything to do with a need, like for what it is you're going to need to accomplish what God has called you to do.

It's kind of like a jet ski or a Sea-doo. You don't have to have one of those, but I've never seen anybody that's not in pure joy when they're out on a Sea-doo; out on a big lake.

You might think, "That's just a toy." Yeah, but it's something that gives you joy. Why wouldn't God provide those kinds of things? I've got my faith out there for a Sea-doo this next year. Now, people say, "Money can't buy you happiness." But it could buy you a Sea-doo and nobody's unhappy on a Sea-doo. It's the idea that God will surround your life with some good things.

A petition is like a list of essential needs, like every human being needs, and prayers of specific desires. You have needs and you have desires. God's desire is to meet every one of your needs so that you have no need; so you can be like the psalmist: "The Lord is my shepherd. I have no want. I should not have any want. I'm not in want of anything. I've got everything I need in order to accomplish what God has called me to do."

It's just like comfortable furniture in your house. Well, it's not necessary. You can survive without that, but if you're going to sit down and spend time with your family, you've got to sit down to eat with them. How about sitting at a nice table with nice silverware and dishes? It makes you feel good. It makes you feel happy to have that kind of provision. Again, it's not a total essential, but God says, "I want to meet your need and do it in a glorious way that you'll know it's from My hand and that I'm providing this."

Ephesians 6:18 says:

praying always with all prayer and supplication in the Spirit, being watchful to this end with all perseverance and supplication for all the saints.

That's why we're going to pray in the Spirit first. Make your supplication of these things. Be in the Spirit. You may say, "Well, how do I know that's happening?" Just keep praying in tongues until you sense: "Oh, my gosh, the Holy Spirit has prayed for all this provision for me. He's prayed for all these nice things to come into my life." So, you realize you have prayed the prayer of supplication by the Holy Spirit first. Then you say, "Well, what is it He prayed?" Pray for the interpretation. Maybe He's prayed for some things that you didn't even think about praying for, that had come. You realize, "Wow, God is one step ahead of me. That's awesome."

He's always one step ahead of you. He always will be, praise God. If you pray in the Spirit, He gets to do that one step ahead of you and cause those things to happen, even in advance. He's able to do exceedingly abundantly above all we could ask or even think to ask (Ephesians 3:20). That's why we pray in the Spirit; so that He can supplicate for us, all these things that are above what we would even think to ask. Then we start coming into agreement and in alignment with Him.

We can pray for ourselves and for the needs of others. A supplication is a humble, earnest entreaty or request. Now, you're not only going to be praying for your needs; you're going to pray for the needs of other people. We get prayer lists all the time from people. "Pray for this." You're going to be praying for people for the need of healing; praying for people for a need of transportation. So, why wouldn't the Holy Spirit be included in praying that for them as well?

If you make yourself a watchman on the wall and an intercessor who prays in tongues long enough, guess what? He will do that. He will start praying through you to meet the needs of other people, and the things that they need to be done in their lives as well. Praise God. We're going to make sure that we're going to supplicate. We're going to offer these petitions by praying in the Spirit enough, that all these things will be covered. Matthew 6:31-33 says:

"Therefore do not worry, saying, 'What shall we eat?' or 'What shall we drink?' or 'What shall we wear?' For after all these things the Gentiles seek."

In other words, the unbelievers seek all these things.

"For your Heavenly Father knows that you need all these things."

Everybody's the same. We all have essential needs in this life.

"But seek first the Kingdom of God and His righteousness,"

By praying in tongues.

"...and all these things shall be added to you."

It stands out to me so often when people say, "How do you seek first the kingdom of God and His kingdom of righteousness?" Well, by stepping over there in prayer; stepping into worship – true worship. If I'm going to just worship the Lord, I usually start out by praying in tongues. I know the Holy Spirit is interceding for me, but a lot of times it's like I'll come to a place where I will just need to sit silently in the presence of my Heavenly Father.

Then, anything the Father needs to speak to me, He will. The Father has spoken to me a number of times. I know His voice. Jesus has spoken to me a great deal of times. He talks to me daily, but it's sometimes very specific and very much concerning the assignment on my life. Every major thing that really came through sounded like an audible voice to me, but I also know when it's coming from Jesus as the Lord and Messiah of my life. But it comes from the Holy Spirit too; the Holy Spirit will speak to you.

The Holy Spirit is the one that's actually delivering the Father's words. It's the Holy Spirit who's delivering Jesus' words. The Holy Spirit's got His own words to speak to you because He's in sync with the mind of the Father and He's in sync with the Word spoken by Jesus, as the living Word. So, the Holy Spirit speaks to you. A lot of times, you just have to get quiet and stop the prayer tongues for awhile, just to listen. And pray that you can interpret what the Holy Spirit's been praying. Then you'll find out whether you're being answered by the Father, answered by the Son, or answered by the Holy Spirit – and what it is the Holy Spirit has prayed.

I'll tell you that this becomes a very supernatural, exciting way to live and walk with God that makes your prayer life exciting. It's not some drudgery. You don't have to say, "I've got to go through my prayer list. I've got to pray all the same things over and over again," and "God never answers."

I remember hearing a story of somebody doing a survey on prayer. This woman had been praying for 35 years. A man said to the woman, "So, how many prayers has God answered?" And she said, "As far as I know, He hasn't answered a single one." And the man said, "Are you kidding me? I would have quit at about fifteen years, if I never got a single prayer answered."

Getting back to Matthew 6:31-33a, we see:

"Therefore, do not worry, saying, 'What shall we eat?' or 'What shall we drink?' or 'What shall we wear?' For after all these things the Gentiles seek. For your heavenly Father knows that you need all these things."

He knows you need everything: the food, the clothing, and the car. We're in a modern world. You've got to have all the modern devices. If you're in the ministry, you've got to have cameras. You've got to have ways to be able to get the gospel out to more people than those that you're going to see in the same room.

"your heavenly Father knows that you need all these things. But seek first the kingdom of God and His righteousness, and all these things shall be added to you."

All these things will come in. Our prayer life should be this supernatural, exciting time of watching God do all these wondrous, miraculous things in our lives. That's why we're Word of Faith people. That's why we believe what we believe from the Word of God. God didn't expect us to withstand this hard life never hearing the voice of God; or, as this woman said, "As far as I know, He's never answered a single one of my prayers." She obviously didn't know how to pray in faith. It's a drudgery for a lot of people. For us, it's an adventure to pray and watch the miracle-working power of God coming into our lives and answering these prayers.

HAVE A GOOD CONSCIENCE

Don't worry, be happy. Ask with thanksgiving, that your Father in heaven will always meet your needs. We're going to find out that we're going to ask with thanksgiving. Where do we find that? In Philippians 4:6:

Be anxious for nothing.

Stop being nervous; stop being full of fear. Remember, this is what Jesus told to Jairus, the ruler of the synagogue in Capernaum, when he came to Him. He says, "My daughter is about ready to die. Would You please come lay hands on her so she'll live?" So, Jesus is on His way and He gets ambushed by a woman with the issue of blood. He suddenly has to stop and He deals with her. "By your faith, you have been healed."

Then people come from Jairus' house and say to him, "Don't bother the teacher any longer. Your daughter is dead." That was the perfect time for a father to just lose it. But immediately Jesus said, "Fear not, only believe." Keep believing. It really literally means: "Fear not, only believe what you just said. If I get to your daughter, your daughter will live. Even though the report is that she's died; fear not, only believe.

What did Jairus do from then on? He just zipped his lip. He didn't say anything. He didn't give into the doubt and unbelief that the devil tried to put in his mind and get him to say. He just went along with Jesus. "I'm just going to go along with Jesus. I'm going to fear not and only believe and go along with Jesus." So, Paul said to be anxious for nothing; fear not about anything, but in everything that you're facing, by prayer and supplication with thanksgiving, let your request be made known to God.

Again, this is prayer and supplication with thanksgiving. We're asking the Father in Jesus' name in faith, and we know it's His delight. He created everything for us to come into our lives. Philippians 4:19:

And my God shall supply all your need according to His riches in glory by Christ Jesus.

Christ Jesus purchased it for you. You hear that name Christ Jesus, as opposed to Jesus Christ. He's Jesus, our Christ; as our representative and as our High Priest to God the Father. But from God the Father, as our High Priest to us, He's Christ Jesus. He provided everything for our lives as Christ Jesus, having paid the price for us to have everything. My God shall supply everything according to His riches in glory by the one who purchased it for you – Christ Jesus – through Him. He's the one who paid the price for you to have everything.

Paul gave Timothy some specific instructions on prayer that we can all benefit from. Paul taught Timothy to wage warfare in prayer to bring prophecies to pass – prophecies that had been declared over him.

Now, listen. I already told you that you can be your own prophet. When you interpret your own prayer in tongues, you become your own prophet. You can hear what the Spirit of God is saying to you. There can be some things revealed to you by the Spirit of God as you get the interpretation of your tongues, that you're going to have to war in the Spirit by praying in tongues even more to receive those things.

But even if a prophecy has been spoken to you by somebody else, you still have to war for that to come to pass. You've got to contend in the Spirit. That's what our spiritual warfare is. We don't wrestle against flesh and blood. It's against all these powers of darkness. We're going to do that in the Spirit.

"This charge I commit to you, son Timothy, according to the prophecies previously made concerning you, that by them you may wage the good warfare" (1 Timothy 1:18).

Prophecy is given to us to wage a good warfare against the devil and what the devil is going to *continually* try to steal from us, continually try to keep us from having, and continually try to stop us from fulfilling the plan of God in our lives. We have to war against all of the things that he would try to do. But the prophecy over our lives says:

No, we succeed in everything God has called us to do. We are more than conquerors through Christ, who strengthens us. We have all of these things God has declared over us. We are blessed among all the brethren; above and beyond everything that anybody can imagine, because the blessing of God rests upon us. He's already declared it over us.

I'm in a war, according to the prophecy that God has spoken over my life. How am I going to win that warfare? By praying in tongues. Now, I'm not going to tell you that there's such a thing as "war tongues," because your tongues is really communing with Jesus and the Heavenly Father, by the power of the Holy Spirit. So, you don't have to "war" in the middle of that communion with God the Father.

When you're anointed by the Spirit of God with understanding, you take authority and dominion. We already saw that. Use the authority over all these mountains and against the kingdom of darkness. That's when you're going to war with understanding of what the Holy Spirit has already prayed through you.

Again, this has many aspects to it that we never even knew were part of what God was saying when He said, "building yourselves up on your most holy faith and praying in the Spirit" (Jude 1:20). It's more than just building yourself up on your most holy faith. It's building yourself up in your relationship with your heavenly Father and the Lord Jesus, and allowing the Holy Spirit to pray through you, all the perfect prayers that need to be prayed.

Then it's to be able to interpret those and take dominion over the kingdom of darkness, because the Holy Spirit has already done that for you. But you need to come into alignment and agreement with it and then suddenly, you are warring a good warfare against the enemy. We're going to see the victory in life when we come into the full measure of this. We have to implement every part of it to get the victory.

Paul first tells Timothy that he's in a spiritual warfare. He says that "prophecies have been previously spoken over you" (1 Timothy 1:18), but he was going to be required to contend in the Spirit and in prayer, to see them come to pass. So, if Paul told Timothy that, we know that it's something that could be spoken to all of us.

Timothy was a great son in the faith. People forget what a powerful man of God he became. He was awesome. He was with Paul through so much. He was with Paul when he wrote all those first prison epistles. He stayed with him in Rome, where he was in his own rented house; and he was Paul's emissary to the church from there. He was Paul's representative. He was like his associate apostle during that time. Later on, he became the pastor of the church of Ephesus.

It's an amazing thing to think; here, where John had been the apostle – and as far as we know – Mary, the mother of Jesus, who was appointed to John, was still there in Ephesus when John was on the Isle of Patmos. And we know that in the process; somewhere in the changeover, Mary might have still been alive and been under Timothy, with him as her pastor when he was at Ephesus. We don't know for sure, but there might have been more family members that were still there. Mary followed wherever John went because Jesus gave both of them that assignment.

There were these awesome positions that Timothy held, so he had to understand this foundation. And, if we're going to do awesome things, we're going to do exactly the same thing Paul instructed Timothy to do. In 1 Timothy 1:18-20, Paul said:

This charge I commit to you, son Timothy, according to the prophecies previously made concerning you, that by them you may wage the good warfare, having faith and a good conscience, which some having rejected, concerning the faith have suffered shipwreck, of whom are Hymenaeus and Alexander, whom I delivered to Satan that they may learn not to blaspheme.

Some people can shipwreck their lives because they depart from the pure Word of God and from praying in the Spirit and walking in the Spirit. Paul reminds Timothy that by maintaining a committed walk, he would not shipwreck his faith or assignment in life.

We find out that Paul used the *prayer of dominion and authority* when he was basically using what's called the *imprecatory prayer*, or a *prayer of justice and judgment*. (We'll examine this in depth in chapter fifteen.) Paul was turning them over to Satan for the destruction of the flesh so they would learn not to blaspheme. What were they doing? Blaspheming. Well, you can blaspheme the Father and you can blaspheme the Son. They were probably doing that, but he wouldn't have prayed for them if they had blasphemed the Holy Ghost – if they had been attributing things to Satan, the things that God was doing by the Holy Spirit. He would not have said that they could have been forgiven. He said, "I'm praying for them..."

that they may learn not to blaspheme.

PRAY FOR THOSE TO BE SAVED

Paul tells Timothy that he has prayed a prayer of justice and judgment over two Christian brothers who have so departed from the committed Christian life that they've begun to blaspheme either God or Jesus or the Word of God. This prayer is so that they can be corrected by the Lord. And there are those who commit blasphemy against the Holy Spirit and cannot be forgiven, so we're *not* to pray for those people.

Let's take a look at 1 Timothy 2:1:

Therefore, I exhort first of all that supplications, prayers, intercessions and giving of thanks be made for all men

We're given an instruction here to be able to pray for others. Of course, this includes women. The terminology in the Bible includes women. When the word "man" is used, it is "mankind" that is being referred to. It's about all people in your sphere of influence and outside your direct sphere of influence.

I really believe that this is going to enlighten many people because they've misinterpreted 1 Timothy 2:2. As Christians, we have to recognize that the leaders, kings, and priests of the kingdom of God are the first ones that we need to be praying for, before we pray for the sinners in the world and the leaders that are sinners in the world.

A lot of Christians waste their time praying for their leaders in government who are not Christians. They say, "Lord, give them wisdom." He can't give them wisdom. They've rejected Him! They have no capability of having any wisdom. You've got to be praying for them to get born again.

"Lord, send forth laborers into the harvest of their lives so that they can be saved. Lord, give us Christian leaders. Let us elect people that will listen to You and that will have wisdom and live by the Word of God. We've had some in the past; we'd like more."

Let me just mention as we go on, that we're going to be praying for everyone as we pray in tongues. Of course, we're going to use supplications, prayers, intercessions, and thanksgiving. We will realize that we're using all prayer, because the Holy Spirit is using all prayer. When we're praying, we're going to include those that we need to pray for, and they will be prayed for by the Holy Spirit. And then we will come into agreement with what the Holy Spirit has prayed. 1 Timothy 2:2:

for kings and all who are in authority, that we may lead a quiet and peaceable life in all godliness and reverence.

Christians are citizens of heaven first, then citizens of an earthly country. Of course, I'm a citizen of the United States of America. We are citizens of another country. The first men and women that Christians should pray for are those in authority in the Church of the Lord Jesus Christ. But who are the kings and the priests that we would see in the Church of the Lord Jesus Christ, that are in this category of leaders?

Ministries that have a global impact are leading the way for the whole body of Christ and should be undergirded in prayer: for their protection, for their provision, and for their continued success in the work of the Lord. We need to be undergirding everybody in ministry first – kings in ministry.

We've got kings in the workplace, and some of us should be kings and priests in ministry, so we're going to be praying for all of them. There are some that have global ministries, that God has given a very clear and concise Word that is a reflection of His will. We need to pray for their continual, ongoing success so that they can continue to influence more people with the truth of the Word of God.

Next, we can pray for the earthly, governmental positions of power so that we can live a quiet and peaceable life of godliness and reverence. Even in the midst of all the crazy chaos of godless, anti-Christ communist governments; there are a lot of Christians that are fulfilling what God has called them to do. So, when they're praying for their government, they can't ask God to give wisdom to communists. They've already declared that "There is no God; the state is God."

That's what communism is. "The state is God above everything." Most of the communist countries are like this. Mao Tse-tung murdered over eight million leaders in communist China – anybody that could be a threat to his government, especially religious leaders. That's because they made and believed that "The state is God."

Everybody who had another religion other than communism was going to oppose everything that they were doing to "try to help the masses of the workers," and had to be eliminated. They were murderers, butchers, Satan's people; demon-possessed people in government. And yet, the gospel still went forth.

There's a movement even in communist Russia today. It's more above ground now, because we've got Rick Renner there, with the greatest Christian television network anybody's ever seen in Russia before. There are so many Christians there now, even if the leader has gone demon-possessed again.

The people are praying against what he's doing, not for him to be blessed with the wisdom of God in how to invade other countries. No, it's for them to survive and fulfill what God's called them to do; to live this peaceable life in godliness and reverence before the Lord.

Many Christians mistakenly pray, trying to control the minds of unbelievers who are in government power. They ask God to give them wisdom, but those who are anti-Christ can never gain the wisdom of God until they become saved. God can however, circumvent them from getting their godless way done, and Christians can still live in peace and freedom, to fulfill God's purposes.

We're going to pray for God to circumvent the efforts of the evil rulers, even in our own country, because there are evil people everywhere in every country. We're the most Christian country there is, but we have less than 50% truly born again Christians in this country.

I knew from the time I got saved 49 years ago, that we were in the extreme minority of people who are actually truly born again. There are a lot of churchgoers, but you can see the way they live. You can tell they do not know the Lord. You know them by their fruits. The reality is that a lot of people don't know the Lord; even in a country that was established to be a Christian country.

A lot of people don't understand this, that in the time of

our founders, they used the term "religion," as synonymous with the term "denomination." So, they believed in the denominational freedom of Christianity. It didn't matter whether you were Catholic or Protestant or in any one of the different Protestant denominations; you had freedom to practice your Christianity. They never intended for us to have all of the false religions here running rampant – demonically inspired religions, taking over in America – but we've got that today.

Obama was right when he said we were no longer a Christian nation. No, we haven't been a Christian nation, where the majority of the people are born again Christians. But he wanted to make that declaration that he was not a Christian. He was going to make sure that everybody in the rest of the world knew that he didn't think we were a Christian nation. He was saying, "We're not going to act like a Christian nation."

It's a sad state of affairs, but we can still fulfill what God has called us to do, in the middle of a bunch of people that are full of demons and that are running things in government. And we can pray for God to circumvent those things that they're doing, that will stop the Church. What they tried to do during the pandemic was stop the Church from getting together and gathering or assembling together. They shut us down from worshipping God. That was in the name of "saving lives," while they were placing people in a medically-induced coma and intubating them. It's hard to use faith when you are in a coma.

Sometimes a righteous indignation will arise. We have a lot of work to do in praying against godless government everywhere. We're going to be praying for godly government and praying against godless government and praying that God will still allow us to have the freedoms to complete everything that He has called us to do. You can pray for God to send laborers into their paths; for these people to get born again by declaring the gospel to them, and giving them the opportunity to be saved (Matthew 9:38).

For this *is* good and acceptable in the sight of God our Savior, who desires all men to be saved and to come to the knowledge of the truth (1 Timothy 2:3-4).

We're going to undergird and pray for people because we want them to get saved, and because God's will would be that nobody would die and go to hell. He wants them all to be saved. That's what our assignment is: trying to get even all these people that we can tell are obviously deserving of hell to actually get saved, and have Jesus wipe away all of their "deserving to go to hell sins" away from them. It's not really those sins. It's the sin of rejecting Jesus Christ as Lord, that sends somebody to hell.

Now, we can recognize a degree of sins – murder is at the top of the list; all the way down through a whole bunch of other things that our civil government is designed to protect us from, with people doing all of these different things that are evil. It's not the doing of those evil things that sends people to hell. They go to hell because *they've rejected Jesus Christ*.

Let's look at Matthew 9:36-38, for we are to offer prayers of supplication for those whom we desire to be saved.

But when He saw the multitudes, He was moved with compassion for them, because they were weary and scattered, like sheep having no shepherd.

These are the multitudes that are following after Jesus and they don't know He's the Messiah. They just know He's a prophet that heals people, and a lot of times, feeds them. So, they're following for the food and for the healings, and they think He's probably good, but they still don't know.

A lot of the ones who were worshipping Him the day that He came into Jerusalem were the same ones that were part of this crowd that said, "Crucify Him! Crucify Him!" But Jesus had compassion; He was moved with compassion for them because they were weary and scattered like sheep with no shepherd. Then He said to His disciples:

"The harvest truly *is* plentiful, but the laborers *are* few."

"We're just a handful to get this message to them. We have to multiply."

"Therefore pray the Lord of the harvest to send out laborers into His harvest."

Well, those original disciples who became apostles prayed that prayer for the Lord of the harvest to send forth laborers into the harvest. If you're pursuing being part of God's harvest and being a laborer in His harvest, you're an answer to that prayer from almost 2,000 years ago. We do know that you're an answer to prayer. You're an answer to *their* prayer. You're the answer to the Father's will, that laborers would constantly be sent forth into the harvest.

When we pray in the Spirit, the Holy Spirit is praying through us, for more laborers to be sent into the harvest. God is able to tap more hearts of believers and say, "I've got a special thing for you to accomplish in being My ambassador and My representative in the earth." So, we're going to keep listening to Him for everything that He's going to be doing concerning sending forth laborers into the harvest.

Again, this request is made with fervency and urgency. What if Jesus is coming back in the year 2030 – 2,000 years from the time He left? Maybe He will. Well, where's the urgency? We need an urgency! I expect to be busier in the next seven years than I've ever been – not because I think He's coming back, but because I think something dynamic is going to be happening. We better be about the Father's business and His kingdom business during the next seven years, in order to be prepared for what's going to come to pass at that point in time.

PRAY FOR RAIN

We can pray for the rain of the Holy Spirit to be poured out for revival and for great moves of salvation. It's amazing. There have been moves of God where people are swept into the kingdom by the millions, throughout the entire earth. We want to see more of those moves of God. Zechariah 10:1 says:

Ask the Lord for rain
In the time of the latter rain.

One of the things the Holy Spirit is praying for you, is for an outpouring in the time of the latter rain; we're in the time of the latter rain.

The Lord will make flashing clouds;
He will give them showers of rain,
Grass in the field for everyone.

James 5:7,16-18 says:

Therefore, be patient, brethren, until the coming of the Lord. See *how* the farmer waits for the precious fruit of the earth, waiting patiently for it until it receives the early and latter rain...Confess *your* trespasses to one another, and pray for one another, that you may be healed. The effective, fervent prayer of a righteous man [or woman]

avails much. Elijah was a man with a nature like ours, and he prayed earnestly that it would not rain; and it did not rain on the land for three years and six months. And he prayed again, and the heaven gave rain, and the earth produced its fruit.

We're praying for that rain of the Spirit of God to come and do a tremendous harvest, in the last days of harvest. The Amplified Bible says this:

The earnest (heartfelt, continued) prayer of a righteous man [or woman] makes tremendous power available [dynamic in its working]" (James 5:16b AMPC**).**

Our prayer is dynamic in its working, because of that power that's available to us — praying in the Spirit — and then of course, getting the interpretation of what we're praying, and coming into agreement and alignment with it. That's why I have no problem praying anything that I sense that the Holy Spirit has prayed through me.

PRAYER FORM 6 – THE PRAYER OF INTERCESSION

When you think about how you answer the call to prayer from the Lord, you can now see yourself as an intercessor. An intercessor is a mediator, a person who stands in the gap where there's something missing. We're willing to take that place. In intercession, it is essential to remember to pray in the Spirit in tongues. You will come into the flow of the Spirit; interceding for yourself and others as the Holy Spirit desires you to pray.

This takes intercession out of the potential of becoming legalistic and rigid. You will also be able to interpret who and what you are interceding for as you intercede in tongues. Then you can also come into agreement with your understanding, and pray and declare in your first language that you usually speak in. Often, more than one kind of prayer will be chosen by the Holy Spirit for effective, successful prayer. Supplication will often merge into and overlap with intercession.

Again, we're going to find out that intercession is standing in the gap for somebody else and interceding for them. But we will also find out that the Holy Spirit is interceding for us. He's standing in the gap for us and interceding. Jesus is interceding; He's standing in the gap and praying for us when we pray in the Holy Spirit. They want us to receive everything God has. And we want others to receive everything God has for them. We find out there's a tremendous need; especially when it's critical to God. It might be a life or death situation. We will be praying for these people in intercession.

Intercession defined is "to stand in the gap and plead the case for oneself or for another." It can include holding back judgment for a wrongdoing that is worthy of punishment. That's standing in the gap for somebody.

What if somebody just goes off course but you know their heart and they've been trying to be good? Maybe there was an intercessor for David when he went off course, but he repented when it was spoken to him. I would say that Nathaniel was an intercessor for him. He spoke to him from God. Maybe he was an answer to somebody's prayer for David to stay on course, and he repented.

We need to make sure that we're going to be doing whatever the Holy Spirit is praying forth. We might be praying for somebody to not get judged for something they were worthy of punishment for.

The *prayer of intercession* can also include issues that are covered – usually in supplication – for deliverance or provision.

We're going to be praying, and while praying, many times angels get involved. Remember, there are deliverance angels. There are not just guardian angels, but ones that deliver people out of trouble.

I've been delivered out of trouble by angels. I know what they do. One kept me alive from a head-on collision that would have probably killed me. I know when those angels show up on the scene by the power of God. My angel must have called them in. Either my angel was able to do that, or I think there were several angels involved in that, who were able to deliver me from death.

In Romans 8:27, we know that the Holy Spirit makes intercession for us, (pleads our case before God the Father) according to the will of God. He is always going to be pleading our case before the Father and before the Son. His will is always going to be for good. Intercession is for the good outcome: for deliverance, for restoration, for restored health, and for restored provision and everything good.

Remember Job? He got everything restored, after his huge trial. And intercession was made for Sodom and Gomorrah by Abraham; to stall God from withholding His protective covering so they would not be destroyed by the destroyer. In Genesis 18:16-33, Abraham failed to ask God to spare them for one righteous man. He stopped at ten. He says, "Lord, would You judge the whole people if there were fifty righteous people there?" He gets all the way down to ten.

God still considered Lot to be righteous. I look at Lot and think, "What were You thinking?" That's because he was actually sitting in the gates with the elders of Sodom and Gomorrah; it was a corrupt place. Of course, you can look at the whole world today, and the whole world is celebrating Sodom and Gomorrah. But Lot was still one righteous man that God would have saved the whole place for at the time, but Abraham didn't intercede to that level. Often, God had no one who would intercede for the land.

> **So I sought for a man among them who would make a wall, and stand in the gap before Me on behalf of the land...but I found no one (Ezekiel 22:30).**

One morning, the Lord woke me up and I was just exhausted. I could barely keep my eyes open, but I knew the Lord, and I said, "Really Lord? I'm exhausted. Do I really have to get up and pray?" The Lord spoke to me and said, "I don't have anybody." It was like I felt this plea coming from Him. "I don't have anybody else who will pray right now." That's why I thought, "Yeah, I'll get up and pray." And I got up and prayed. But afterwards, I started realizing: could there be times where there's nobody that will stand in the gap and intercede?

He's calling us as Christians. It's like He's saying: "I've got something going on." It might have been for one person; maybe they were facing death, or expulsion from a ministry, or whatever, I don't know. But nobody would pray, and the Lord asked me to pray, so it was critical to Him. If it's critical to Him, it should be critical to us.

If He says, "I've got nobody else but you guys to pray, will you please pray?" Take your place. He'll probably let you know what you were praying about, later on. I still don't know; I just know that it was critical for somebody and He didn't have anybody else, so I said, "Okay, yeah, I will." We have to come to that place where we're willing to do that.

PRAYER IS GOD'S WILL

God's will concerning all people is expressed by the Apostle Peter. He said:

The Lord is not slack concerning *His* promise, as some count slackness, but is longsuffering toward us, nor willing that any should perish but that all should come to repentance (2 Peter 3:9).

I'd say that's why Jesus hasn't come back yet – it's because God's long-suffering. He realizes when He sends Jesus back, that it shuts the door for everybody else. They're going into judgment. And there are seven and a half billion people on the planet today. God is not in a hurry to send five and a half billion of them into the devil's hell for eternity, so He's long-suffering. He's putting it off as long as He possibly can.

I don't know; it might be some number that He's got in mind that will fill all of heaven and all His purposes. Every believer that's on the earth – there's probably more born again believers on the earth today than there actually are in heaven. That's because there were so few for the longest time, and the population of the earth has so increased. With just the numbers that are here, we might already match the numbers of those that are in heaven.

I don't know if there's going to be a point or some divine number that God has in mind, and He says, "That's it," and He'll send Jesus back. He's longsuffering until then, because He knows what's going to happen for all those that are left on the earth after He extricates the Church from the earth and brings judgment.

Again, repentance has changed the people's minds about what they believed about Jesus and God the Father. God was moved by Moses' intercession for the nation of Israel (Numbers 14:11-19; Exodus 32:7-14).

God was done with Israel and He says, "I'll just wipe them all out Moses. I'll start all over again with just you. I'll do what I did with Noah and his family. I'll just wipe everybody else off the planet, and start all over again."

Moses interceded, "But You've put Your Word out there; the whole world is watching this nation that has come up to be Your blessed people by Your Word." He was interceding for the people. God listened to Moses' intercession and He did not turn them over to the destroyer. In Psalm 106:23 (NASB), He said he would have done that.

Therefore He said that He would destroy them, If Moses, His chosen one, had not stood in the gap before Him, To turn away His wrath from destroying *them.*

Jesus, our great intercessor, was called forth by the Father because He had no intercessor. Now, He always had the plan. Jesus was not "Plan B." Jesus was always "Plan A," from the very beginning. Even when He created Adam, He knew He was going to have to have a second Adam or the last Adam, who was going to be the one who redeemed mankind.

He had to give Adam the ability to have a choice, or he would not have been created in God's image. God has the ability to choose, but He always chooses perfectly. He always chooses Holiness. Sure, God's got a choice. He could have chosen, but He never chooses wrong; He always chooses right. He had to make Adam with the same faculty that He had; the ability to choose.

Now, on Adam's part, he was there when Eve misquoted God to Satan. "You can't eat or touch the fruit." She saw that it was good. "This is good fruit. It must taste good too." She ate of it and then gave it to her husband. He was right there. Here's the deal: Adam knew that whatever she was going to go through – if she was going to be separated from God, that he would be too.

He knew that if she was going to die, he wanted to die. He had so gotten his eyes on his bride, who he's now one flesh with. He's so gobsmacked by her that he's willing to listen to her, rather than to God. If he had not eaten, she would have died spiritually.

God would have had to give him another "Eve," if he'd have just stuck with the plan. But God knew. He'd given him the choice. He knew Adam was going to choose wrong, so He always had a plan. Jesus was always "Plan A," but He had no intercessor before Jesus, to be able to stand in the gap for him and to be his high priest to represent them to the Lord.

He saw that *there was* no man, And wondered that *there was* no intercessor; Therefore His own arm brought salvation for Him; And His own righteousness, it sustained Him (Isaiah 59:16).

For *there is* one God and one Mediator between God and men, *the* Man Christ Jesus (1 Timothy 2:5).

He's our intercessor, our mediator.

For Christ has not entered the holy places made with hands, *which are* copies of the true, but into heaven itself, now to appear in the presence of God for us (Hebrews 9:24).

That's to represent us before God. He's constantly before the Father as our intercessor.

Who *is* He who condemns? *It is* Christ who died, and furthermore is also risen, who is even at the right hand of God, who also makes intercession for us (Romans 8:34).

Twice we have seen Paul tell us, in both Romans 8:34 and in Hebrews 7:25, that Jesus *ever* lives to make intercession for us.

But He, because He continues forever, has an unchangeable priesthood. Therefore He is also able to save to the uttermost those who come to God through Him, since He always lives to make intercession for them (Hebrews 7:24-25).

Jesus is our great intercessor. The ministry that Jesus now has in heaven is to perpetually intercede for His family, the royal priesthood, the holy nation of believers. That's you and me. But just like the Holy Spirit, Jesus can't intercede for us until we pray in tongues. When we pray in tongues, the Holy Spirit prays through our spirit, and Jesus then comes into intercession. He is praying for us and it's all completely dependent upon us praying.

The Lord Jesus will stand in the gap for us. He would intercede for us anyway, but He doesn't get to do the real intercession that we need, until we come into agreement with what the Holy Spirit is interceding for us. Remember, it is always intercession for you first; then it goes into intercession where you now start taking the place as an intercessor – one standing in the gap for somebody else to pray and intercede for them. Then, just keep praying through until the Holy Spirit reveals that.

So much of the time, you get these encounters with the Lord and you realize: "Wow, I just got to pray through one of our family's needs. I just got to pray through one of the ministry's needs. Now it's activated. It's on its way." You come into agreement with it when it's revealed to you about what it is. Sometimes you don't even know. You have prayed through and you come into agreement with it, having prayed through regardless of what it is. You just know it's good. It's on its way, so praise God.

CHAPTER THIRTEEN

THE WALK OF FAITH

PRAYER FORM 7 – THE PRAYER OF AGREEMENT

The *prayer of agreement* is when two or more people are praying in complete spiritual alignment with one another. I use the term "alignment" because most people are familiar with their cars and when you have to take your car to have your wheels aligned. Of course, you steer with your front wheels, but if your front wheels are not completely in alignment with each other, your tires will wear out; both of them have to be straight. One of them could be toed-in or -out from the other one, and it's going to be pulling the car to one side. Your front wheels have to be in alignment with your back wheels, and vice-versa so they are completely straight.

When we come into alignment with the Lord, it's like we are completely lined up with the Father, the Son, and the Holy Spirit – and us; and we make a majority. That's what it is to really come into agreement. It is to come into complete alignment; we're in a straight line with what the Father's will is, that He has passed on through the Lord Jesus to the Holy Spirit. He comes to us and we're in total agreement with everything that They will for us. So again, we're to come into alignment with one another.

The prayer of agreement is praying with other people to

come into this same alignment. Both people must be relatively at the same spiritual level of understanding the promises of God in His Word. You have to find people who are spiritually mature on the level that you are, so you can come into alignment together.

There's always going to be different levels, but you can find a place to be in agreement with other people at the highest level of spiritual maturity that they're at, that you know of. You can come into agreement with them in understanding our authority given in the name of Jesus, to petition the Father in heaven. We're all going to be coming into agreement together to ask the Father in Heaven in Jesus' name, to meet a certain need.

In Matthew 18:18-20 (TPT), He says:

"Receive this truth; whatever you forbid on Earth..."

He's speaking about the authority of *binding and loosing* on earth. You can only do this with somebody else when you both come into a true alignment.

"Whatever you forbid on earth will be considered to be forbidden in heaven,"

This is from *The Passion Translation:*

"and whatever you release on earth will be considered to be released in heaven. Again, I give you an eternal truth: If two of you [two human beings] agree to ask God for something in a symphony of prayer,"

That's the prayer of agreement. You know what a symphony is; that's where there's harmony. It doesn't use the word here, but a symphony of prayer is so that all the requests are harmonious. They sound right. One's not out of key or off the note they're supposed to be on.

"If two of you agree to ask God for something in a symphony of prayer, my heavenly Father will do it for you. For wherever two or three come together in honor of my name, I am right there with them."

Jesus is saying, "I'm going to be there with you when you're asking the Father in My name. I'm going to come up; I'm going to show up." When two people agree together, all of a sudden, Jesus makes you the Church. He says, "I'll be there in the midst of you. My anointing will show up. I'll be there when you come together to worship me; when you come to gather to worship and pray and seek the Father on behalf of somebody else.

Verse 18 is referring to the authority that we discussed, concerning demanding the powers of darkness to be stopped, and the natural circumstances to be changed, to match the good will of God. That's John 14:12-14; taking authority in the name of Jesus.

The *prayer of agreement* will sometimes take the form of the *prayer of authority* when you're agreeing to come against the works of darkness. But it's also going to come into the prayer of agreement when praying to the Father in Jesus' name, to be able to receive. Again, that's the whole idea of forbidding something – that's going to be the authority that is used. You are going to be forbidding the devil; forbidding the mountain to stay in that place, by casting it into the sea.

It's an amazing thing when two people are able to be in a prayer of agreement. First, they usually need to pray in tongues together for a long time. You find that these people are prayer partners. My wife and I are prayer partners, and we both pray and always compare the things that the Lord is showing to both of us in our prayers. So, we both pray in tongues a lot. You will find that God will give you a prayer partner where you can come into alignment and agreement with them.

Sometimes you're going to be taking authority and dominion over things. Two people will be binding something on earth and stopping it from happening. And they will be loosing the power of God and the answers to come from the Lord. Sometimes, the two of you are going to be asking in a request, a supplication to the Father, in Jesus' name. So, both prayers get used here in the prayer of agreement.

Again, Matthew 18:18 is referring to the authority that we discussed. Verse 19 is speaking about two or more people who are coming into harmony spiritually, and their prayers are sounding like a symphony as it rises up to the Father in Jesus' name.

Now, your individual prayer obviously does extremely well for you and for so many things, but it also seems totally unlimited. When we dig into the prayer of agreement, we find out – *anything* is possible when two people can really come into alignment. Again, this is two or more people coming into harmony – spiritually. Their prayer sounds like a symphony as it rises to the Father.

Verse 20 is speaking to the reality that the Lord Jesus manifests His presence when just two or more people are assembled in prayer; making it a gathering of the Church. The Church of course, is not the building. It's the living stones (1 Peter 2:5). It's the Christian human beings, when they gather together, so two people can make up a church. You can start a church with just two people. A husband and wife can be a church. They can start a church, if they know how to pray together.

So many churches have started that way. I don't know

how many people that I know of, that have pioneered churches.

We decided to start the church, and that first Sunday it was me and my wife and our baby kids. I just preached to them and then we just kept inviting people and some people came over. We started this ministry in our house, when the Lord told us to start it. We left the seminary that we were ministering at, and we started both the church and the university in our house.

We had our office together. We put two desks together and purchased a computer on a credit card, to get started. We started putting the university together and holding services in our house. We outgrew it in about two weeks, so we had to rent a place. We were able to rent an office space and we moved everything there. Then we were able to rent a Taekwondo Dojo for holding church services. There was another church in the same business complex there that had some offices and a couple of meeting rooms, so we used those for the children's ministry. I always joked, calling it the "First Church of the Taekwando."

Anyway, you don't despise the days of humble beginnings, because you will say, "Who knew that in just a few years..." I remember thinking that at the very beginning, I would do this for thirty years and we would finally be up to one hundred campuses. We hit that number in the seventh year!

Starting at that point in time, I had no idea that in the seventh year we would hit one hundred campuses. It suddenly lunged way ahead and we've actually opened well over two hundred campuses in the process of time. And, we've always maintained over one hundred active campuses from the time that we hit one hundred.

Some churches that were operating campuses would run to a point of saturation. Everybody in their church that wanted to get an education in ministry did that, and they'd say, "We kind of ran out of students," so they would go on what we call a "hiatus" and they would shut down. Over the last ten years, so many of them have come back and started up all over again. We even relaunched in places where we had campuses because the church kept growing and more new people came in.

They'd say, "Hey, the same people are here to teach this and we've got enough students to start all over again, so can we do that?" "Yes, absolutely; start them up all over again." It's been a very exciting and interesting venture. People say, "Well, how did you figure out how to do it?" God gave us the idea and then we had to invent things as we went.

That's *the walk of faith.* You find yourself praying for God's wisdom and understanding and He imposes that on you and you just act on that. It's almost like inventing because you're doing things that have never been done before.

I used to teach that before starting a new endeavor, to look for somebody that has done what you want to do before you do it, and learn from them. You get good guidance and counsel from somebody to be able to do something, and then you started realizing, "God told us to do something we've never seen anybody do before." We had to get it strictly from Him. So, when people say, "How did you do it?" I say, "Well, I just had to listen to God, because I didn't have anybody else to look to." We were doing something unique.

It's been a very exciting journey to be on: just fearing God and wanting to educate people that wanted to have a ministry education that could not go to some school. They didn't have that opportunity. So, God put us in campuses in churches where people were unable to go off to *Rhema* or to *Christ For The Nations.* They might say, "I'm a businessman with five kids at home, so it'll be thirty years before I can do that." But God was able to bring an education to them.

Now, with online education, anybody anywhere in the

world that can speak English can get our ministry education program; and for some of them, English is not their first language. So again, LCU came about because my wife and I came into agreement to birth a university as the Lord has directed us in.

OUR PRAYERS ARE UNLIMITED

It seems that the *prayer of agreement* is unlimited in its usage. There is *nothing* that can't be prayed for and received when two or more are truly in one accord. This kind of praying should be especially powerful in Christian marriages. It will still require both of you to be on the same level spiritually, and on the same page in agreeing with the promises of God.

I went to Rhema in 1980 and graduated in 1982. I came back to Tampa and was pastoring my first church. Then, when I met my wife, we started dating and then we got married. After that, the Lord told me, "Your wife's going to have to have the same ministry education that you have." He didn't say that she needed to go to Rhema; He just said she has to have the same ministry education I have. I knew that He meant that she needed to go to Rhema, so we packed up again and went out to Rhema in 1988.

I left the church we were pastoring and went out to Rhema for her to get a ministry education. She graduated in 1990, and of course, we launched into ministry together from there. It's a whole lot easier to do things in agreement; you get more done that way. I just have to testify that it will work for married couples.

A hindrance to praying the prayer of agreement is when you are attempting to agree with someone and their faith is not where your faith is – and is often opposite of where your faith is. Not everyone is going to have the same understanding of the Word of God. Not everyone's mind has been renewed to the will of God, so you can't come into the prayer of agreement with everybody.

You can locate them in where their faith is at, and come into agreement with where their faith is at, but it might be a lower level than what you're used to praying on – and that's okay. You'll help them get to the next level. They need to find out that God will still answer their prayers, so you locate them and find out what level of faith they're actually at.

If you want to pray with someone for their needs, you must locate them spiritually and find out what they can believe for. Quite often when it comes to healing, their faith may be that the work of the doctors and medicine is what's going to bring about the desired results. In such a case, simply come into agreement with what it is they can believe, and pray that the doctors will be anointed to do the best job they have ever done.

You can still get the miraculous outcome by praying the prayer of agreement with somebody, at the place where they are at in faith. Now, if their faith is for them to be able to be healed supernaturally; praise God, that's what you want to agree on. A born again believer has been given authority over Satan and every fallen angel and evil spirit, but we don't have the authority over another person's spirit. To try to manipulate people or pray to overcome one's spirit is witchcraft. We can't fall into this ineffective deception of the devil, and cross over to copying his ways.

In 1995, my wife and I started *Life Church* and *Life Christian University*. We pastored for the first five years and then the Lord enabled us to move out of pastoring and just do the university ministry. For the last twenty-three years, that's what we've done. The university went global during that time. I'll never say "never" to the Lord, so if He says "pastor" again, I'll certainly do what He says to do.

An amazing thing happened involving the *prayer of agreement*. One of these healings involved Deb Smith, who's been our main campus director for many years; she has a number of children. One of her children at the time – a grown adult child named Marchant — was pregnant with her second child (a daughter), and she was in the hospital. I didn't realize what was going on, but she was probably five months pregnant I believe; certainly not full-term.

You know, there would be some great complications if she was to have the birth that early. She had developed toxemia. Toxemia creates poisons in your system and this was causing her to go into contractions, which might have forced an early birth of the child.

I got a call from Deb and she said, "Pastor Doug, can you possibly come to the hospital? I'm up here with Marchant right now, and she is in a bad situation." So, I went to get my associate pastor at the time, Brother Terry. I called him at around three in the morning and I said, "What are you doing?" He said, "I was sleeping."

Anyway, he let me come and pick him up. We both went to the hospital and when we walked in, we saw Marchant. She had a tube in her nose that went into her stomach. They were trying to pump the poisons out but nothing would come out. They had her on a monitor and it was monitoring the contractions that she was having. I think she had IVs in both arms and she looked exhausted and kind of desperate.

I said, "Marchant, what is it you're believing for? I want to pray with you, but I need to know what you're believing for. Do you believe that what the doctors are doing is going to work and you'll be able to go full-term and that you'll get over this toxemia? Or, are you believing that Jesus wants to just heal you and be done with this thing?" And she said, "I believe Jesus is my healer. By His stripes I was healed. I'm standing on that Word."

I said, "Okay, that's exactly how we're going to pray." So, Brother Terry and I and Sister Deb gathered around and we were praying for her. We laid hands on her and prayed for her. We prayed a prayer of agreement with what she was believing for. We believed exactly what she was believing in: Jesus was going to minister to her right then.

It was interesting, because after we stood back for a second; Brother Terry, the associate pastor, backed up to the wall. Apparently he got a little bit nauseous from looking at all of the tubes and IVs. He nearly passed out and just slid down the wall. His legs were kind of buckled underneath him. I said, "Brother Terry, do you want me to straighten your legs out so that you can be more comfortable? Do you want me to help you stand back up?" And he said, "Help me stand up," so as he pushed a little, I pulled him up the wall.

Well, as soon as he rose up, Marchant is looking at him and suddenly sees Jesus. Now, I don't know why she saw Jesus when she saw Brother Terry, because I wore a beard at the time, and I thought I looked more like Jesus than he did, but she was seeing in the Spirit. She saw him; She saw Jesus, so she reached her hands out and said, "Jesus, You're here." She was seeing Jesus in the room.

Brother Terry didn't know. She was looking right at him, so he just walked over and grabbed her by the hands. All of a sudden – and I believe it was our prayer of agreement that had done this – but she was now having an encounter with Jesus.

We watched, and all of a sudden, the machine kicked in and all those toxins in her body were being pumped out of her body. We watched the monitor that was monitoring her contractions suddenly go flat. That's the only time you want to see a flat line: when it's monitoring contractions that need to go away.

We watched the actual hospital equipment register the healing being manifest in her body at that time. And she went full-term and eventually delivered a beautiful baby girl. Of course, the baby grew up, and today she is in the Air Force.

The prayer of agreement is powerful! Again, there are so many things that my wife and I have come into spiritual agreement over, concerning this ministry, over the years. We've seen miracles happen over and over again – so many, that I can't even remember all the details.

PRAYER IS NOT MANIPULATION

Let's examine what happens when people cross over into trying to manipulate a human spirit, a human person. What we know is that we have been given authority over Satan and every fallen angel and every evil spirit, but we do not have authority over any other person's spirit. That's why it requires the teaching and preaching of the Word of God. It requires the gospel to come to people who are not saved and who are being ruled by Satan.

They don't know that they've surrendered to him. They're just a puppet to the devil and they are living completely murderous and horrible kinds of lives. That's because the devil will take people and just twist them around and make them completely insane.

As a matter of fact, we've had so many different shootings; mass shootings of people, like when they go into a school and some 18-year-old shoots a bunch of second graders. People try to figure it out psychologically and they say, "We don't know what set them off. We don't know what the mental state of that one was."

They will never understand it because they won't understand demon possession. They don't understand when unsaved people have been manipulated by the devil, and that yes, there are some bad circumstances in their lives that led them to mental instability, but that just means they're right on the verge of giving in to total demon possession. When they do that, a lot of times they confess afterwards, "Well, I heard these voices tell me to do it." They've given in to demon possession, and that's why they do those kinds of things. One of the things that people say is, "We're going to have to find the solution."

Well, secure the schools. Just like you finally secured the cockpits of the airplanes; secure the schools. It's going to take that when you have a demonized culture. I mean, all the nations of the earth are having the same kind of demonized culture everywhere. And until we – in America at least – are sensible enough to secure the schools; you're not going to have another way to be able to stop these demon-possessed people from coming in. They have to be stopped from the outside.

When we talk about people trying to manipulate other people; quite often we've had intercessory groups get together to pray for the church. Then, all of a sudden, you find a couple of leaders in this intercessory group that disagree with the pastor about this or that, or whatever. Now, the pastor may be wrong about something. They may be wrong about some doctrine, but that doesn't mean you have authority over the pastor's spirit or you can try to pray against him in some way, without stepping over into the area of witchcraft.

It's an ineffective deception of the devil and it's copying his ways. We don't want to do that. Many prayer groups in churches that have been very ignorant of the Word and the Spirit, have unknowingly attempted to use witchcraft to manipulate pastoral leadership to do what they think is best.

Now, maybe they were completely wrong in what they think is best, and maybe they are right, but we do know that you can't use witchcraft to change it. That will ruin a church.

It will sow seeds of all kinds of division.

Even if they have the right ideas, they can destroy the spiritual health of the church by unknowingly using witchcraft. Prayer groups should certainly pray for the pastoral leadership of the church; that God would give them wisdom in all things and keep them strong in the Spirit, and blessed in their family life, with all the good things from the Lord and any other good blessing that they can think of.

If you surround a pastor with prayer – one who's searching and seeking the Lord – then He will come into this place of always being strong in the Spirit; his family life's going well and he's not going to be distracted. He can hear from the Lord concerning the church. And if He's undergirded that way, God is more than able to speak to the pastor or to the pastoral leadership, or whoever it is you're praying for and undergirding. He will correct them if necessary, and guide them as well.

When you have a born again, Spirit-filled leader; when you pray for them to be blessed of the Lord, it's more likely that God is able to speak to them and keep them on the right path. That's one of the reasons I believe we should pray so much in intercession for the spiritual leadership. We should intercede for people that are world-changers and history-makers with their global ministries. There are leaders in the body of Christ throughout the entire earth, and also those at the local level, which is the most important level where we live.

That's why it's so difficult for so many people who are trying to find a spiritual home church. I understand that after this whole pandemic, we've had so many people doing their live-streaming of their church services online. They've picked up a lot of people that have found that this or that church is really balanced in the Word and totally full of the Spirit.

So, where they couldn't go to church at some other

place (physically), they start following the streaming of this particular church and they become church members, even if they live in another state. They get connected; they get hooked up.

I believe in people pastoring churches where you have people from all over the planet that are members of your church. There's no guarantee in their local area that they're going to find anything like what it is you would have in a totally Word-based church – *proclaiming the life-transforming power of God's Word.* That's the slogan for *Life Christian University;* a church that is Holy Spirit-led and empowered to bring the people into the place where they're always hearing from the Lord. They're hearing Him. It is always based on the Word. It comes into alignment with the Word and they're solid.

God's not bound by space or time, so He can reach people who are watching television. They're watching recorded programs or courses. They get transformation happening in their lives because it's based on the whole counsel of God's Word and the move of the Spirit of God. As we're talking about intercession, it's very, very important that we come into alignment for intercession for the spiritual leadership. And when you're praying against ungodliness in the world, we're going to find something completely different. I need to make sure you understand that when we talk about the prayer of agreement, we also ought to talk about what we are binding and loosing. Let's look at Matthew 18:18:

"Assuredly, I say to you, whatever you bind on earth will be bound in heaven, and whatever you loose on earth will be loosed in heaven."

Whatever you are forbidding on the earth will be considered to be forbidden in heaven. Whatever you release on the earth will be considered to be released in heaven. There is an element of the authority of the believer that is in that Word.

You're using the prayer of authority in Jesus' name, and Jesus is doing it.

It's like what we saw mentioned in Mark 11:23, where you're casting the mountains out of your life. Then in verse 24, you're believing in the prayer of faith to replace whatever the obstacle was: the opposition of the devil, that mountain out of your life, and to replace that mountain or obstacle with the provision of the Lord. A lot of times they work hand-in-hand; where the authority and the dominion in life, in agreement with the Lord over those opposition forces, happens first. Then, the prayer to the Father in Jesus' name – for the provision that only God can provide – comes in to replace and meet the need.

CHAPTER FOURTEEN

THE POWER OF ONE ACCORD

PRAYER FORM 8 – UNITED PRAYER, AND PRAISE AND WORSHIP

United prayer is simply praying together as a group, and can be done with everyone praying in tongues or with their understanding, at the same time. In the New Testament, it also seems to be the beginning of group singing; singing praises or worshipping together.

These two kinds of prayer: *united prayer* and *praise and worship* kind of segue together. At the time of the early church, they sang some hymns. When Jesus had the last supper with His disciples; right before He was about to be arrested, everybody was going to pray together (at the Garden of Gethsemane). Jesus was trying to get them to pray for an hour with Him there. But before they even left to do that, they sang a hymn together.

We know that we're in the Spirit-filled Church. Those hymns have turned into something where there's praise and adoration of God, and extolling His magnificence. Praise songs are not always necessarily the fast songs, but it's fun to use the faster tempos in praising our God.

Worship is where you enter into communing with our

Heavenly Father all together, as a group of people. It's where you're all singing *unto* Him. We're not just singing *about* Him. We're singing *to* Him about His magnificence and His splendor and glory.

I believe we see a pattern in the New Testament, in the Word of God, where they came into the place of united prayer, and which led to what we know of today as *praise and worship*. Then you add the music and the singing and everything to that united prayer. Praise and worship really comes together when people are really on the same page spiritually. They all come into that place.

I remember when I was a new believer – maybe two years in the Lord – but it was at the very pinnacle of the Charismatic Renewal, when so many people were being swept into being baptized in the Holy Spirit, from all different denominations. By the second year or so, my mom told me about this Charismatic conference that was being held in Montreat, North Carolina.

Montreat, North Carolina is the place where Billy Graham actually lived. To enter, you had to come through the gates of the property, which was owned by the Presbyterian Church. They had a retreat and campground, with a retreat center in the middle and a big auditorium. You had to come through that gate to go up the hill to Billy Graham's house.

So, we were going to go to a Charismatic retreat there. We did, and of course, we drove up to the top of the hill to see Billy Graham's house. The first year that I went was the first time I heard 2,000 people singing in tongues at the same time – with just a piano. The pianist was doing these arpeggios (rolled chords) up and down the keyboard.

I thought that I must have gotten saved just in time to get raptured with the Church. I thought, "This is it. We're going." I mean, the presence of God was so strong. I expected the building to just open up at the top and Jesus to be there, and all of us would just float up and we would all be raptured right there. It was just this incredible unity of the Spirit and this incredible worship.

Interestingly, the second year that I went to the Charismatic conference; Billy Graham actually came down from the mountain and came into the place and said, "My wife and I were just feeling the love of God coming up the mountain and I just had to come down to be able to greet all of you." He continued, "And besides, one of my favorite Bible teachers is here." It turns out that Billy Graham was listening to these Spirit-filled teachings. I think he was a closet Charismatic.

The reality was that he was powerfully anointed for evangelism. But of course, most of his followers were evangelical-only. He did not want to disrupt that assistance that he got from all of them, that made all of those crusades available. Of course, they would get the people in, and the Charismatic Renewal would occur. Well, a lot of them got baptized in the Holy Spirit along the way. So, worshipping together in the Spirit in true unity is so powerful; it's incredible.

Now, we're going to look at a couple of places where the early church prayed and came into the place of unity. We're going to find out that's where they got baptized in the Holy Spirit, on the Day of Pentecost. Again, this is united prayer and praise and worship. To unite is simply to pray together as a group. This can be done with everyone praying in tongues or with their understanding, at the same time.

In other words, the 120 gathered in the upper room were simply praying according to their understanding; but after ten days of prayer, they were in total agreement. It tells us here in the New Testament, it seems at the beginning that the group were singing praises and worshipping together.

UNITED PRAYER BEFORE GOD EMPOWERED THE CHURCH

Before the power of God had been given to the church, they still came into one accord. Let's look at Acts 1:14:

These all continued with one accord...

That means one alignment and agreement with the will of God. Jesus says, "Don't leave Jerusalem until you're endowed with power. Do not try to be My ambassadors without this power; you'll mess it up terribly if you try to represent Me without the power." And for 300 years, the Church did it right with the power. You would think it would be great that the Emperor of Rome got born again. That was fine and good, except that he made it the state religion.

After 300 years, everybody had to claim to be a Christian or you were in violation of the rules of the government. So, everybody claimed to be a Christian and they weren't. The Church got completely watered down. The doctrines got watered down and the people stopped listening to the whole counsel of God's Word and started coming up with things. They were representing the Lord and being His ambassadors without the power, and certainly made a mess of so much of it. It's such a shame.

But we have seen a return to power. We are living in the time of the return of the power of the Day of Pentecost; where the Holy Spirit has been again able to fill us up. People have been born again throughout all of that other time, but when you get filled up with the Spirit, there's an overflow into your soul. And your soul gets transformed by the renewing of your mind. You come into this place where, spiritually, your soul begins to resemble your spirit, and they come into complete agreement and alignment. That's where the power of God starts being unleashed.

The 120 in the upper room came into one accord. Acts 1:14:

These all continued with one accord in prayer and supplication, with the women and Mary the mother of Jesus, and with His brothers.

Other translations mention his "brothers and sisters." We know Jesus had four brothers. We see in Matthew 13:55-56 and Mark 6:3 that Jesus had four brothers, named James, Joseph, Simon, and Jude; and at least two sisters. There might have been three or four; we don't know. Mary might have been very prolific in giving birth to all the family of brothers and sisters of Jesus. It might have been that there were nine kids: Jesus, and then four brothers and four sisters. We do know that the family was there, and Mary, the mother of Jesus, was there.

Whenever I meet a Catholic that is not baptized in the Holy Spirit, I mention that Mary was there. She's *not* deity, but she certainly should be respected. She is certainly greatly chosen of God, for the Father to say, "I'll be the Father; you be the mother, and we'll bring forth My Son. He'll be the Son of God and Son of Man." So, yes, she's very important to the Father, and has a great, honored place in heaven, but again, she is *not* deity. She didn't become part of the Godhead.

But at the same time, I like to tell Catholics that Mary was there on the Day of Pentecost and she prayed in tongues. And I ask, "Don't you want to be like Mary?" It's plainly in the Bible, but they don't really read the Bible. You have to look at it and see that of course Jesus had brothers and sisters. They had the whole family business that He had been running.

And of course, that's one of the reasons James was upset that Jesus suddenly left the family business. They were prospering. If there was anybody who was going to do business God's way, it was going to be Jesus. I'm sure they were the wealthiest family in the whole city, and James says, "What? Now you're going to saddle me with this whole thing?"

I have a lot of teachings on James, because I really believe that he probably worked side-by-side with the Lord Jesus, for about eighteen years. I know Jesus practiced a lot of sermons on James and his brothers and sisters over those years before He stepped into His ministry. That doesn't mean that He was anointed yet to do all of that ministry and step into His high priestly role, but He still knew the Word and probably preached the Word to the family.

It turns out that after these other disciples that have been with Jesus full-time for three and a half years; James didn't even believe in Jesus' ministry – not until His resurrection from the dead. Jesus showed Himself specifically to James, just to convince James that, "It's Me. I'm here." And can you imagine what James must have felt like? Because Peter had denied Jesus three times, then he was just crestfallen until Jesus was raised from the dead. But Jesus forgave him of all of that and said, "Peter, I called you to feed My sheep. You're going to be the apostle to the lost sheep of the house of Israel."

Could you imagine what James felt like? It probably went something like this, "I worked next to the man for eighteen years, and I heard Him speak the Word of God, over and over again. And I didn't even believe in His ministry when He launched out, until He showed me Himself after His resurrection." I'm sure James said, "I will be His best disciple and His best representative."

He became the pastor of the church of Jerusalem; from which all the other apostles came in to answer to, and went out from. It's reasonable after all those years of listening to Jesus, that James would have been that man that God would have chosen to be the pastor of the church of Jerusalem.

Let's look at Acts 2:1:

When the day of Pentecost had fully come, they were all with one accord in one place.

Twice it says they came into one accord in their prayer and one accord spiritually, in believing God was going to do something to launch them, as He said. "Jesus told us not to leave until we're empowered with that gift from the Father." Once they had that empowerment, they were ready. Now, they're in an upper room; there's 120 of them.

They obviously had open windows. Some people would have heard all that commotion that was going on. But I believe they just kind of started stumbling out. The power of God was probably hot in that room, after the Holy Spirit had filled them all. All the other people outside were able to hear them. They didn't stop praying in tongues. They didn't stop speaking in tongues. They walked out into the streets and they're speaking in tongues. All these Jews that had come back for the Feast of Pentecost from all over the world heard them all speaking in their own tongues.

When Charles F. Parham in Topeka, Kansas was seeking the power of the Holy Spirit; he asked the students to look through the Word of God and find what was missing in the Modern Church. It was the beginning of 1901. On New Years Eve, at midnight in 1901, they discovered that the Church had been baptized in the Holy Spirit, with the evidence of praying in other tongues, and they thought that was probably what they were missing.

Parham was really excited about that because he thought as missionaries, they could go out and they wouldn't have to learn foreign languages. They could just speak in tongues to the people and they would understand them, because they would just speak the Word of God. Well, it doesn't work that way. It did on the Day of Pentecost, but that was for a sign for all those who were part of the diaspora – Jews who had left Israel.

GOD EMPOWERS THE CHURCH
WITH THE HOLY SPIRIT

The disciples that had been praying in one accord were anointed. They were in complete agreement while following the directions of the Lord Jesus. The power of this united prayer is what enabled God to send the anointing without measure that had been on Jesus, and was now able to fall on them, and to continue in the Church that was gathered and waiting before the Lord, in prayer.

Now, I don't know why it took ten days. Did God just have foreknowledge it was going to take them that long to get into one accord? I think that if you pray with anybody over a ten-day period of time, you're locked up in one room and you're eating meals together and spending time together; they probably did.

I'm not exactly sure how they did it. Maybe they didn't sleep there. Maybe they had other lodgings around and they slept there and then came back. At any rate, at that point of the day of the Feast of Pentecost when so many people were going to be in Jerusalem; there, by the power of the Holy Spirit, they could have this great demonstration and speak in the tongues of all these other people, as a sign and a witness to them: "We're empowered by God. We didn't even learn his language."

They heard them glorifying God. They were truly worshipping Him in Spirit and in truth, when the people heard the languages. So, the power of this united prayer was what enabled God to send that anointing on that day. It had to be at that place and God knew it was going to happen on that day.

After the Day of Pentecost, the Church was empowered. Immediately after the Church had been filled with the Holy Spirit on the day of Pentecost, and Peter preached his first sermon to the masses there; the Church began to spread the gospel everywhere. In Bible times, they always counted the heads of families or the men. The men had their families with them. In all likelihood, more than 3,000 people got saved on the Day of Pentecost at Peter's first sermon.

I love his first sermon. He started off by defending all of the rest of the 120 that got baptized. "They are not drunk like you suppose" – because the people were accusing them of being drunk at nine in the morning. He says, "They're not drunk like you suppose. They're drunk by the Holy Spirit."

They must have acted inebriated by the power of the Holy Spirit. If you've ever been in the joy of the Lord and drunk on the Spirit of God – I have been, many times – then you know what I'm talking about. It's the presence of God, and after giving out the Word and ministering, you're almost loopy for a little while. It's great to stay in that presence of God, where you're enveloped in His presence. Peter stands up to defend them and he says, "It's not what you think. Wait a minute."

I always like to say that Peter did not have a chance to make sure he had a sermon prepared that was homiletically, hermeneutically, and exegetically perfect. No, he was suddenly filled with the Spirit of God and he got it by a revelation from heaven. "We just experienced what Joel had prophesied about: 'In the last days, I'm going to pour out My Spirit on all flesh'" (Joel 2:28).

Now, nearly two thousand years later, He's still pouring out His Spirit on all flesh that want to receive it. For those who want to receive the power of God; He's still pouring it out. That's why we want to keep this ministry going – getting people filled with the Spirit so they can come into this Holy Spirit-empowered prayer experience.

Later, Peter and John go to the temple to pray. It was their pattern. They were good Jews. If they were in Jerusalem, they were going to go to the temple to pray. When they were at home, they were going to go to the synagogue on the Sabbath. They're going to go. When they are in Israel; especially at a time of a great feast like the Feast of Pentecost, they're going to be in there at the time of prayer. But on the way, they see the beggar, the crippled man, who was sitting by the Gate Beautiful.

Some Christians believe the apostles were poor, just because Peter said, "Silver and gold we don't have," but if you read the previous chapter, they had just given away all their silver and gold. They gave generously because the Church was in one accord. They wanted to make sure the people who didn't have enough, now had enough.

Others believe God wanted to set up socialism. The Church should be the ones to look out for one another and take care of the needy. When the government tries to do it, they ruin it because they are always corrupt, because they don't know the Lord. It becomes a corrupt system of trying to meet the needs of the government. They become extremely rich, while the people who have the needs, have close to nothing.

RESURRECTION AUTHORITY

After Peter preached to the masses there in the temple; because of gaining so many new converts to Christ, he and John were arrested by the Jewish leaders. When they asked by what authority they healed the man, they declared to them:

"let it be known to you all, and to all the people of Israel, that by the name of Jesus Christ of Nazareth, whom you crucified, whom God raised from the dead, by Him this man stands here before you whole" (Acts 4:10).

When the leaders of Israel threatened them to never

preach in the name of Jesus again, Peter and John replied:

"Whether it is right in the sight of God to listen to you more than to God, you judge" (Acts 4:19).

Then they returned to their company and reported all that was told them by the leaders of Israel, and then they prayed this prayer. Somebody prayed it and they all heard these particular words. They all came into agreement with this prayer. We're going to find out they all start praying together. This is a Spirit-filled gathering now, praying together; and something really wild and radical happens. (Acts 4:24,29-32):

So when they heard that, they raised their voice to God with one accord and said:

They were in agreement and one accord.

"...and said: "Lord, You *are* God, who made heaven and earth and the sea, and all that is in them...Now, Lord, look on their threats, and grant to Your servants that with all boldness they may speak Your word."

You see, that's the proper prayer when you're under the pressure of the devil:

"Lord, grant us the power to speak Your Word, with greater boldness in the face of the devil and all of his minions and all of his servants on the earth. And grant our petition as we speak this Word, with signs and wonders. Let the signs and wonders follow the Word that we're going to declare."

"...that with all boldness they may speak Your word, by stretching out Your hand to heal, and that great signs and wonders may be done through

the name of Your holy Servant Jesus"

Wow, they said "in Jesus' name!" When we preach in that name, we know God will always punctuate it with healings and signs and wonders, and it's going to be glorious, so empower us to do that. Wow, if the Church prayed for that – praying in the Spirit for that all together – you'd see tremendous things.

Today, we have pockets of revival and pockets of people praying this way. The work of God that is going forth in the earth is usually coming from people that know how to pray this way; and then pray in the Spirit and then interpret their prayers.

"...And when they had prayed, the place where they were assembled together was shaken; and they were all filled with the Holy Spirit, and they spoke the word of God with boldness."

Well, you know, that's pretty powerful when you come into the place of unity and agreement and you find that the Lord has actually shaken the place. It's a move of God; it's not an actual earthquake but it seems like an earthquake. The whole place shook, so God certainly answered their united prayer with a demonstration of power. He punctuated their prayers, "Yeah, when you go out, I'll be there with healing signs and wonders. I'm giving you this as a sign, as well."

I love signs from the Lord. I'm not looking for the signs, but when He punctuates a place of unity of the Spirit with a sign and a wonder, praise God. I mean, most every move of God that's been a great move of God, is a sign and a wonder. People ask, "How did this come about?" It's because there was a bunch of people who prayed for it, and prayed and prayed. Every move of God was prayed in by intercessors first, and then it is received by the yieldedness of those instruments that God uses for that purpose.

When we get to heaven, we're going to find that it was the intercessors who are going to get the reward for starting up a lot of churches, and for every great move of God. And to the people that thought they were going to get the credit for it, He's going to say, "No, this got prayed through long before you showed up on the scene. You need to be humble and recognize you were just part of it." Praise God, you get rewarded for being obedient to what you were called to do, but the intercessors prayed this thing in.

GOD USES PRAYER AND WORSHIP
TO START A CHURCH

In the letter to the Philippian church, we find that God uses Paul and Silas through their prayer and worship, to begin the church in Philippi. When Paul and Silas were ministering in Macedonia at Philippi, they were arrested for casting a spirit of fortune telling out of a young damsel. Now, remember, they're there because Paul kept praying for the next assignment they were supposed to go to, and the Holy Spirit forbade them to go into several places. Then, in the middle of the night, he has a vision. This man from Macedonia is calling to him, "Come over here and help us." So, they knew to go to Philippi.

Well, they get up there and they find Lydia, the seller of purple; she was a Christian. She took them into her house, but she couldn't be the man from Macedonia. Then, they go out to preach, and see this maiden – who is a fortune teller – a slave girl who is owned by these men, who are making a lot of money off of her telling fortunes, by the power of the devil. Well, she couldn't be the man from Macedonia, either.

They cast the devil out of her, and all of a sudden, these slave owners suddenly lost their income from this little girl. They stir everything up, and of course, the magistrates had them beaten with rods and held fast in the lowest parts of the prison, with their feet in stocks. It's a dire condition. This is the second missionary journey.

Remember that Barnabas was with Paul on the first missionary journey. We find out that John Mark, who wrote the Gospel of Mark, was a young cousin of the Lord Jesus. He went with them. He was called by a good friend of Barnabas in Antioch, and of course, he wanted them to go with him. But he deserted them before they really got started doing very much, so Paul got into an argument with Barnabas about that. He did not want to take Mark with them the second time. The disagreement they had was enough that they parted ways. Barnabas launches out with Mark and Paul launches out with Silas.

Paul and Silas have now been beaten with rods. Their feet are in stocks and they're in this prison, in the lowest part of the prison in Philippi. Silas had just joined Paul in the second missionary journey. If I had been Silas, I might have been tempted to say, "Paul, I haven't been traveling with you that much, but if this is the way most of your missionary trips go, I'm not sure I want to keep going with you."

You realize that something miraculous is happening. They're in pain but Paul says, "Silas, let's get our eyes off the pain. Let's get our eyes off of the disgrace of being arrested and beaten." Now, it's interesting because Paul is a Roman citizen and he could have prevented this beating if he had used his citizenship at that point in time, but he didn't. I'm not exactly sure why, because he did strategically at other times.

Let's read here from Acts 16:25a,26-28, where we see:

But at midnight, Paul and Silas were praying and singing.

They were singing hymns to God so they're probably praying in tongues. They're singing. These prisoners had never heard anything like this. When these other prisoners were brought into the prison, they were beaten and stuck in stocks. They were probably cursing and screaming at everybody around them, but this was completely unique to hear these new prisoners singing.

They see these new guys, who come in and are beaten and put in stocks and they just start praying to their heavenly Father in the name of Jesus. They are praying in tongues, in this language they have never heard coming out of people. The prisoners might have said, "Whoa, these guys know a bunch of different languages and they're singing hymns unto God."

Paul and Silas go into that place of worship. I have a feeling that they were kind of translated into that place, like when I thought we were going to be raptured; the first time I heard 2,000 people singing in tongues at the same time. Paul and Silas were sitting there in the presence of God, even though in the flesh it looked diametrically-opposed to that.

When you juxtapose the two situations together, they're sitting there in pain. They're bleeding and their feet are in stocks, but in the realm of the Spirit, they're caught up. They're glorifying their heavenly Father and praising Him with hymns, and praying to Him.

Then, suddenly in the middle of this, all of the prisoners are listening to them. I think they're getting caught up in the praise and worship. They're probably thinking: "I've never heard anything like this before. It's the strangest thing. I've never heard any of these psalms that they're singing; but man, they sure love their God."

Suddenly there was a great earthquake, so that the foundations of the prison were shaken;

The building actually shakes. The prison shakes. The

building shakes, and immediately all the doors were opened. It shakes the doors – whatever way they were locked – and broke that apart. Everyone's chains were loosed. That means that all the prisoners are sitting there when this shaking of the prison happens. The chains that are binding them fall off of them.

Now, that's a radical thing. They had to have known that the doors flew open. There had to be noise from this. They had to have heard the chains falling off of them, but they're sitting there in shock because they hear Paul and Silas praying.

They are honoring God and worshipping Him with these hymns; caught up in the Spirit. The prisoners are kind of caught up too and they're still just sitting there. They haven't moved a leg or an arm. Maybe some of them stood up, but it's like they're in shock. They're all still in the prison.

and immediately all the doors were opened and everyone's chains were loosed. And the keeper of the prison...

Now, the keeper of the prison obviously had a house that was right next to the prison and he hears this noise. He hears the earthquake shaking the building. His building is probably sitting there not shaking at all. It's ten feet away but this one's shaking. All of a sudden, the door is open and he hears chains falling. He realizes this as he awakens from sleep. He hears the noise and awakens from sleep. Acts 16:27 (AUTHOR PARAPHRASE):

and seeing that the prison doors were open, he supposed now that all the prisoners are gone.

Well, he knows as a Roman Centurion, that he's going to die. If the prisoners escaped, you paid for it with your life. Don't let anybody tell you that life in Rome was a peaceful time. It was debaucherous. It was demon-possessed. In the time of their glory, it was not glorious.

Thousands and thousands of people were murdered in their Colosseum as gladiators; and just for being Christians, and who were torn apart by wild animals. Rome was demon-possessed. They were openly having sex in the stands while people died! You'd have to read a little bit more into history to find out how perverse these people really were. It was a fallen culture, as far as you can fall. I don't care what they built; they were fallen.

supposing the prisoners had fled, drew his sword and was about to kill himself.

Now, you can hear what's happening with these open windows in his house, a few feet away from the prison building. Paul hears the keeper draw his sword and knows he's ready to kill himself because he probably walked over far enough to see that the doors were open. The Centurion thinks, "So that's it. All the prisoners have escaped."

But Paul called with a loud voice, saying, "Do yourself no harm, for we are all here."

Every single prisoner is still in the building; nobody left, even though it's like when Peter got set free and he walked right out of the prison. There was that earthquake and he was loosed by the angel to get him out and set free because the church had prayed. They forgot to pray for James, the brother of John, and he was executed by Herod. At least Peter gets out so the church and the leadership are able to go on. But Paul said:

"Do yourself no harm, for we are all here."

First, we must take note that even though Paul and Silas were in great pain, they prayed and sang hymns all night until midnight. They must have been very much in the Spirit with a powerful anointing, to do this. We notice that the other prisoners heard them and were most likely affected by the anointing filling the prison, along with the worship songs being sung, so they were still sitting there.

Next, we must take note that God punctuated their prayer and worship with the demonstration of delivering power which manifest as the earthquake, and which opened the doors of the prison, and everyone's chains fell off of them.

When the prison keeper awakened, he immediately assumed that all the prisoners must have escaped, but they were all still just sitting there. Could it be that they were caught up in the Spirit along with Paul and Silas, and it had not yet dawned on them that they'd been set free by the earthquake? I don't know. It's one of those stories. One day, I'll get to talk to Paul and Silas and I will ask them both about this. Maybe I'll go to Silas first, as I'll probably get a different rendition from Paul. "Let me ask it from your perspective."

When Paul called out to the prison keeper, he ran into the cell with a torch and came right up to Paul. Perhaps this was the first time that Paul recognized the jailer as the man in the vision in the night, who had beckoned him to come to Macedonia to help them. I really believe that was the case. I believe this was the man. I believe that eventually, this jailer became the pastor of the church at Philippi. Let's follow along in Acts 16:30-34:

And he brought them out

The jailer brings them out and serves them. Now, you see, he had all of these soldiers under him that were probably the ones that put Paul and Silas into the prison. So, this is the first time that Paul is able to see this man's face; it's just in the light of this torch as he came up to him. But he brings them out and asks:

"Sirs, what must I do to be saved?"

This is right outside the prison. He probably locked the prison doors and kept the prisoners there because he didn't want to be executed. He's still trying to figure all of this out. He says:

"Sirs, what must I do to be saved?" So they said, "Believe on the Lord Jesus Christ, and you will be saved, you and your household."

A lot of people see this and believe they can claim their whole household, without them hearing the gospel, but that's just not the case. He knew that his whole household was going to hear the gospel and he says, "You and your whole household will be saved by the hearing and receiving of this gospel of the Lord Jesus Christ."

Everybody could claim that, but you have to understand. You better start praying for your family members after you're saved; that God would send forth laborers into the harvest of your family member's lives so they can hear the same gospel. God will send somebody to them that they will listen to, if you'll pray. And if you'll pray in the Spirit, the Holy Spirit will be praying that for them, so that's why we need to pray in the Holy Spirit.

A lot of people don't pray in the Holy Spirit enough to get their family members saved, but this is what will happen. That's what the Holy Spirit will do. He'll send forth laborers into the harvest of their lives. You will get the interpretation of that as you pray. You will interpret your own tongues. Then, you can come into agreement with what the Holy Spirit is already praying through your spirit – about them being saved.

Then they spoke the Word of the Lord to him and

to all who were in his house.

They all heard – everybody. There were other soldiers with him in his house.

And he took them the same hour of the night and washed *their* stripes.

The jailer washes them. He doesn't put them back in the prison. He's going to answer for them himself. He's just going to keep them in his house.

And immediately he and all his *family* were baptized.

They allowed Paul and Silas to baptize all those who had just received Jesus as Lord.

...having believed in God with all his household.

So, we know that all in the household that heard the same gospel received. They experienced a tremendous miracle. The church of Philippi got started with the power of God, but Paul and Silas had to pay the price of being beaten and arrested. They were put in this place where they actually stay in the Spirit; and pray and sing and worship God in Spirit and in truth – and the miracles happened. At Philippi, the church gets established.

Notice a few points about the story that makes a more complete picture, based on what we know from the rest of Paul's writings. First, when the jailer took them out of the prison, he immediately asked what he needed to do to be saved; knowing that he would be executed if he let the prisoners escape.

He surely secured the jail with all of the other prisoners inside. But again, he lives right next to them so they're hearing the gospel preached to the family. He was right outside the prison when he and his family heard the gospel preached to them by the Apostle Paul; and surely the other prisoners heard the gospel as well.

It stands to reason that a good number of the prisoners accepted the Lord Jesus as Savior, at the same time. Only the family of the jailer was able to be baptized that night, but it does not prevent the prisoners from having the genuine new birth experience. So, I believe the church at Philippi got started this way. This new church that has just been birthed in Philippi started with the jailer, his family; and most likely, they were joined by the prisoners that were saved and later released.

Can you imagine that you're in jail and you get saved but you've gone through this incredible, miraculous experience? And you say, "But we found the truth and now our jailer is learning the truth of the Word of God and is preaching it to us, so this is a great place for us to be part of the church."

We also know from Paul's writing to the church at Philippi, that they were the only church that continued to share with him in giving and receiving, in partnership with his ministry. It was like they received him as an angel sent by God and they said, "Whatever we can do to help this man. Eternal life came to us because he got arrested here and thrown into prison, but he didn't let that move him. He prayed seriously to God and worshipped God, and we all came into the kingdom because of it."

They didn't receive any admonition from Paul, but only praise for the way that they conducted the church. We might even assume that the jailer became the pastor of the church at Philippi. I believe that's how it really all began. How long it stayed that way, I don't know.

Sometimes they would move these Centurions; sometimes they would stay for the rest of their life in part of their assignment, because they have to learn the culture of the people. The Centurion that came to Jesus built the people a synagogue, so he's probably a proselyte to Judaism. He gets this assignment to come to Israel and he meets the one true God through the people there.

He wasn't born again until later on, but we know that at that point in time, he'd become a proselyte to Israel. He believed in the one true God that these people worshipped. He realized that back in Rome, they were worshipping all kinds of gods that were really weird. This one true God has a completely different set of standards of holy importance. Anyway, they received no strong admonition.

Also, in 1 Corinthians 8:1-5, we find Paul using the Philippian church as the example of giving to the needs of the church in Jerusalem – a church that was in the midst of a famine. He says, "Listen, these men showed us how to do this, and I bragged to them about you Corinthians; that you'd follow suit the same way." He told them in many places. He was telling a lot of people about the church at Philippi, and he would brag about the churches that he knew wanted to be like the church of Philippi.

He had first identified when the Macedonian church began, that they were all in a great trial of affliction and deep poverty. But they gave themselves first to the Lord, and then in submission to the apostles. They became the wealthy church that always gave, and that had enough to give to Paul's ministry, every time they could locate where he was. You know, they always wanted to give, but they couldn't always find out where he was.

They didn't have cell phones. They didn't have GPS. They didn't have *FedEx* to be able to *FedEx* the money or to wire some, so it was difficult. They had money and feelers going out all of the time and people that are traveling and asking the questions, "Do you know where Paul is? Where was Paul when you last saw him?" "Oh, he's gone to spend a number of months in this other place." So, the Philippian church would ask, "Can we send money back with you?" And they'd respond, "Okay, I'll go back there and take this." Or some would just travel themselves when they knew where he was going to be, and they would bring the funding to him.

Paul told the Corinthians that the Philippians gave way beyond their ability, every time that they gave. It seems that they really experienced what Paul told them in Philippians 4:19:

"And my God shall supply all your need according to His riches in glory by Christ Jesus."

This church was birthed in this miracle of worship and the agreement of prayer and the earthquake that was shaking the building. I'm sure that message and the stories got passed on for generations afterward. "Here's how the gospel came to us. This is why we're so appreciative. We feel like it was just a miracle that God was able to get the gospel to us, so we've always been supporters and partners with those that were in the ministry that came to us."

All of this came to pass because Paul and Silas prayed and worshipped God, even while in pain in the prison. Of course, they had to overcome what they were going through, in order to be able to bring glory and honor to the Lord. So, a great miracle happened in establishing the church there. You can see that in that case, as Jesus told the disciples, "When two or more are gathered in My name, there I am in the midst of you."

In this idea of united prayer and worship and the prayer of agreement where they were all in one accord – at least Paul and Silas were in one accord – all these things work together.

They dovetail together in all of this; even in forms and patterns of prayer. They all dovetail in with one another. That's why when you're praying in the Holy Spirit, He's praying the exact prayers necessary to get the need met for someone; first for you, then those around you, and then further out for somebody else.

Of course, it's exciting to see what God brings to pass when people come into this place of agreement and in united prayer and worship. I wanted to tie that in. I think that's where the true worship really began and where people started seeing the power of praying together – in united prayer and in worshipping God together.

They were singing those hymns and it started spreading. They probably experienced the same kind of things. Sometimes they were able to use the synagogue or "so-and-so's" house, where the church was meeting. They would listen to the Word and say, "Well, let's all pray; and here's some needs that we know. Can we all agree in prayer?"

They came into this prayer of agreement. At some point in time, they're praying in agreement and they're worshipping God. They must have experienced something all of a sudden. There was no earthquake or anything every single time, but the presence of God came in and they were overwhelmed with the glory of God.

They understood this empowering revival power of God; where, when they meet, they do the right things with the Word and the Spirit, and worship and prayer, and then the presence of God manifests. I'm sure many, many people were healed in their services and they kept seeing signs and wonders, because they expected those to follow the Word being preached, and for the people's lives to come into alignment with the will of God.

CHAPTER FIFTEEN

IMPRECATORY PRAYER

PRAYER FORM 9 – PRAYERS OF JUSTICE AND JUDGMENT

The next form of prayer is one that a lot of people are dubious about, because they don't think God would do this anymore. It's the *prayer of justice and judgment.* I want to share with you that I know the Holy Spirit prays this perfect prayer of justice and judgment. Why? Because God is a just God.

And guess what? One day, He's going to settle all the scores. He's going to give justice to those who have been taken advantage of and abused, and everything else. He's going to bring justice to everybody who's been abused in any way. He has already brought judgment to those who were the abusers. What we're seeing is that the Holy Spirit is always going to pray in agreement with the will of God. We see that through the rest of the Word of God.

If you read the *Book of Revelation*, it's all going to be poured out. We're going to come to a final reckoning day. God is still the God of justice and judgment, so when we pray in the Holy Spirit, the Holy Spirit is praying that through our spirit. Let's just break it down a little bit. I want to explain some things that I've learned concerning all of this.

These prayers are also known as the *imprecatory prayer*. This kind of prayer is also in the category of the *prayer of authority*. We saw Jesus, who says, "There are going to be prayers that you pray to Me in My name and I'm going to do it; or that you demand in my name." We're going to realize in justice and judgment, that we're demanding the circumstance to change and the judgment to come; sometimes in order to preserve the Church and to keep it holy. Sometimes it's to preserve the gospel itself, to keep it pure and holy and not defiled and so error-laden that you can't even recognize it anymore.

God has to do that. He has to do that to preserve the Church and preserve the Word. Why? So that it can continue to go forth and the Holy Spirit can still empower the Church to complete the assignment the Church has – to keep bringing in the sheaves, bringing in the lost; and maturing the saints and having everybody fulfill what God has called them to do within the Church and be blessed in their doing of it. That is, until Jesus is able to return for the whole Church and bring on the final judgment and justice for us.

Prayers using the authority over demonic forces will affect the people that have yielded to demonic power. So, a lot of the prayers of judgment are going to be against people that don't know the Lord and that are being used by demon spirits. Many of them are demon-possessed and God says, "I'm not going to allow them to destroy."

I believe it's just like when Paul was on his way to Damascus to arrest people that were believers and take them back to Jerusalem and have them executed. When Jesus showed up to him on the road to Damascus; I believe Jesus had foreknowledge. The Father had the foreknowledge that he would yield to this, but They were not going to allow Paul to keep killing Christians. Either he bowed his knee to Jesus and surrendered, or it was going to be death for him. He immediately recognized when Jesus spoke to him. He said,

"Who are you, Lord?" He knew it was God. He knew it was God that knocked him off his horse and blinded him.

Paul said, "Who are you, Lord?" but it was not the God he expected. He heard, "I'm Jesus whom you're persecuting." Jesus spoke to him. I believe Paul would have died if he had not yielded to the Lord. God would have had to choose somebody else. But He also knew Paul was a zealot for the truth of the Word of God. He thought Christianity was trying to take away the one way of salvation that God had given to the nation of Israel, so he was a defender of salvation given by God.

Later on, Paul had to become the defender of the real salvation given by God, through the Lord Jesus, and he was just as much a zealot for that. That's why he ran his course with the passion he had for the truth of the Word of God! So, when he got transformed, he escaped justice and he got a judgment and justice and he was used greatly by the Lord.

Again, prayers using authority over demonic forces will affect the people that have yielded to demonic powers. This prayer of authority is designed by the Lord; often to bring justice to those who should be vindicated. Also, the use of this authority is needed to keep the Church pure. Even some believers have fallen into the devil's traps and have been used by him to do evil. Many unbelievers have so yielded to the devil, that they have become servants of Satan themselves.

A believer can't be possessed by the devil, but unbelievers can be. A believer can be totally *demonized* and do some really stupid things, but they can't be *possessed* because Satan would have to possess your spirit. If you're still born again, the devil cannot possess your spirit. The Holy Spirit possesses your spirit, so long as a person is truly born again. I've known some really dumb Christians doing some really dumb things over the years; so you realize they're squandering all the grace and the authority and power that would have been given to them to complete a great assignment.

The early church had great reverence for the Holy Spirit because Jesus laid the foundation for their understanding. The Chief Cornerstone laid the foundation of their understanding. "You're going to be empowered by the Holy Spirit. He's going to be the Comforter. You're going to be so happy when He is able to manifest Himself. Right now, that's the anointing without measure that's on Me, but I'm going to pour it out on you and you're going to realize you didn't have this power before. Even though you were born again, you did not have *this* infilling until I was able to release it on you. Then you'll say, 'We are certainly comforted now. We've got the goods. Jesus gave us the goods that rested on Him: that anointing without measure, so whatever God's called us to do, we can do it.'"

THE UNPARDONABLE SIN

The early church had this reverence. Jesus warned the disciples about blasphemy against the Holy Spirit. I have to break this down a little bit for people, because a lot of people don't even pay attention to this being in the Bible, but this is in reference to what's considered to be the "unpardonable sin." I've heard a lot of preachers say, "Oh, there is no unpardonable sin. God pardoned every single one of them." Let's just break this down from what happened to Jesus, and let's look at the words of Jesus and what He happens to say is "unforgivable." I'm reading from Matthew 12:22-27:

Then one was brought to Him who was demon-possessed, blind and mute; and He healed him, so that the blind and mute man both spoke and saw. And all the multitudes were amazed and said, "Could this be the Son of David?"

You see, they recognized Jesus as a healing prophet, but

they didn't all recognize that He was the Messiah. But they started wondering, "Could this man be the Messiah? I mean, could the Messiah do any greater works than what we're watching Him do?" As soon as the Pharisees heard that, they said:

"This *fellow* does not cast out demons except by Beelzebub,"

Which is Satan.

"the ruler of the demons."

They said, "This man is casting out demons by the power of Satan." So, this is what they said about what the Holy Spirit had just done, with the anointing without measure through the Son of the living God operating as the anointed Son of man. "Oh, He's doing that by the power of Satan." Wow, what a stupid statement.

But Jesus knew their thoughts, and said to them: "Every kingdom divided against itself is brought to desolation, and every city or house divided against itself will not stand. If Satan casts out Satan, he is divided against himself. How then will his kingdom stand?"

He basically said, "Your statement that you're making is just stupid." We always want to say, when people ask a question, "No question is a stupid question." Actually, I've heard a lot of really stupid questions. This statement was not thought through whatsoever. He said: "If I cast out devils by the power of the devil, then Satan's kingdom is divided against himself." Enough said.

"If Satan casts out Satan, he is divided against himself. How then will his kingdom stand? And if

**I cast out demons by Beelzebub, by whom do your
sons cast *them* out?"**

They actually had exorcists in Judaism. Remember the
seven sons of Sceva (Acts 19:14)? They were trying to cast
out devils by the name of Jesus, whom Paul preaches. They
weren't born again. The devil just speaks up and says, "Jesus
I know, and Paul I know; who do you think you are?" And he
jumps on them. The man who was demon-possessed whips
them all and rips their clothes off of them. They run for their
lives. Matthew 12:27-32:

**"And if I cast out demons by Beelzebub, by whom
do your sons cast *them* out?"**

You see, they thought they could do this. Maybe there
were some demons they were successful with. Was it the Spirit
of God that was helping them when they were trying to help
other sons and daughters of Abraham?

**"Therefore they shall be your judges. But if I
cast out demons by the Spirit of God, surely the
kingdom of God has come upon you."**

Jesus may have thought, "I'm doing this by the anointing,
because I am that anointed One. I am that Messiah, the Christ,
and you're trying to call Me anything but Him."

**"Or how can one enter a strong man's house and
plunder his goods, unless he first binds the strong
man? And then he will plunder his house."**

He says, "I'm plundering the devil's kingdom while I'm
here. Here's an analogy for you. How could you plunder a
strong man's house unless you bind the strong man first? If he
can resist you by himself, he's going to do it and you've got no

way to plunder his house."

"He who is not with Me is against Me, and he who does not gather with Me scatters abroad."

Verses 31-32 – This is the important part:

"Therefore I say to you, every sin and blasphemy will be forgiven men, but the blasphemy *against* the Spirit will not be forgiven men. Anyone who speaks a word against the Son of Man, it will be forgiven him; but whoever speaks against the Holy Spirit, it will not be forgiven him, either in this age or the *age* to come."

In other words, anybody who blasphemes the Holy Spirit or attributes the works of the Holy Spirit to Satan is saying, "That's Satan doing that, not God." *That's* blaspheming the Holy Spirit. He says, "You won't be forgiven in this age or in the age to come." Let me read Mark's account of this. We're going to go to Mark 3:22-30, where he says:

"And the scribes who came down from Jerusalem said, "He has Beelzebub," and, "By the ruler of the demons He casts out demons."

So He called them to *Himself*...

...and said to them in parables: "How can Satan cast out Satan? If a kingdom is divided against itself, that kingdom cannot stand. And if a house is divided against itself, that house cannot stand."

"And if Satan has risen up against himself, and is divided, he cannot stand, but has an end. No one can enter a strong man's house and plunder his

goods, unless he first binds the strong man. And then he will plunder his house."

"Assuredly, I say to you, all sins will be forgiven the sons of men, and whatever blasphemies they may utter;"

Jesus was saying that all kinds of blasphemies will be forgiven. You can blaspheme the Father in heaven. He's saying, "You can blaspheme Me, the Son of God. All of the blasphemies can be forgiven."

"but he who blasphemes against the Holy Spirit never has forgiveness, but is subject to eternal condemnation"

He said this:

because they said, "He has an unclean spirit."

Well, Jesus is the only person who's never had anything unclean in His Spirit. He was filled with the anointing of the Holy Spirit of the living God. He says, "Don't come against this anointing that's on Me that makes me the Messiah and the Christ, and that will rest on and fill My Church and make them the fulfillment; the body of Christ on the earth while I'm the head in heaven, orchestrating the operation of My body in the earth, to complete the assignment the Father has for us."

"And anyone who speaks a word against the Son of Man, it will be forgiven him; but to him who blasphemes against the Holy Spirit, it will not be forgiven" (Luke 12:10).

And He says, "...and not in this age or the age to come" (Matthew 12:32 AUTHOR PARAPHRASE). That means if a person that's a born again Christian blasphemes the Holy Spirit, it's the one place I've been able to find, where you can lose your salvation.

In every other place, Jesus says: "The devil can't pluck you out of My hand. The devil can't pluck you out of the Father's hand. There's no way you can lose your salvation." You would have to be convinced that Jesus is not Lord and renounce Him as Lord and say, "I do not believe that Jesus Christ is the Son of the living God. I don't believe He is Lord. I don't believe He is raised from the dead."

You'd have to do this in order to give away your salvation, but if you blaspheme the Holy Spirit, you lose your salvation. That's the only way I know that you can lose it. There are a lot of people who have been blaspheming the Holy Spirit since this whole Charismatic Renewal started, and even before, going back to the outpouring of Pentecost, from the turn of the 20th century.

They have told people that those who pray in tongues in the modern age are praying in tongues by the power of the devil. That is blasphemy against the Holy Spirit! You can only pray in tongues by the power of the Holy Spirit if you're a born again Christian.

Now, there might be some demon-possessed people that are not born again Christians; they've never been baptized in the Holy Spirit – obviously – that might have some sort of "tongues" in manifestation, that they have by the power of the devil, but that's because they're not part of God's kingdom.

They're not even born again, so they could have some deception there; but if you're a born again Christian and you get baptized in the Holy Spirit, the peace of God comes over you. It's the Holy Spirit of the living God that is praying through your spirit as you're praying.

In Matthew and Mark, Jesus had been accused by the

religious leaders of casting out demons by the power of the devil. Jesus replied, "Then the kingdom of Satan would be divided against itself." Then He told His disciples that men would be forgiven of blasphemy against Him, but not against the Holy Spirit in this age, or in the age to come. Blasphemy against the Holy Spirit would be to attribute to Satan or to demonic forces, that which God is doing through the Holy Spirit.

We know that when someone is baptized in the Holy Spirit and they begin to pray in other tongues; if someone says that that person is praying in tongues and is doing so by the power of demons, that is blasphemy against the Holy Spirit and it will not be forgiven in this lifetime or the next lifetime, for eternity. This is known as the "unpardonable sin."

If this message ever happens to get to somebody who's been doing that, listen. I don't care if you refuse to get baptized in the Holy Spirit; that's your business. If you believe that it has passed away and it's "not available to us," that's your business; that's fine.

But the minute you tell anybody that a Christian who prays in tongues is doing so by the power of Satan, you have just lost your salvation and will not be forgiven in this life or in the next life to come. So, I'm warning you, reverse that! *You repent of that* so that you don't go to hell for eternity and lose your salvation. That is the unpardonable sin. That is blasphemy against the Holy Spirit.

Why would God do that? He's going to protect the power of the Holy Spirit and the people who desire to be baptized in the Holy Spirit. Then He's going to have the Holy Spirit pray through their spirit, the perfect prayers for everything. And if you're going to try to rob them of that, God will get you out of the way, so you better repent.

I want to make sure people understand that reasoning.

The Father is saying, "I've got to protect the baptism of the Holy Spirit and the ability to pray in tongues, like nothing else. That's the one sin that will take a Christian and send them to hell for eternity. They won't be forgiven in this age or the next age, if they attribute the ability to pray in tongues to Satan." People have done it for generations and I know that a lot of them went to hell, because they never repented of that blasphemy. People are still doing it today! I pray that they hear and get this message.

I've got a little bit of steam in my heart about this, for protecting the sanctity of the Holy Spirit's prayer language through us when we pray in tongues. Even if the person committing this blasphemy is a born again Christian; this is the one known way that a person can lose their salvation and go to hell.

I hope that everybody who teaches this course will preach this. I will have to have a precursor that I write to each one of the faculty members that is going to teach this. I will tell them they need to start praying in tongues at least an hour a day, before they teach this. This is going to orchestrate a new level of life and existence for you with God, in your assignment. I hope they listen and get how vital I think this is.

JUDGMENT IN THE EARLY CHURCH

We're still going to deal with these other issues that we see: judgment in the early church. Here, we are going to see judgment where people actually drop dead, but there's no indication that they lost their salvation; they just simply lied to the Holy Spirit. It didn't say they blasphemed the Holy Spirit; they lied to Him.

The reverence for the Holy Spirit was great among the apostles while they walked with Jesus, but when they believed on Jesus' resurrection from the dead, the Holy Spirit took up residence in their spirit. When Jesus breathed on them, they came to realize that He had dwelled in Adam and Eve before they lost that relationship for the whole human race.

Then, on the Day of Pentecost, they experienced the same power that rested on Jesus; the anointing without measure that had been on Jesus before He was seated in heaven. So, they were very grateful for this heavenly gift. They were grateful for being born again first; and then this heavenly gift came to them on the Day of Pentecost: the anointing without measure.

The power without measure came upon them that had been on Jesus, and He released it on the Church once He took a seat as King of Kings and Lord of Lords. It was an earthly anointing. He didn't need that anointing for earthly ministry any longer; His earthly ministry was complete. And He knew the Church needed that anointing without measure, in order to complete their assignment.

None of us are individually going to have as much of the measure that was on Jesus. That's what made Him the Messiah, the Anointed One, the Christ. But we'll have a portion of that measure; and that portion that we have can constantly increase all the days of our life, if we live this life correctly. Nobody's ever done it perfectly. Even the Apostle Paul never did it perfectly. He says: "I'm still just seeing through a glass darkly. But one day; one day I'll be able to see face-to-face" (1 Corinthians 13:12).

We're always going to be in that place of slight deceptions or a lack of knowledge and understanding of everything. Paul says, "There's one thing that I'm going to do though. I'm going to strive for that mark of the high calling in Christ Jesus. I'm going to run this race to hit that point; to achieve everything that God has for me."

He did it with His prayer life; he did it with his study of the Word. He did it with the preaching of the gospel to as many as he could, and being useful to the Lord; even to the point where he was so brutalized by the Jews who didn't believe that Jesus was the Messiah.

During the great supernatural growth of the church at Jerusalem, the Holy Spirit inspired the wealthy believers to sell extra houses and lands that they possessed, to meet the needs of the less well-off. Ananias and Sapphira wanted to be recognized like Barnabas. Barnabas was one of the first persons who sold everything.

Ananias and Sapphira decided to sell some land, but held back a portion of the profit from the sale for themselves. Then they reported that lesser amount as the total amount they received from the sale. Well, Peter knew by a word of knowledge that they were lying about this.

You might say, "Well, why would it make a big difference?" Listen. Maybe it wouldn't make as big a difference today, in some barely-saved church where they're just evangelical and they don't believe in being baptized in the Holy Spirit. But at the beginning of the Church, they were walking in a place of holiness that God had to preserve. The power couldn't be in this kind of resident manifestation in the Church, if they weren't all walking in the holy power of God.

I like referring to the Holy Spirit the way Paul does in Romans 1:4, as "the Spirit of Holiness," because that's ultimately what God wants to produce in a sinner's life. Once He puts the Spirit of Holiness in us and Spirit of Holiness is there, He will cause us to be continually transformed into walking a holier, more sanctified, set-apart life, every single day. It's like the song we used to sing at the beginning of the Charismatic Renewal:

"Turn your eyes upon Jesus.
Look full in His wonderful face.
And the things of the earth

will grow strangely dim,
in the light of His glory and grace."

(Original hymn written by Helen Howarth Lemmel, 1922)

You see, we need to see the things of the earth growing strangely dim, and our focus on Jesus and our assignment that He has given us, and the preservation of the holy nature of that assignment. Each one of us can only fulfill it if we allow Holy Spirit to be Spirit of Holiness through us.

He will not only pray the perfect prayer through us, but live the perfect life through us. Nobody ever becomes perfect except Jesus, but we can strive for it and have a greater measure of that anointing without measure resting upon us, as we come into that place of "yieldedness" to the Lord.

I remember the day the Lord told me, "Walking in My kingdom is all about *yieldedness*." I started looking it up; it's not even a word that I can find. I mean, the computer always tells me when I try to type it in, that I'm misspelling it. I'm not misspelling it. It just doesn't exist in the dictionary. But God told me, "It's all about yieldedness; keep yielding to what I'm leading you to go into and I'll empower you for it."

So, Peter knew by a word of knowledge that Ananias and Sapphira were lying. Acts 5:3-4:

But Peter said, "Ananias, why has Satan filled your heart to lie to the Holy Spirit and keep back *part* of the price of the land for yourself? While it remained, was it not your own? And after it was sold, was it not in your own control? Why have you conceived this thing in your heart? You have not lied to men but to God."

When you lie to the Holy Spirit, you're lying to God. You're lying to Jesus. Now, Ananias was a born again member of the Church. Ananias and Sapphira both were born again. They were probably baptized in the Holy Spirit, but for some reason, they were not allowing Holy Spirit and Spirit of Holiness to cause them to drive out lying.

Peter says, "Listen, you own the land. You could have sold it and said, 'We're keeping back part of the money,' but don't tell us you're giving all of it and then keep back part of the money. You're lying to the Holy Spirit."

Peter knew this because he had that by a word of knowledge. He realized, "You're trying to fool the Spirit of God. If you're trying to fool me, you're trying to fool the Spirit of God, because you're thinking that the Holy Spirit won't tell me and tattle on you and tell on you," but that's exactly what He did. When Ananias heard these words:

...he fell down and died (Acts 5:5a NIV).

There's no indication that he blasphemed the Holy Spirit. He did not attribute to the devil, the things that the Holy Spirit was doing. He just decided to lie to Peter. He thought he could just lie to Peter and still look like a big man on campus. "Yeah, I sold a bunch of stuff and gave it, just like Barnabas did." Ananias dropped dead; he physically died. Now, it's better actually, that the two of them and what they did just got wiped out from the church. You know that a great fear hit the rest of them, because it's really strange. Here are these words:

...he fell down and died.

The same thing happened to Sapphira when she came to the church several hours later. She comes hours later. It's either some long church service or they're conducting a whole bunch of other business for the benefit of all the Christians there. But hours later, she comes in and Peter just asks the question. He sets her up. I mean, it wasn't very pastoral at all, if you ask me. He could have said, "Listen, I need to warn you. Ananias already died when he came in and tried to lie to us."

He didn't even do that. He just let her tell the same lie and she dropped dead too. He even prophesied to her. "You know, the people that just carried out your husband are about ready to carry you out." Bam! She falls over. Well, that's judgment. They're not allowed to live and continue to bring that kind of demonic activity – even as born again Christians – into the holy operation of the founding of the Church. It's important that the Church start off pure and holy, with a reverence.

Again, many questions arise due to this violation of lying to the Holy Spirit. Did God kill them? No, God is the giver of life, but He can remove His hand of protection from someone who lies to the Holy Spirit. In essence, it's turning them over to Satan for the destruction of their flesh. We're going to deal with that in just a little bit.

Did Ananias and Sapphira go to hell when they died? Well, if God only considered it lying to the Holy Spirit and not blaspheming against the Holy Spirit; then of course as born again believers, they would have gone to heaven. Remember again, that blaspheming against the Holy Spirit would be to attribute something that the Holy Spirit does, to the works of Satan.

We didn't see them do that, so I think they just lied thinking they were lying to Peter. Either way, the Holy Spirit, the Father, and Jesus certainly desired to keep the Church spiritually pure at such a critical time for establishing the gospel and the Church. Purity had to remain in the early church for the Lord to continue to bless it.

APOSTOLIC AUTHORITY IN THE CHURCH

The Apostle Paul wrote to the Corinthians about purity in the Church, in his first letter. Paul had many good things to say to them as well, but he was addressing a sin among them that he said wasn't even numbered among the unbelievers.

Now, Corinth was an exceptionally sinful city. Of course, the Greek temple of Diana – which is the goddess of fertility – was there and it was filled with temple prostitutes. They celebrated sex in the city of Corinth. Of course, once the Church is saved, God is trying to showcase coming out from the world and the sins they were living in. They were so totally given in to the sensual lusts, without any kind of a bridle whatsoever from the Lord, that would need to be there to protect their lives. God's not trying to take our fun away from us; He's trying to protect us.

Paul says that the marriage bed is blessed of the Lord. It's undefiled, but there are certain parameters. What is the marriage bed? Well, it's between a husband and a wife. God wants us to be able to have sex for enjoyment as well as procreation, because the only two people that can procreate are a man and a woman. God only created two: a man and a woman, just like the original creation. That's the only ones that can procreate or continue the human race, but the people were worshipping all kinds of foul things in Corinth.

This man in Corinth, as a member of the church – a born again and maybe even spirit-filled member of the church – had taken up with his father's new wife or his stepmother. And she has left the father and is now living with the son in sin; like a married couple, but they're not married. Paul is addressing this and he is telling them how to be able to deal with them. Paul says something very interesting.

Of course, he preached the gospel first to the Corinthians. He is truly their apostle. He brought the gospel to them when nobody else had brought the gospel to them before. There are a number of churches he addressed, almost as though he was their founder, even though he acknowledged that he wasn't –

like the church at Colossae.

Paul tells the Corinthians something very interesting about how to deal with this man who is unrepentant. He brings his stepmother to church. They might still have a seat on the front row and the church is just not dealing with it; they're not saying anything. They're just sweeping it under the rug. "Nothing to see here. Move right along. These are not the 'droids' you're looking for." That's just a Star Wars joke.

They're just like ostriches hiding their heads in the sand. But the message of what's going on gets to Paul, so he writes to them. Now, Paul is praying for all of the churches. He has made it real plain. He's laboring in the Spirit over all the churches that are being established. He's praying hours on end over all of them. He's so connected to them, there are times when he is actually joined with them in the Spirit and he knows what's going on there; even the things that haven't been told to him. He says this in 1 Corinthians 5:4-5:

In the name of our Lord Jesus Christ,

We do all things that we do in the name of the Lord Jesus, because He's our salvation. Life is not about us; it is now about Jesus. Christ is our life. So, he says, "when you are gathered together..."

In the name of our Lord Jesus Christ, when you are gathered together, along with my spirit,

He says, "When you gather, my spirit comes along with you, so my spirit's going to be with you this next time that you gather."

...with the power of our Lord Jesus Christ,

When you sense the power of the Lord is in manifestation; you know, we understand about the difference between the omnipresence of God and the manifest presence of God. You begin to worship the Lord, meditate on His Word; you worship Him to receive all the glory and the honor and you extol Him for all of His Majesty. All of a sudden, He manifests His presence. So he says, "...in the presence, when the power of the Lord Jesus Christ is there, deliver this man..."

deliver such a one to Satan for the destruction of the flesh, that his spirit may be saved in the day of the Lord Jesus.

Paul is saying, "I want this man to be saved, but you're going to have to deliver him over to Satan for the destruction of his flesh." Well, why would you do that? You can't turn him over to God for the destruction of his flesh, because God doesn't destroy flesh. He's the source of life; but He's also the One who has an umbrella of protection over everybody – even unbelievers. And yet, when you take the authority in the realm of the Spirit and you remove that umbrella of protection over someone, suddenly Satan has free course to absolutely go after him.

That's what Paul was telling them. He says, "Just turn this one over to Satan for the destruction of his flesh." That doesn't necessarily mean for him to die. It doesn't necessarily mean for him to have a disease that he comes down with and he's just going to be maimed with it for the rest of his life, or any such thing. It just means that somehow, something would go badly for him – bad enough for him to recognize and know: "The church did this. They released me to Satan."

They basically said, "We're not going to pray for you and keep the umbrella of protection of the Lord over you. We're going to turn you over to Satan so that whatever happens to you happens to you so that you'll repent; change your mind. (*Metanoia* is the Greek word, meaning "to change your mind.") Then you will come back into a right relationship with the church. That means not living with your father's wife; your stepmother."

It's an amazing thing that this can actually be going on, but Paul says, "Listen, I'm asking you to do this as the Church, and my Spirit will be with you and the presence and the power of the Lord Jesus will be with you." So, this is something that God is demanding of us, in order to keep the Church pure. Paul desired to keep each one of these newly-established churches, like the Corinthian church, pure and holy. Paul was praying over them. He was laboring in the Spirit for them to remain established.

If there was anything Paul was afraid of, it was that he had run his race in vain; that any part of what he had done laboring unto the Lord would have turned out to have been done in vain. If it didn't last, he would have felt like a failure. Paul was concerned about that. He wanted every one of the churches that were established, to remain established. And it turns out of course, that 300 years after Paul's death, every church he established was still in existence.

I'd say that that "thorn in the flesh," that demonic force that was trying to rip down his ministry and get him executed, was not successful. So, when the Lord told Paul, "My grace is sufficient for you Paul; your work is going to be established. It's going to make it all the way." I believe there are two aspects to God's answer. Paul came to realize that he could take authority over the devil and stop the persecution. Part of it ended when he stopped going to the Jews first. He stopped going to the synagogue when he got to a city. He started going to the Gentiles when he realized, "I'm the apostle to the Gentiles, so why go stirring up a hornet's nest with the Jews?"

Now, Paul loved the Jews and wanted to minister to the Jews. He was probably envious of Peter being the apostle to the Jews because he had been such a zealot for Judaism, yet it wasn't his assignment. That's one of the reasons why I really believe Paul is the author of the *Book of Hebrews*. I believe he published it as a book without his name so that he could actually have a ministry to the Hebrews. It's so in-line with all the rest of his writings.

I don't believe there's anybody but Paul who could have written Hebrews. He had the insight about the better covenant based on the better promises. He had the insight about all the heroes of the Hall of Faith. These people changed the world. They rewrote history by believing God. They gave us so many foundational truths so that we realize we can follow in their footsteps. We can walk in faith and make a difference in our lifetime, in this world that we live in.

Paul didn't want people to reject the book because it was written by him. A lot of Jews didn't want to have anything to do with him. They didn't want to listen to him so he didn't sign that letter, but he wrote it so that the Jews would read it. It's plainly a letter to the Jews – and of course, it's to the Christian Jews, but it is also written to draw in any other Jews.

As a logician, somebody who uses logic, this is being "apologetic." That is not apologizing but laying out the entire case for believing in Jesus as the Messiah. He did that for the Jews in the *Book of Hebrews*.

We're going to find out there are a couple of other people that Paul turned over to Satan so they would learn not to blaspheme. The word "deliver" is *paradidōmi* [Strong's G3860]. That is a judicial act of sentencing. Paul was saying, "We have to serve a sentence here on this sin that the man has committed against the church. The man is expecting to be able to attend the church without anyone saying anything to him about the sin that he is living in."

The word "destruction" is the Greek word *olethros* [Strong's G3639]. This word may refer to death or sickness. It was something that was going to be happening in his flesh and that was going to be enough of an alarm to him, to want to repent. The man, who is the subject of the command by Paul, is the one who had stolen his father's wife and who was living with her in sin. However, no one in the church did anything to attempt to correct the man and preserve purity in the church membership. They acted as though there was nothing wrong.

Having established the church, the Apostle Paul had authority to correct the church. Some pastors pioneer a church. Some of them pastor a church they pioneered, for forty or fifty years. They're actually the apostle of that church. If you pioneer it and you're the one who established it, you have that authority over that church.

I believe in apostles and prophets, but no pastor of a church should listen to somebody who comes in and says, "I'm an apostle. I think the Lord has called me to be the apostle of this church." No, you can't be the apostle of that church. No apostle just walks in and says, "I'm the apostle of this church." Either you have established the church and that gives you an apostolic right, or you haven't. Even if you stand in the office of an apostle, you would only be the apostle of the churches you have established.

Again, they hadn't done anything to correct this. Paul had the authority to correct the church. He admonished them to receive the man back into the fellowship in the second letter to Corinth, because the man had repented.

In this case, they dealt with it; they must have done what Paul asked them to do. Something happens when the man repents. He stops living with the woman, but the church wouldn't let him back into the church. They were still rebuking him for having sinned, after Paul brought it to their attention.

In 2 Corinthians, Paul said, "Now that the man has repented, you've got to let him back in. Listen, God forgives sins, even the worst of sins – even something that would have disrupted the purity of the church here. Once the man is repentant and wants back in, you have to be like God and forgive and let the man back in." So, he repented. Apparently, turning him over to Satan for the destruction of his flesh happened to have worked.

Paul gave further instructions to his son in the faith, Timothy. He said in 1 Timothy 1:18-20:

This charge I commit to you, son Timothy, according to the prophecies previously made concerning you, by them you may wage the good warfare, having faith and a good conscience, which some having rejected, concerning the faith have suffered shipwreck, of whom are Hymenaeus and Alexander, whom I delivered to Satan that they may learn not to blaspheme.

Let me break this down a little bit, because the first thing Paul says is: "I charge and commit to you, son Timothy, according to the prophecies previously made concerning you." There were a number of people that were prophets, that you could take their word of prophecy as real. Paul had probably prophesied to Timothy himself. Timothy may have even interpreted his own tongues and received things that the Holy Spirit had prayed for him, as a prophecy to himself.

The reality is that you can be your own prophet. You can interpret your own tongues and your prayer in tongues. Then of course, you can get direction from the Lord. The number one part of a prophet's office is to be able to hear from God. God intended for every believer to be able to hear from Him; making us the prophet of our own life. In other words, you're the one responsible. You're the steward. You've got to hear directly from the throne of God's grace.

The Father can speak to you. Jesus can speak to you. The

Holy Spirit can speak to you. Your own spirit, where the Holy Spirit dwells, can speak to you and give you guidance and direction. But sometimes you need very specific words and illuminations of Scripture so that your faith comes alive, such as when it has to do with a promise from the Lord. But you can also get a direct revelation from the Holy Spirit, where He's revealing things to you out of His truths in life that you can walk by. But some of the prophecies may have to do with a word of wisdom concerning your future ministry.

So, Paul was telling Timothy what he was going to have to do with these prophecies that had been prophesied over him:

previously made concerning you, that by them you may wage the good warfare.

I believe that you wage this warfare by praying in tongues.

OUR VICTORY IS CONDITIONAL

There are times when I'm praying in tongues and I realize – especially during the first hour – that I'm getting pushback from the kingdom of darkness. A lot of times, it takes praying through that first hour, to pray back that opposition from the kingdom of darkness. You feel like you are praying against the darkness that Satan's trying to specifically target you, through certain demon spirits. Many people have said, "The devil's really after me." They're thinking it's Satan himself. There might be a whole lot of other bigger names in ministry that he's really after and trying to stop, than you and I.

Satan has a lot of demonic forces on his side, so yes, there might be some demons that are assigned directly to you, but it's probably not Satan himself coming after you. At any rate, we've got to push back against all opposition in the kingdom of darkness. And we find out that when we're doing that, a lot of the attacks have to do with prophecies over our lives and our ministries, and things that we're supposed to be completing.

Over the years, I have heard people saying strange things about intercession. People have done some goofy things in intercession. I can intercede for four hours in the middle of the night, at my house. I just walk around for several hours and sit for several hours and just pray in a whisper. I don't wake anybody up, yet I can actually do spiritual warfare. But I've heard people talk about "war tongues." They say, "You've got to pray in your war tongues," and they'll get real loud and real violent.

Praying in tongues is allowing the Holy Spirit to pray through you. There might be some times that He will have you raise your voice. There may be some demonstrative actions where you're taking dominion and authority over some mountain in your life, in opposition of the devil. But you can still do warfare much of the time with just a normal voice. It's not like it's always going to be loud and screaming at the top of your lungs. A lot of times, people add a lot of drama to our walk with the Lord – drama that's really just not necessary.

In 1 Timothy 1:18-20, Paul was telling Timothy that, "You're in a warfare and you've got to pray over the prophecies and wage a good warfare, for these prophecies to come to pass."

There are many prophecies over our lives; even that the Lord would give us directly, that are *conditional*. We have to meet the conditions according to the Lord's plan for our life, to be able to fulfill many of them. Unless we do certain things, these prophecies will not come to pass.

There are many things that I've heard prophesied to people, that have not come to pass. I realize that the people weren't very faithful to the Lord in much. Some of them I know have even shipwrecked their whole lives and ministries because they were just unfaithful to the Lord and His assignment to them.

It's one thing if people feel like they've never heard the Lord giving them any direction, but you've got to pursue Him to find out direction for your life. Then, once He gives you direction, you need to revere the call of God that's on your life.

You must approach this as the most holy directions you could ever get. It's the most holy opinion of the Creator of the universe that He has for you, and where you fit into His scheme of things while you're here on this earth. A lot of people do not revere the calling on their lives. They put no attention to it; no prayer, no study in the Word, and no preparation to fulfill what the Lord has shown them or has even prophesied to them from somebody else.

Again, we have to wage that warfare against the kingdom of darkness. Many times, just praying in tongues the first hour; you're pushing back the kingdom of darkness. The second hour, you go into breakthroughs. You start hearing from the Lord; all these directions are being sent to you.

In this category of prayers of *judgment and justice*; I'd like to share an illustration. I started realizing something when I was praying for Ukraine. That will date the time I'm telling this story, because this is something I'm teaching in August of 2022. This story is from around February, when Russia invaded Ukraine.

I know the ministry that's been going on there; I have so many friends who have done much ministry in Ukraine. There is a wonderful group of Christians there. At the same time, my good friend Rick Renner is in Russia and he has won millions of Christians to the Lord in Russia and in all the Russian-speaking parts of the world. They watch television programs in Ukraine that Rick has produced in Russia. There's a lot of wonderful Russian Christians and a lot of wonderful Ukrainian Christians.

All of a sudden, Putin comes along and invades Ukraine. If you watch his life over the last few years, he has been breaking down, as far as mental faculties go. I think He's delusional. He thinks he's the greatest leader since Peter the Great – the greatest, brutal, murderous dictator since Peter the Great.

I started praying for Ukraine. After awhile, I started to sense that I'm praying for all the Ukrainians; especially for all those that have become refugees. They had to run away. They had to get out of Ukraine to survive all the bombings there. Now they are refugees. There's a couple million in Poland.

My friend Mike Francine has gone over and preached the gospel. He delivered a couple semi-trailers of food to Ukraine and preached the gospel over there. Then, he went into Poland and preached because there are so many refugees there. His goal is to win a million Ukrainians to the Lord, while they're in the middle of this crisis.

I noticed after awhile (praying in tongues), that I could sense I'm praying the *imprecatory prayer*. The Holy Spirit is praying it through me. He's praying judgment over Putin, and over all of those that are in alignment with him, and willing to be murderous butchers and dictators. They're brutal.

Listen, the unsaved Russians are as easily demon-possessed as anybody I've ever seen on the planet. That's the same as any place, but they have a long history of evil. A lot of countries have a history of being barbarians, so they're doing that again.

I realized the Holy Spirit was praying through me, the *imprecatory prayer of judgment* over these people. The next thing I started noticing in the news, is that Putin's having all kinds of health issues, and I'm thinking, "Holy Spirit, if you're turning him over to Satan for the destruction of his flesh, I'm all on board with whatever it would take for him to repent or get out of the way, to stop this whole insanity." Of course, they're delusional, thinking they have an army and the ability to actually take over Ukraine. Before it's all over, Ukraine is probably going to be moving into Moscow and taking over there.

You have to understand that when the Lord is using us in prayer, the Holy Spirit will actually be doing the imprecatory prayer of judgment against some, and justice for others. So, I knew the Holy Spirit was praying for justice for the Ukrainians. He had now also moved into the place of praying judgment over the Russian military.

What you have to understand is that if you pray in tongues long enough, that's what is going to be prayed through you. You can't say, "Well, I'm not going to pray for somebody else to die."

Listen, it's just turning them over to Satan for the destruction of their flesh. If they're not believers, they're already on their way to hell for eternity. When does it matter how soon they get there? That is such a long, long, long time. Any 120 years on this earth is just a vapor; so the sooner they get there, the better for all those that are still left on the earth.

The reality is that I'm going to be in agreement with what God will do to preserve the Church and save people's lives and preserve nations that want to serve God – those that want to be a predominantly Christian nation. That is one of the things we are going to see that is happening here. Paul was dealing with this when he was talking to Timothy about what he was doing: turning Hymenaeus and Alexander over. He says:

whom I delivered to Satan that they may learn not to blaspheme (1 Timothy 1:20).

These were Christians. These were men who were supposed to be teaching the truth. Paul was addressing

Christians. He says again in 1 Timothy 1:19-20:

that by them [by these prophecies] you may wage the good warfare, having faith and a good conscience

You know, there's nothing like having a good conscience. If your conscience is pure and clean – that is, you've already repented. Repentance is something we need to do every day.

"Lord, in anything I've done to offend anybody today, I repent. Please, forgive me. I want to represent You as an ambassador and always represent You for a blessing to the people, and salvation to the unsaved."

We do that – repent – all the time, to keep a good conscience. He says:

which some having rejected, concerning the faith

In other words, they reject having a good conscience; they do bad things and they know it, and they don't repent of it. Therefore, they come to this place of having suffered shipwreck. They suffer shipwreck: of their lives, of their ministries. These were Christians he was talking about. He says:

of whom are Hymenaeus and Alexander

Now again, we'll find out. There was Alexander the coppersmith. We're not sure if he's the same one. Paul also mentioned Alexander the coppersmith in 2 Timothy, as doing him much harm, but it's unclear if this is the same Alexander. At any rate, this name shows up several times. How would you like to have been the person whom Paul named in one of the letters and now we're reading about it 1,900 and some years later?

Now, if they corrected themselves and got saved, you'll

probably meet them one day. You'll get a chance to talk to them and they might say, "Praise God that Paul did turn me over to Satan for the destruction of my flesh, so I could learn not to blaspheme God the Father, or the Word of God," or whatever it was they were blaspheming.

They might say, "It got me straightened out. It got me corrected. I wouldn't have made it into heaven if Paul hadn't done that. I would have shipwrecked my entire life and come to the place of giving my salvation back; not believing. I was close to not believing that Jesus Christ is the Lord."

They might say that; we don't know. We do know that Paul understood how to get people corrected. That's why I'm spending the time here on this prayer of the *imprecatory prayer* or the *prayer of justice and judgment*. That's *justice* for the person being offended or abused in some way, and then *judgment* for the abusers.

Timothy is now pastoring the church in Ephesus. Paul mentions two men who have departed from true faith. Paul mentions that he has turned them over to Satan so that they would learn not to blaspheme.

Hymenaeus is mentioned along with Philetus, in Paul's second letter to Timothy (2 Timothy 2:17) – as still spreading false doctrine. Maybe Hymenaeus didn't get it right and Alexander did. Again, we don't know if it's the same people he's talking about. It's unclear.

Again, he mentions Alexander the coppersmith, whom he says "did much harm" to him. This sounds like Alexander the coppersmith was not a believer. He was a Jew who made his money creating idols.

A lot of times, silversmiths and coppersmiths; even people that work with stone, created idols, and of course, they were not part of Israel. It was probably Gentiles that were making idols for all the different idol worshippers; all the different foreign gods and false gods that were part of Greek culture and religion and Roman culture and religion, that kind of replaced the Greek and blended the two together.

Either way, the apostle Paul had no problem protecting the purity of the Church through prayers of justice and judgment. I have no problem protecting the purity of the Church in the modern era, through prayers of justice and judgment.

When I pray in tongues long enough and I get the interpretation of those tongues, I'm going to allow the Holy Spirit to do the prayer of justice and judgment. Then I'm going to come into agreement and alignment with it.

There are still all kinds of warfare going on throughout the earth, but we're not as cognizant of it. I have very close friends who have done a lot of ministry in Ukraine. And of course, I've been to Russia and done ministry there, and I've got lots of friends who have done a lot of ministry in Russia. Thank God we know the people are praying. Christians are praying against what their nation is doing.

We have LCU graduates who ministered in their home country of Venezuela. The country was turned from the most profitable South American country that had democratic principles, to what is now is a totally Socialist dictatorship. And we found out that Chavez's daughter has $3 billion.

What does that tell you about what happens with the corrupt people that get power and who rob the people of all of their money and keep it in their family?

One LCU graduate tried to go back and pastor in Venezuela. He said, "What wonderful, marvelous Christian churches they had there," but then he said that the opposition of the Socialist government was so great that he could not stay there – and he was a citizen!

He was going back to his own country, but he couldn't stay there and keep ministering because he was so oppressed by the demonic government of socialism in Venezuela.

We know there are marvelous Christians all over the place. What we have to believe is that they can still fulfill what God called them to do; just like Jesus did and the apostles did when they were living in Israel, which was an occupied nation. It was occupied by demon-possessed Rome, yet they were still able to conclude what God had called them to do.

You may have received the interpretation of your prayer in tongues while praying for the justice of God to be demonstrated to those who are being oppressed by evil men; and the prayer of judgment being prayed by the Holy Spirit, over the evil men who are the oppressors. Abusers are oppressors.

We do not know what the effect would be if every Christian prayed in tongues. I'm talking about just those who have been baptized in the Holy Spirit and prayed in tongues once. You'd be shocked to find out how many people have only prayed in tongues when they first got baptized in the Holy Spirit.

They didn't know there was any continual prayer in tongues. It was essentially, "Well, I've got it now. I've got the power. I've got the Holy Ghost." They never, ever tap into all the benefits, the privileges, the power, and the anointing that comes from praying continually in tongues; and allowing the Holy Spirit to do your perfect praying for you, through your spirit.

So much grace is squandered by people. What if everybody who's ever been baptized in the Holy Spirit – if every single one of us prayed in tongues at least an hour a day? Perhaps all wars would cease because God would have enough intercessors to pray the prayers of justice and judgment throughout the entire earth.

I believe that's why we're going to have a revival of praying in the Spirit before the Lord comes back. There's going to be a revival that is so sweeping of so many Christians into the kingdom in the very last hours.

It will be like the last great demonstration of God; of what His power and His might can do when the Church becomes pure and focused and does everything that we know to do from the Word of God. That's praying in the Spirit, studying and meditating on the Word of God, and praying through, and doing everything the Holy Spirit shows us to do.

That's waging a good warfare over all the prophecies of our lives and standing in that place where God can use us to bring opposition to Satan's kingdom – even the demonic governments all over this planet.

It may cause all wars to cease before God would say, "Okay, Jesus. Go back. Bring home the Church; the final number has finally come in. The revival has finally hit its peak. It's time to bring the Church home and the judgment can fall after that." That is in the Word of God. We're going to see the justice and the judgment of the Lord in manifestation.

OLD TESTAMENT PRAYERS TO DESTROY GOD'S ENEMIES

If we're in Christ, our enemies in the New Testament are God's enemies. I listed a long list of Scripture passages from Psalms that were Old Testament prayers to destroy God's enemies. David prayed those prayers over and over again. They include:

Psalm 3:7-8 Psalm 5:10 Psalm 10:15 Psalm 35:1-8 Psalm 56:5-8 Psalm 59:12-13	Psalm 68:1-4 Psalm 69:22-28 Psalm 137:8-9 Psalm 139:19-22 Psalm 140:6-11

Just for your own interest, I also wanted to give you a list of the Roman leaders that persecuted the early church and that had a dire death experience. Quite possibly, it was due to the prayers that were being prayed in the Spirit, by the early church members. I believe that they were actually praying these imprecatory prayers.

Whether they really understood it all or not, they were praying in tongues a lot, for the first three hundred years. So, here's what happened to all of those Roman rulers that oppressed the early church:

Tiberius: He was smothered and that was arranged. (A.D. 14-17)

Pilot: Suicide or beheaded (A.D. 16-37)

Caligula: Stabbed to death. He was a dirt bag. (A.D. 37-41)

Claudius: Poisoned (A.D. 51-54)

Nero: Committed suicide. Here was another demon-possessed, evil guy. (A.D. 54-68)

In other words, all of these people are burning in hell right now because they were evil and did evil against the Church. They never received Jesus as Lord, even though we find out that after 300 years, Christianity became the state religion.

Here are some others:

Galba: Beheaded (A.D. 68)

Otho: Suicide (A.D. 68)

 Vitellius: Tortured to death. (A.D. 69)

That's a tough way to go.

Domitian: Stabbed (A.D. 81-96)

We find out in history, that every single one of these emperors of Rome were worshipped after their death, as though they were a god. Domitian was the first one to say, "I'm a God while I'm living; I have to be worshipped as God while I'm here now." That's when it started getting really, really offensive to the Lord; when men were claiming to be God in the flesh – men who were serving Satan.

CHAPTER SIXTEEN

ALL THINGS ARE POSSIBLE WITH FAITH

PRAYER FORM 10 – THE PRAYER OF COMMISSIONING ANGELS

This is the tenth form of prayer that I've found. You won't find this in anybody else's books. This is something the Lord has revealed to me. It's the *prayer of commissioning angels.* How do I know this? I discovered this as we were working on our course on *Angelology*. At the very beginning of this university, God plunged our little church – in the second year – into a great revival. Now, it wasn't a revival that drew in lots of other people, but we had incredible experiences. I had so many angelic visitations around that time, that I had to come up with a course on *Angelology*.

The Lord had pointed out something very interesting to me. A minister friend of mine and I were sitting in one of Kenneth Copeland's meetings and he just made a simple statement. It was just a side statement around the major theme and thoughts that he was talking about, and it just dropped out of his mouth. I thought about it and told my friend, "Wait a minute; that is a major power bomb he just dropped! I want to hear the rest of it." I thought, "Brother Copeland, can you go back and teach on that? That was so powerful!" It was just one of those nuggets he just kind of tossed off.

I believe that oftentimes, we need to study the words of the apostles of the Lamb and the founding apostles, the same way. For example, in 1 Corinthians 13, when Paul is writing the "love" chapter, he places it between chapter twelve, where he's talking about the gifts of the Spirit; and chapter 14, where he's also talking about the gifts of the Spirit. He just happens to drop this at the end of the chapter:

"And now abide faith, hope, love, these three; but the greatest of these is love" (1 Corinthians 13:13).

As Word of faith people, we would think that it's *faith*, right? No, it's not. The greatest of these is *love*. We find out it is the love of God that gives us the promises. Then we find out that faith is *us believing the covenant promises*. So, now we pray the prayer of faith – the whole thing.

We use God's faith; we take authority over the mountains. We believe and pray to God to replace the mountains with the things that we need. Then we walk in love with everybody. We're in that place of faith but then you don't always see an instant answer to your prayer.

So, you have to have *hope* to be able to sustain you through that time, before you can say, "Amen, it has finally arrived" – the healing of the body, the provision, the peace in my family, the restoration of this relationship, or whatever it is. Before you can say, "Praise God, it has finally arrived," you have to have hope to stand there; and then you will see a full manifestation of the love of God.

Now, Paul said something at the very beginning of this chapter in 1 Corinthians 13:1. "Though I pray in the tongues of men and of angels..." When you're praying in tongues, sometimes your prayer is in *the tongues of the angels.*

I know a bit about the angels; about our individual angel, and about the diversity of all the different types of angels, and purposes for all the angels and their various assignments. The word "angel" means messenger. It's *angelos* [Strong's G32] from the Greek, meaning "a messenger." Of course, there are messenger angels, and some of the ones that were involved in the Old Testament brought messages from heaven. Gabriel brought the messages about the Christ, the Messiah, to Mary, and visited Joseph in his dreams.

I know we have already mentioned the archangels. There are three that we know of: Gabriel (Gabri-"el"), Michael, and Heylel. I believe those three archangels were each assigned to one of the three persons of the Godhead. Heylel was probably assigned to the Word, and was envious of the Word's position and wanted to take over God's whole throne. We also find out that all of us have been assigned an angel. These are Jesus' own words. As children, we are all assigned an angel.

"Take heed that you do not despise one of these little ones, for I say to you that in heaven their angels always see the face of My Father who is in heaven" (Matthew 18:10).

"one of these little ones"
Other translations say it this way:

"...For I can assure you that in heaven each of their guardian angels always sees the face of my heavenly Father" (Matthew 18:10 TPT).

"...You realize, don't you, that their personal angels are constantly in touch with my Father in heaven" (Matthew 18:10 MSG)?

It is clear that each of us have personal angels that guard and minister to us.

For He shall give His angels charge over you, To keep you in all your ways. (Psalm 91:11).

Are they not all ministering spirits sent forth to minister for those who will inherit salvation (Hebrews 1:14)?

You may say, "Why aren't these angels able to save children that get murdered or that die in an accident when they're young?" If everything was coming together in a faith atmosphere around them, they would be able to. Children are innocent, and as they grow, they have to be taught the Word of God and how to pray the prayer of faith. Satan can take advantage of the ignorance of those around them, and the protection not being there, through those who have authority to protect them.

Boy, did my guardian angel have a job! He saved me from so many things. It's amazing I survived my childhood growing up out here in the country north of Tampa, Florida, on the lakes; swimming in a lake with alligators in it. He saved me from all kinds of things. Yes, we have guardian angels and there are healing angels; there are provision angels. There are many different angels. We're going to take a look at what they're able to do as we pray in tongues, and the angels are able to hear and exactly understand what it is that we are saying.

The *prayer of commissioning angels* is a prayer that can only be prayed in tongues. As I said, it is based on the beginning of Paul's "love chapter," in 1 Corinthians 13. Why is it that it's only prayed in tongues? Well, when Paul began this statement concerning the pure love of God and all that it does in the lives of committed believers; he began with a statement that opens a discussion of what really happens when we pray in tongues:

"Though I pray in the tongues of men and of angels" (1 Corinthians 13:1 AUTHOR PARAPHRASE).

When the Apostle Paul mentioned that our prayer in tongues is sometimes in the tongues of angels, it brought me to the realization of a profound truth about the angel that is on assignment for each one of us. We all have a guardian angel. There's no indication that the guardian angel leaves you when you become an ornery teenager or an even more ornery adult. They stick with us for life, so praise God that they are there and on assignment.

That's why we have to learn how to be in faith – so they can get their job done. We have to pray in tongues enough that they hear what we're praying and they can get their job done for us. Each one of us has a guardian angel that can hear us praying in tongues. They understand what Holy Spirit is praying, when it happens to be in the "language of the angels."

The Holy Spirit is always praying the perfect will of God for our lives, including all of our necessities. A commissioning of the angels to provide that which they are authorized to do is being given to them while we are praying in tongues. In other words, the commissioning that the Holy Spirit wants to commission them to do can only happen when we pray in tongues and they hear it coming out of our mouths.

As I said, I believe you can pray in tongues in your mind. Psalm 139 tells us that God knows all of our thoughts. So, when you're thinking in tongues, God can "read" your mind. He hears your tongues, He knows your thoughts and He knows what you're praying in tongues. And of course, you can do that before you are falling asleep. You might even pray in tongues all night long while you're doing it. It's a good practice to get into.

But when you're praying in tongues out loud, that's when the angels can hear. I believe that our guardian angel has the ability to call in all of the other angels that have all of these other assignments – the provision angels and the healing angels.

What if the commissioning of your own healing for your body *only* comes when you pray in tongues out loud long enough that your angel says, "That was the commissioning I needed to hear coming out of your lips. Now I can call in the healing angel that's assigned to you to heal your body, but I couldn't do it until you prayed in tongues long enough"?

How about the provision of the finances that you need? Your angel, your guardian angel is there saying, "Okay, I can call in the provision angels now." Listen, provision angels have to move a whole bunch of things around to be able to start getting money to you. But when it arrives, you realize, "Man, that's so supernatural. Thank God for what He's doing in answer to our prayer."

I believe that so much of the answers to our prayers are prayed in the spirit. What about people in your family that you've been praying for and you don't know how to pray for them? Or, how do we fix your brother-in-law and sister's marriage that's coming apart, when they're on the verge of divorce?

Well, when we pray for them in tongues enough, all of a sudden, a peace angel can be assigned to them. Then they will have to draw near to this peace that comes into their presence. And of course, you're also praying for the Lord of the Harvest to send forth laborers into the harvest for them.

They might be Christians, but they're not having the harvest of a harmonious relationship, so they need the peace angel to come there and then somebody to speak wisdom and counsel to them. Then they will suddenly come into a place of forgiving one another and coming back into harmony.

What about completely estranged relationships? Family members haven't talked to each other for years, yet when you're praying in the Spirit, the Holy Spirit is trying to pray a commissioning through you. It comes out of your mouth and your angel picks it up and says, "Oh, good. I can get these angels assigned to that and to the both of them." Then people come along too, as laborers in the harvest. All of a sudden, estranged people come back together.

Or, even when no human beings are involved, the angels themselves can get it done. They're able to just hang around them and suddenly bring their attention to certain things. They suddenly start feeling, "You know, I was really unjust when I refused to forgive this or that; because I needed to be forgiven of half a dozen things myself." They come to a realization that it's ridiculous to remain estranged when we're blood family and God wants us to be able to be a support to one another.

In our course on angels, we discovered there are many different types of angels, with varying assignments. We do know that our guardian angels have authority to call along the assistance of any other angel that is necessary; just as Jesus had the authority to call 10,000 angels to Himself to rescue Him, but He refused to do that. He could have done that, but He refused because He didn't come here to live before us and survive, and we'd never have salvation. We'd never have the perfect sacrifice made for us. No, He came and His purpose was to die.

I don't know if you ever saw the music video *Secret Ambition*, but it's just amazing. The secret ambition of Jesus was that He came to die on our behalf and nobody really understood that or knew that until the very last moment – and of course, until His resurrection from the dead. It's an awesome Michael W. Smith music video; Stephen Yake produced it.

My wife Susan and I were working at *Willie George Ministries* while she attended Rhema. Stephen Yake had produced the *Gospel Bill Show* and the *Fire by Nite* TV programs. He started producing all these music videos. This was one of the most powerful music videos I've ever seen done. It's just incredible. Look it up.

As we have said, our personal angel may be getting marching orders from the Holy Spirit through our spirit, when we pray in tongues. They may be standing by, waiting for the commissioning to call a healing angel when they would be needed. If we're praying in tongues out loud enough for them to hear, they may be waiting for the command to call forth provision angels to provide all that we need, in order to complete our divine assignment.

Again, all these good things God wants in our life are so that we can run our race all the way to the finish line and complete exactly what He planned for us to do. If we're praying in tongues out loud long enough, the Holy Spirit is able to get around to praying that through our spirits. He's going to pray the most important things, but some of those things have to come through us by praying in tongues long enough. We've already talked about this concept of "praying through."

I don't usually stand in the pulpit to minister until I've prayed through in tongues at least two hours beforehand; especially when it's a ministry time, like with one of our classes. I want the same anointing for the classes because you're to be trained up to do the exact same things when you step into the ministries – continually – that God has for you.

There are times when you realize that the Lord will have you up; when He just wakes you up in the middle of the night. You start praying and then you look at your watch or your clock and you say, "I have been here for five hours, praying in tongues." But you finally feel that release. It's an amazing thing when that much time is given to prayer.

Many times people say, "Well, I'll be exhausted the next day, if I did that through the middle of the night." Well, He might have you just turn off the TV and pray a couple of hours in tongues before you go to bed. Then, in the middle of the night, you may wake up and pray a couple of hours. The next day, you just hit the ground running and you pray in tongues as you're running along.

There's no law on this. I can't tell you how much to pray except what I have sensed from the Lord. We need to be able to tarry at least an hour in tongues. It's something I just assumed as a believer that is born again and empowered by the Holy Spirit; that I need to be able to do this. The original disciples weren't born again yet and they weren't empowered by the Holy Spirit, so they couldn't even last an hour while Jesus was facing the cross to pay the price for our sins.

I believe that once we have the power and the ability to do it; let's just do it. Many times, we'll find ourselves praying through. A lot of times, even if it's just right in the middle of the day, you've got to take a break from what you're doing and just pray. Sometimes you've prayed through and it's just fifteen minutes and you really sense: "I had an unction to pray, I prayed through, and I felt released by the Holy Spirit. I prayed through whatever God wanted me to pray."

The Holy Spirit revealed to me, if it's the will of the Lord, if it's the Father's will, if it's Jesus' will for that to be revealed to me (what I prayed for); then I can ask:

"Please give that to me because I want to come into agreement."

I want to find out what form of prayer these were that I

have prayed through, because I know it's going to fit into one of these areas and categories. This will hopefully inspire you to pray in tongues much more than you have been because of the benefits, which may produce incredible, miraculous results in your life and your divine assignment from God.

THE POWER OF PRAYER

We have seen that God knows our thoughts and we can pray in tongues in our minds, where our Father and our Lord Jesus can hear us. Our prayer life in communion with the Triune Godhead can be very effective, even when we're praying in tongues in our mind. There is no indication that the angels can read our mind, so we probably need to pray in tongues out loud enough for them to hear the Holy Spirit praying for us and through us.

We can pray even in a whisper, as they can hear the whisper. I believe your angel is the one who picks the prayer up and who is able to call in whatever other angels are needed, but he needs that commission. Now, why do I say "he" instead of referring to female angels? There may be female angels, but I believe God only sends male angels into the war zone, which is planet earth, where Satan and all the demon forces of hell – the fallen angels and everything evil – are all warring against the Church and against humankind.

If I was God, I wouldn't send the females into combat either. I can't believe our own government would do that. These women who say, "I'm going to prove I can die for my country just like the men," well, okay, go ahead. They're trying to prove something. Now, I believe when it comes to fighter pilots, that a lot of women are going to be so much more capable. They have the dexterity and sometimes the instincts.

There may be guys that grew up playing video games and who developed the same thing. It turns out that a lot of surgeons today are using laparoscopes and robots to do surgery. They're watching the screen and they do all this amazing surgery. A lot of times, the best surgeons today in this era are the ones who grew up playing video games. Who knew? There's actually a positive use for video games.

One final note on prayers that the Holy Spirit prays through our spirits, is found in the prayer that Jesus prayed for His disciples and for all the disciples, including you. It is found in John 17. I like to say that a thorough reading of that great prayer is greatly encouraged. Let's just read part of it, just to hear the tone. Remember, this is the prayer that Jesus is praying for His disciples and for us; but there was nobody around Him to hear it. But John wrote it by revelation of the Spirit of God because John was asleep while Jesus was praying this. All the disciples were asleep. Jesus was praying this over us and over the Church.

Again, it's interesting to see that this was revealed to John the apostle, just like The Revelation was given to John. It says in John 17:9-17:

"I pray for them. I do not pray for the world but for those whom You have given Me, for they are Yours."

He's talking about the Church and praying for all those in the Church, but especially those disciples that He brought to Himself in the time of His earthly ministry.

"And all Mine are Yours, and Yours are Mine, and I am glorified in them. Now I am no longer in the world, but these are in the world,"

They're going to be left here.

"...and I come to You. Holy Father, keep through Your name those whom You have given Me, that

they may be one as We *are*."

Keep them in unity and keep them flowing with us in the Spirit so that they can be one with us and always act out everything that we want them to act out in their ministries.

"While I was with them in the world, I kept them in Your name. Those whom You gave Me I have kept; and none of them is lost except the son of perdition, that the Scripture might be fulfilled. But now I come to You, and these things I speak in the world, that they may have My joy fulfilled in themselves. I have given them Your word; and the world has hated them because they are not of the world, just as I am not of the world. I do not pray that You should take them out of the world, but that You should keep them from the evil one."

Jesus was praying this over all the Church, so this is a prayer that's prayed over you and I, as born again believers, and as somebody who represents Him as an ambassador.

"They are not of the world, just as I am not of the world. Sanctify them by Your truth."

Remember, Jesus said in John 14:16:

"I am the way, the truth, and the life. No one comes to the Father except through Me."

That truth that you receive from Jesus sanctifies you. It sets you apart for holy purposes. You are a sanctified vessel.

John 17:17b-26:

"Your word is truth. As You sent Me into the world, I also have sent them into the world."

Every single one of us that fulfills a ministry God has for us, is sent by the Lord Jesus, who is the head of the Church.

"And for their sakes I sanctify Myself,"

I set Myself aside for their sakes.

"...that they may also be sanctified by the truth."

Jesus then went on to say:

"I do not pray for these alone, but also for those who will believe in Me through their word;"

In other words, almost 2,000 years later, we're still believing Jesus through His Word that was passed on from His disciples.

"...that they all may be one,"

Every believer is to be as one.

"...as You, Father, *are* in Me, and I in You; that they also may be one in Us, that the world may believe that You sent Me."

It's through looking at the Church that's doing it right that has power, that the world will look on it and say, "Jesus really did get sent by the Father. These people are still following Him and they're getting the same results."

"And the glory which You gave Me I have given them, that they may be one just as We are one: I in them, and You in Me; that they may be made perfect in one, and that the world may know that You have sent Me, and have loved them as You have loved Me. Father, I desire that they also whom You gave Me may be with Me where I am,

that they may behold My glory which You have given Me; for You loved Me before the foundation of the world."

As the Word of God, He was just as loved then as God was going to (in the future) send Him to take on human flesh and become the Son of God in the earth – the Son of man and His Son of God. He wasn't the Son, even of God, until He took on human flesh. Until then, it was the eternal Father, the Word, and the Holy Spirit. Now it is the Father, Son, and Holy Spirit.

"Oh, righteous Father! The world has not known You, but I have known You; and these have known that You sent Me. And I have declared to them Your name, and will declare *it*, that the love with which You loved Me may be in them, and I in them."

It's a powerful prayer that Jesus prayed over us, the whole Church; that we would walk in the power all of our days.

FEAR NOT, ONLY BELIEVE

There is one final thing that I want to teach you concerning a foundation for your faith, and some key things to continually believe in, that Jesus said. I extract a few things out of what He said because they're so powerful in and of themselves. And I'm going to tie two different stories together here and tell you the things that He said, that were so powerful in each of these two stories so that you can hold onto these truths.

I'm looking in Mark 5. It's interesting, because at the end of chapter four, we find that Jesus is crossing over the Sea of Galilee to a place for a ministry assignment. It turns out that He's on His way to deliver the demoniac named Legion, who had over 2,000 demons in him. A Legion of demons is 2,000.

We're going to find out that they go through this storm in the sea that is about ready to sink them, but Jesus already made the statement, "We're going over there," so He falls asleep in the boat. He's asleep, and all of a sudden, they're about ready to sink. The disciples wake him and say, "Lord, we're going to perish." Jesus just rebukes the wind and the waves. Well, it was obviously a storm of demonic origin, so He was able to stop it right away.

Guess what? That storm was there because of Legion. He knew Jesus was on His way over to get him set free, so the demons were trying to stop Him. But then when Jesus comes into his midst and they land on the shore; the man himself – even though he is demon-possessed – comes running to Jesus. The man falls down and worships Him because he knows that Jesus is the one that can set him free.

Most of the time, the demons are speaking through the man, but Jesus sets Legion free. Now free, of course the man wants to follow Jesus and be one of His disciples. The man was from the area called Decapolis. It was a ten-city region to the northeast of the Sea of Galilee, and everybody in those ten cities knew all about this man. Jesus says, "Go back to your people and tell them all the great things God has done for you."

The people found the man clothed in his right mind. You know the story from the Word of God. Upon Jesus' resurrection, this man probably heard about it and was probably the first one to get born again there and baptized in the Holy Spirit and it would have been powerful.

Jesus goes back to Capernaum, which is His headquarters. As soon as He lands on the shore; Jairus, who is one of the rulers of the synagogue, has a daughter who's about ready to die. (Mark 5:21-24):

Now when Jesus had crossed over again by boat

305

to the other side, a great multitude gathered to Him; and He was by the sea.

In Capernaum.

And behold, one of the rulers of the synagogue came, Jairus by name. And when he saw Him, he fell at His feet and begged Him earnestly, saying, "My little daughter lies at the point of death. Come and lay Your hands on her, that she may be healed, and she will live."

Jairus made a faith declaration there; He knew. He was in a room of the synagogue, in the town where Jesus set up His headquarters. Miracles are happening there all of the time. He knows that Jesus is either the Messiah or He's the prophet who can definitely heal his daughter. So, Jairus comes and is begging for Jesus to come so that his daughter can be healed. He knows that as soon as Jesus touches her, she's going to be fine, so he's made that faith declaration, and Jesus says, "Well, sure, I'll do that."

So *Jesus* went with him, and a great multitude followed Him and thronged Him.

That means they're pressing in on Him from all sides. They're thronging Him. All of a sudden, Jesus gets ambushed by the woman with the issue of blood. Now, a lot of times, we focus so much on her story because Jesus says, "Daughter, your faith has made you whole." When we study the faith that she had, she had been saying continuously – over and over again – "If only I may touch His clothes, I shall be made well."

Even though she's had this issue of blood for twelve years, it is unlawful for her to be in a crowd of people; just like when somebody had leprosy. By the Law of Moses, she could have been stoned for being in a crowd, but she had the ability to keep going to doctors and she had to stay out of the public. It could have been contagious, so they don't know. That's why God put it in the Law, just like leprosy. "Don't mix with the people."

She doesn't know what is wrong, but she just keeps getting worse and worse, and she realizes everybody's touching Jesus, every place He goes. She also lives in Capernaum. She knows all this information about Him. I believe she was the first one to think she could actually just touch His clothes so that He would not notice her touching His body. But she believed she could draw the power of God into her body and be healed of her plague, and He would never even know it. Jesus would just keep going along and she'd be healed and she could just draw back (Mark 5:25-27).

> **Now a certain woman had a flow of blood for twelve years, and had suffered many things from many physicians. She had spent all that she had and was no better, but rather grew worse. When she heard about Jesus, she came behind *Him* in the crowd and touched His garment.**

One of the gospels says:

> **she touched the hem of his garment (Matthew 14:36 WBT).**

She was down all the way to the bottom; probably crawling through the crowd, to not be noticed. There was no pride left in this woman, whatsoever. She just needed her healing. She grabs hold of His clothes, thinking she can get the power to be healed and He won't notice. She had been saying over and over again (Mark 5:28-36,41-43):

> **"If only I can touch His clothes, I shall be made well."**

Then, from the time she gets healed by touching His clothes – that's what all the people were asking for – "If I could just touch His clothes." The word got out on her about what happened.

Immediately the fountain of her blood was dried up, and she felt in *her* body that she was healed of the affliction.

She says, "Glory to God," and she starts backing up.

And Jesus, immediately knowing in Himself that power had gone out of Him, turned around in the crowd and said, "Who touched My clothes?"

Wow! Jairus is on the way with Jesus back to his house, to take care of his daughter. Now, all of a sudden, He's been ambushed by this woman, and Jesus turns around and says:

"Who touched My clothes?"

And His disciples say, "Lord, are You kidding me? Everybody's touching You."

But Jesus says:

"Who touched my clothes?"

He knew the power had gone out, just through His clothes. She wasn't one of those people who were touching Him with a touch of curiosity. There are a lot of curious people who don't have any faith at all.

But His disciples said to Him, "You see the multitude thronging You, and You say, 'Who touched Me?'" And He looked around to see her who had done this thing.

The woman is fearing and trembling. She knows she can't hide from Jesus. I think she believes He's the Messiah; I think she has that much trust. "This man is that special. He's probably the Messiah among us. I have to tell Him everything."

But the woman, fearing and trembling, knowing what had happened to her, came and fell down before Him and told Him the whole truth.

We don't know how long it took. Jairus is there saying, "My daughter's dying. We're on our way. Now this woman's got to tell her whole story. Jesus, You want to listen to her whole story?" He's probably growing impatient, but he came there saying, "If you just come touch my daughter, she'll be healed."

And He said to her, "Daughter, your faith has made you well. Go in peace, and be healed of your affliction."

As soon as He says that, these friends or relatives of Jairus come from the house, with a terrible report.

While He was still speaking, *some* came from the ruler of the synagogue's house who said, "Your daughter is dead."

"We're sorry."

"Why trouble the Teacher any further?"

As a father – I've got a daughter, just one daughter, a 22-year-old cutie. I love her with all my heart. If there was any place for a father to just break down and lose it, it had to be with that word. "Your daughter has died." But Jairus gets an intervention. Jesus intervenes when He hears them say that to Jairus, and He immediately responds:

As soon as Jesus heard the word that was spoken, He said to the ruler of the synagogue, "Do not be afraid;"

I really believe it was like "Fear not!" In so many places, the King James says, "Fear not!" That's said 167 times in the Bible: "Fear not." That's because fear is completely opposite of faith. Jesus is saying, "You came to Me with faith that if I lay hands on your daughter, she'll be fine. Why does it matter what's being said? What does it matter, even if she has already died? *Fear not. Only believe.* Here's your assignment in life."

After I really got this, that's when I felt like the Lord told that to me. I was concerned about some things that were starting to cause some fear to creep up. When I was meditating on this, I heard the Lord say, "Fear not!" And I swear, I heard it in Kenneth Copeland's voice, because he's my spiritual dad now. It was like, "Oh, my, that command." I could almost see his blue, piercing eyes. "Fear not!" It just arrested me. "Fear not! Only believe."

When I heard that "only believe," it was like, "That is my assignment in life: to fear not and to only believe above everything else." It is just to be delivered of fear. If you're delivered of fear and you only believe, you are translated out of the kingdom of the darkness of fear; you're translated into the kingdom of faith, the kingdom of His dear Son, the Son of His love. And yes, it will work that much. "Fear not."

"only believe."

Notice that Jairus never said another word. Why? Because you can undo your faith with all kinds of murmuring and complaining. He didn't say. "Yeah, but Jesus, You heard that message. She's already dead. It's too late." He didn't say a word. He's saying, "Fear not, only believe what you were saying." Only believe what you had been saying when you came with that declaration in your faith, that if I touch your daughter, she's going to be fine. One translation says:

"Do not be afraid; only keep on believing [in Me and my power]" (AMP).

We know that He went on with Jairus to the house. It's amazing. He put everybody out of the house because the wailers and the even the professional wailers were already there. There are certain cultures that think you have to wail over people that have died. Well, they were never going to see them again, but born again believers; we're going to see everybody again. This life down here is temporal, but the one we're going to have there is going to be for eternity. We will see everybody who's born again.

So, Jesus puts all of those wailers out and says, "She's just asleep." He's putting it in a frame of reference for Jairus to see. "Oh, it's just like she's asleep." He puts everybody else out. He only allows Peter, James, and John to go in. Jesus did that a number of times, and I asked, "Lord, why was it that only Peter, James, and John were able to go in?" And He said, "Really, only those three qualified to see a manifestation of My love on that level." In other words, *you can disqualify yourself from seeing the great works of God.*

I said, "Lord, I see that now, but would you please help me to never disqualify myself from seeing a manifestation of Your love on the greatest levels? I cannot be eliminated from that. I don't want to eliminate myself. If I would start to do that and bring a reproach to Your name, please let me die rather than do that – don't let me disqualify myself."

We know that Jesus went there and touched her and she was raised. As a matter of fact, in verses 41-43 it says:

Then He took the child by the hand, and said to her, "Talitha, cumi," which is translated, "Little

girl, I say to you, arise." Immediately the girl arose and walked, for she was twelve years *of age*. And they were overcome with great amazement.

Actually, even Peter, James, and John are kind of shocked. The parents are kind of shocked, because it's still awesome when God manifests Himself. We want to act like, "Oh, yeah, we were really expecting that," you know? But we're all still amazed.

"But He commanded them strictly that no one should know it,"

Every place that the word got out on Jesus, the crowd tripled in size. He couldn't even go to teach and He couldn't make it into the next town. He had to minister to everybody that showed up, because they all needed to be healed. Then Jesus said, "Now, give the girl something to eat." Why? Because she's so healed that she's hungry. Healed people get hungry. She was healed and she was hungry.

Now, the next passage I want us to look at is in Mark 9. To set this up, I have to share this story. Again, Jesus took Peter, James, and John up onto a special mountain and He was transfigured before them. What it really means is that He revealed the glory that was actually on the inside of Him – past this disguise that He was wearing as a human body. They saw Him in His *shekinah glory* and they were blown away. It's like looking at the sun but it doesn't hurt your eyes.

He's transfigured before them. Peter makes this brilliant statement, "Oh, let's build three tents: for You and Moses and Elijah." He talks out of his head. These three are coming down the mountain with Jesus, and they come to where the other nine disciples are, and there's this big throng of people around them. There are a bunch of scribes and Pharisees there that were making fun of the disciples, so Jesus was wondering what was going on. These are saying, "Oh, you guys think you're so full of faith?" Remember, these guys had great success when Jesus sent them out two-by-two. They came back and said, "Lord, even the demons are subject to us in Your name." They were amazed.

But this man came to them with a son who, from all description, looks like he's got epilepsy. He has seizures that cause him to foam at the mouth and go rigid. Sometimes it throws him into the fire – it's a demon spirit in this case, that casts him into the fire. It casts him into the water to try to drown him; it's trying to kill this kid.

The man brought his son to Jesus' disciples to cast the demon out, but they couldn't do it. They tried; they did everything they knew to do, but it didn't work. Later on, they asked the Lord Jesus. "Lord, why couldn't we cast out this demon?" And He says, "It's because of your doubt and unbelief." In one translation, it says that Jesus also says not without fasting and prayer:

"This kind can come out by nothing but prayer and fasting" (Mark 9:29).

You see, they hadn't fasted and prayed enough to be in that level of belief. That's why it's so important now. It's interesting to see if, on this side of our prayer (post-resurrection), it's not as much about fasting. We're still going to fast some. We're going to pray a lot. The Lord actually corrected me on fasting and praying: *the only reason to fast is to take the time strictly for praying.*

Sometimes I've prayed straight through a meal, so I'll fast for that meal, but one time I did eleven days. God didn't build me to fast, because I dropped down to 103 pounds; fasting for eleven days. I got my answer from the Lord, but I also got a rebuke when He told me, "Don't ever do that again." So, I knew never do more than a three-day fast. I could do some partial fasts and a liquid fast; but the whole purpose of fasting is *to get tuned up to be in the Spirit.*

Jesus tells them, "because of your unbelief and you haven't fasted and prayed enough to be in this level of belief." Again, the crowd was around Him (Mark 9:17-20):

> **Then one of the crowd answered and said, "Teacher, I brought You my son, who has a mute spirit."**

He was deaf and dumb; he couldn't speak. Jesus is talking to this father as he is describing what goes on. He says:

> **"And wherever it seizes him, it throws him down; he foams at the mouth, gnashes his teeth, and becomes rigid. So I spoke to Your disciples, that they should cast it out, but they could not."**

They could not cast it out.

> **He answered him and said, "O faithless…"**

He rebuked his disciples. The only time He rebuked His disciples was because of a lack of faith. He said:

> **"Oh, faithless generation, how long shall I be with you? How long shall I bear with you? Bring him to Me."**

"I'll get this thing fixed. I can't believe you guys did not believe enough to get it fixed."

> **Then they brought him to Him. And when he saw Him, immediately the spirit convulsed him, and he fell on the ground and wallowed, foaming at the mouth.**

Jesus is watching this seizure happen. I can just see Him standing there.

"And often he has thrown him both into the fire and into the water to destroy him. But if You can do anything, have compassion on us and help us" (Mark 9:22).

It's interesting that he says, "If You can do anything. Your disciples couldn't do anything. If You can do anything." This man's faith is not there. "I don't even know if You can help, but if You can; I've heard that You could, but I don't know that. If You can do anything, please have compassion on us and help us." Now, Jesus didn't say, "Oh, sure, okay, I'll have compassion." He threw it right back at the guy. Jesus said to him, "It's not just *if* I can do anything." He says:

"If you can believe, all things are possible to him who believes" (Mark 9:23).

Wow. What an endorsement for faith. He just rebukes His disciples for their lack of belief and He tells the man, "Listen, if you can believe, all things are possible to those who believe." So, that's why I couple: "Fear not, only believe," with: "If you can believe, all things are possible to those who believe." So, "Fear not, only believe, *because* if you can believe, *all* things are possible to those who believe."

Faith is totally unlimited. Praying in the Spirit long enough takes you into a place where your faith is in this place that Jesus wanted His disciples to be at. Don't be part of the faithless generation where Jesus says, "How long do I have to bear with you" (Mark 9:19b)? He was saying, "I want you to believe. I want you to have this level of belief."

"Immediately the father of the child cried out" (Mark 9:24).

315

He heard that from Jesus, like a rebuke, but he cried out, "Lord, I believe! You said it, so I believe! Please help my unbelief." Yet, that is a massive problem because it is possible to have belief and unbelief at the same time. You've got some faith, but the devil always has an argument against it, and demon spirits come to try to take you out of faith. You listen to that, and sometimes you actually encourage the demons by saying, "Yeah, but..."

The Lord says this, and you say, "Well, yeah, Lord, I heard you say that. Yeah, but I heard the devil say this, and I'm really used to listening to the devil, so I think I can believe him easier than I can believe You." That's the problem.

This doubt and unbelief is always believing input from Satan's kingdom. It's going to try to rob us of this faith of God's kingdom; that is a totally supernatural realm. Praying in tongues enough takes you into that supernatural realm. So, hear these words: *the Lord had compassion on him.*

He rebuked the unclean spirit, saying to it, "Deaf and dumb spirit, I command you, come out of him and enter him no more" (Mark 9:25).

"Then *the spirit* cried out, convulsed him greatly" (Mark 9:26),

Then the man became dead, so that many said, "Oh, he's dead. Jesus just killed him. He pulled the spirit out of him and the boy died." It's kind of like when Smith Wigglesworth would punch somebody in a tumor because the Holy Spirit told him to. Then they'd fall out and people thought they were dead.

There were times when there were doctors in the audience that wanted to jump up and pull Wigglesworth off the platform. "This guy's a heretic. He just killed that guy!"

316

Then, all of a sudden, the guy jumps up, completely healed. There's no tumor. That big old lump is suddenly gone. He's running up and down in a hospital gown. "I'm healed! I'm healed! I'm healed!"

Jesus is doing the same thing. The spirit cries out and convulsed him greatly, and it comes out of him and he becomes like one dead. Then Jesus takes him by the hand and lifts him up and He arose. And of course, then all these people come in to throng around Jesus. Later on, His disciple says, "Why couldn't we cast it out?" And Jesus says, "Because you haven't entered into that realm." He wanted so much for them to enter into that realm, He empowered them after He took His seat at the right hand of the Father, and released the Holy Spirit without measure upon the Church.

It was that which John the Baptist had told us about. Jesus had this anointing without measure that makes Him the Messiah, the Christ; and He gave it to us, the Church. It arrived on the Day of Pentecost. It was probably A.D. 30.

TAP INTO THE POWER

Jesus paid the price for our sin, and was raised from the dead and ascended to the right hand of the Father in the year A.D. 30. Here we are some 1,993 years later. The Church hasn't turned 2,000 years old yet. We've still got seven years to go (as of 2023). I don't know what's going to happen. Something dynamic is going to happen.

All I know is that the Lord is saying, "Pray in tongues. Tap into this power. Tap into the full measure of the anointing without measure. Keep increasing in that anointing without measure that rests on your life; for your ministry's sake, for your family's sake, for the kingdom's sake around you, and for all those under your purview."

Believe me, when you pray in the spirit, it matters. LCU

has over 21,000 graduates (and counting) around the planet, in twenty-four foreign nations, on five different continents. When I pray in tongues, that's sometimes why I have to pray for five hours. I'm praying for all of these ministries and graduates of LCU that I know. There's a seed of truth in them and I feel responsible, like a father, to pray over them. I don't even know them all. They didn't sit under my classes. They had other professors, but we made the way for them to have their ministry education, so I feel responsible to pray for them.

I know the Holy Spirit prays for them through me. You see, what God will use you to cover in prayer is unlimited. You might be praying into the next generation. You might be praying for grandchildren and great-grandchildren, and great-greats. I don't know how long the Lord's going to tarry. It's whenever the Father says, "Jesus, go back for the Church." None of us will know the time.

I know something dynamic is going to be happening in seven years, so I'm going to be incredibly busy over the next seven years. Then I'm going to hit eighty years of age. Maybe it will be like Moses. Maybe that's when my real ministry is going to start; I don't know.

The promise is 120 years. Don't give up! I always knew that I was going to live to be 105, at a minimum. I keep getting the sneaking suspicion that God's going to say: "You're going to have to push it out. You're going to have to push it out."

I've always said He may require that of some of us, to prove His Word is true. The power of God is true. This realm of the kingdom of the miraculous of God is available to us. It's the kingdom of His anointing without measure, that we activate when we pray in tongues and we pray all the way through.

How much are you going to need to pray? I don't know; that's up to you and the Lord. How much am I going to have to pray in the future? I don't know, but I do know this. I love my intercession ministry probably now today, as much as anything that I do.

And I do know that even at 105 or 110, if nobody wanted to hear me preach – I think, though, if I was preaching on longevity, I'd get somebody to want to hear something about that – but I know I'll have this ministry of intercession until my last breath on earth. Each one of us can have that. Right before graduating to heaven, you can be praying in tongues.

I've heard so many people say so many times, that the angels take you to heaven and then you get to see things. You get to see Jesus or maybe a bunch of Christians before that. I just prayed one day; I said, "Jesus, when I graduate to the other side, I want Your face to be the first one I see." And He said, "Okay, it's granted." I'm looking for that, but I'm going to pray my way to it.

As I said before, I just know that God is going to inspire you. This is Holy Spirit-Empowered Prayer. You're going to be praying and the Holy Spirit is going to be praying through your spirit, all of these different forms of prayer. You are going to fulfill major divine destinies, and it's going to happen in the mighty power of the name of Jesus. We do all that we do in the name of that mighty name. The King of Kings and Lord of Lords is represented in the name of Jesus. All the authority and dominion under Heaven and in Heaven is in the name of Jesus, so we do it all in that name.

It's a joyous journey, and it's going to be a glorious entry into our eternal life. Life on this earth is not about life on this earth. This is just a test. We need to fulfill what God has called us to do here so that we can move into the full measure of our rewards and assignments we're going to have, that will go on and on for all of eternity. I only have this one little life that is described in the Word of God as a breath or a vapor. It's one breath. In the mind of God and in His timeline, it's like one breath of God – one whole 120-year life, at the max.

Let me pray.

Father, in Jesus' name, I just pray for each and every person that takes our courses and each one that reads or hears these words. Lord, I pray that the anointing will be upon every person and that they will be inspired by You to press in; praying in the Spirit. Lord, that they will get used to praying without ceasing and praying in their minds continually, between things of responsibility that they have to think on and be focused on.

Lord, I pray that they will take every moment that can be idle time and either pray in the Spirit silently, or in their mind. They will pray in the Spirit even with a whisper or out loud, where the angels can hear, and the commissioning of angels can take place as we pray in the Spirit. And Lord, bless each and every person and every disciple of the Word and take them into the supernatural, powerful Holy Spirit-empowered prayer that they can move into, in Jesus' mighty and matchless name, I pray. Amen and Amen.